The BIG
THREE *in*
ECONOMICS

OTHER ACADEMIC BOOKS
BY MARK SKOUSEN

The Structure of Production

Economics on Trial

Dissent on Keynes
(editor)

The Investor's Bible:
Mark Skousen's Principles of Investment

Puzzles and Paradoxes in Economics
(co-authored with Kenna C. Taylor)

Economic Logic

The Power of Economic Thinking

Vienna and Chicago, Friends or Foes?

The Compleated Autobiography by Benjamin Franklin
(editor and compiler)

The BIG THREE *in* ECONOMICS

ADAM SMITH

KARL MARX *and*

JOHN MAYNARD KEYNES

MARK SKOUSEN

M.E.Sharpe
Armonk, New York
London, England

Library of Congress Cataloging-in-Publication Data

Skousen, Mark.
  The big three in economics : Adam Smith, Karl Marx, and John Maynard Keynes /
Mark Skousen.
    p. cm.
  Includes bibliographical references and index.
  ISBN-10: 0-7656-1694-7 (cloth : alk. paper)
  ISBN-13: 978-0-7656-1694-4 (cloth : alk. paper)
  1. Economists—History. 2. Economics—Philosophy. 3. Economists—Biography.
4. Smith, Adam, 1723–1790. 5. Marx, Karl, 1818–1883. 6. Keynes, John Maynard,
1883–1946. I. Title.

HB76.S58 2007
330.15092′2--dc22   2006020466

Printed in the United States of America

The paper used in this publication meets the minimum requirements of
American National Standard for Information Sciences
Permanence of Paper for Printed Library Materials,
ANSI Z 39.48-1984.

BM (c)   10   9

Dedicated to
The Big Three in my life,
My editor, my friend, and my wife,
Jo Ann Skousen

Contents

Introduction   ix
Photos follow page 104

Chapter 1. Adam Smith Declares an Economic Revolution
          in 1776   3

Chapter 2. From Smith to Marx: The Rise and Fall of
          Classical Economics   46

Chapter 3. Karl Marx Leads a Revolt Against Capitalism   64

Chapter 4. From Marx to Keynes: Scientific Economics
          Comes of Age   105

Chapter 5. John Maynard Keynes: Capitalism Faces Its
          Greatest Challenge   133

Chapter 6. A Turning Point in Twentieth-Century Economics   163

Chapter 7. Conclusion: Has Adam Smith Triumphed Over
          Marx and Keynes?   191

Bibliography   219
Index   231
About the Author   243

Introduction

During the past three centuries, three economists stand out as archetypes, symbols of three distinct approaches to economic philosophy. In the eighteenth century, Adam Smith, a student of the Scottish Enlightenment, expounded a "system of natural liberty" (what we might term a liberal democratic order consisting of an unfettered market and limited government), and elucidated how a nation flourishes and advances the standard of living of its citizens. In the nineteenth century, the German philosopher Karl Marx attracted and inspired workers and intellectuals who felt disenfranchised by industrial capitalism and sought radical solutions to inequality, alienation, and exploitation of the underprivileged. Finally, in the twentieth century, the British economist John Maynard Keynes sought to stabilize a crisis-prone market system through activist fiscal and monetary government policies.

The Pendulum and the Totem Pole

The stories and ideas of these Big Three economists are told in context of a larger history I have described in greater detail in *The Making of Modern Economics*. In the introduction to that work, I describe two possible approaches to writing about the lives and ideas of economists, what I term the *spectral* versus the *hierarchal* approach.

The most popular method of analysis I describe as a pendulum, by which historians place each economist somewhere along a political spectrum, from extreme left to extreme right. Figure A illustrates the pendulum approach used in many economics textbooks.

The Pendulum Approach to Competing Economic Theories

Simple though it is, I see several problems with the spectral approach. First, it treats Karl Marx and Adam Smith as coequals, that is,

Figure A   **The Pendulum Approach to Competing Economic Theories**

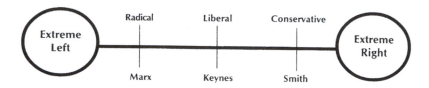

"extreme" in their positions and therefore equally bad. By implication, neither man's position is sensible and must be rejected. The result is a pendulum-like swing between the two extremes, eventually coming to rest in the middle. Consequently, the moderate, middle-of-the-road position held by John Maynard Keynes appears to be the more balanced and ideal. But is his system the way to achieve growth and prosperity? Or is the middle of the road simply the path toward big government and a cumbersome welfare state?

I suggest as an alternative the "hierarchal" approach. In Indian folklore, the higher one's placement on the totem pole, the higher the rank of significance. Instead of comparing economists horizontally on a pendulum or spectrum, we might choose to rank them by height according to the same standard of achievement. Using this totem pole structure, I would reformulate the diagram according to Figure B.

The Totem Pole of Economics

I have chosen a ranking system consistent with the opinions of most economists. A large majority of economists and historians of economic thought consider Adam Smith the greatest of the Big Three. His model of competitive markets constitutes the "first fundamental theorem of welfare economics," what George Stigler called the "crown jewel" of economics, the "most important substantive proposition in all of economics" (Stigler 1976, 1201).

Next on the list is John Maynard Keynes. Despite substantial criticism of the Keynesian model, it continues to endure as a macroeconomic model in institutional analysis and policy matters. As a defender of bourgeois values, Keynes supported individual liberty, but on a larger scale, he thought that macroeconomic intervention is

Figure B The Totem Pole Approach: The Ranking of Three Economists (Smith, Keynes, and Marx) According to Economic Freedom and Growth

essential to stabilize the economy, a view still held by many economists today.

The third man on the totem pole is Karl Marx. Although his endorsement of centrally planned command economies at both the micro and macro level has been largely discredited, Marxist interpretations of class conflict and economic crisis still draw the attention of sociologists, historians, and economists.[1]

The story of modern economics can be told through the eyes of the Big Three. I have added vital transitional chapters between the three biographies to complete the story. As you will see, it is a cunning plot that has many unexpected twists and turns. Let us begin.

---

1. Those radical economists who take issue with my ranking of Marx as "low man" on the totem pole may take comfort in the argument made by some experts in Indian folklore who claim that the figure on the bottom may in fact be the founder or most significant chief in the history of the tribe.

The BIG THREE in ECONOMICS

1

Adam Smith Declares an Economic Revolution in 1776

Adam Smith was a radical and a revolutionary in his time—just
as those of us who preach laissez faire are in our time.
—*Milton Friedman* (1978, 7)

The story of modern economics begins in 1776. Prior to this famous
date, 6,000 years of recorded history had passed without a seminal
work being published on the subject that dominated every waking
hour of practically every human being: making a living.

For millennia, from Roman times through the Dark Ages and the
Renaissance, humans struggled to survive by the sweat of their brow,
often only eking out a bare existence. They were constantly guarding
against premature death, disease, famine, war, and subsistence wages.
Only a fortunate few—primarily rulers and aristocrats—lived leisurely
lives, and even those were crude by modern standards. For the common
man, little changed over the centuries. Real per capita wages were
virtually the same, year after year, decade after decade. During this

3

age, when the average life span was a mere forty years, the English writer Thomas Hobbes rightly called the life of man "solitary, poor, nasty, brutish, and short" (1996 [1651], 84).

1776, a Prophetic Year

Then came 1776, when hope and rising expectations were extended to the common workingman for the first time. It was a period known as the Enlightenment, which the French called *l'age des lumieres.* For the first time in history, workers looked forward to obtaining a basic minimum of food, shelter, and clothing. Even tea, previously a luxury, had become a common beverage.

The signing of America's Declaration of Independence on July 4 was one of several significant events of 1776. Influenced by John Locke, Thomas Jefferson proclaimed "life, liberty, and the pursuit of happiness" to be inalienable rights, thus establishing the legal framework for a struggling nation that would eventually become the greatest economic powerhouse on earth, and providing the constitutional foundation of liberty that was to be imitated around the world.

A Monumental Book Appears

Four months earlier, an equally monumental work had been published across the Atlantic in England. On March 9, 1776, the London printers William Strahan and Thomas Cadell released a 1,000–page, two-volume work entitled *An Inquiry into the Nature and Causes of the Wealth of Nations.* It was a fat book with a long title destined to have gargantuan global impact. The author was Dr. Adam Smith, a quiet, absent-minded professor who taught "moral philosophy" at the University of Glasgow.

The Wealth of Nations was the intellectual shot heard around the world. Adam Smith, a leader in the Scottish Enlightenment, had put on paper a universal formula for prosperity and financial independence that would, over the course of the next century, revolutionize the way citizens and leaders thought about and practiced economics and trade. Its publication promised a new world—a world of abundant wealth, riches beyond the mere accumulation of gold and silver. Smith promised that new world to everyone—not just the rich and the rulers, but the common man, too. *The Wealth of Nations* offered a formula for emancipating

Figure 1.1 **The Rise in Real per Capita Income, United Kingdom, 1100–1995**

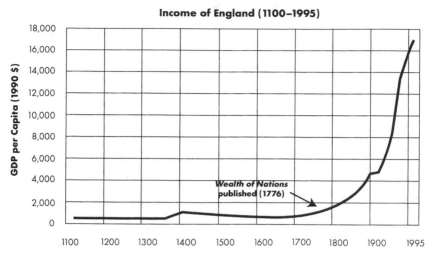

Income of England (1100–1995)

Courtesy of Larry Wimmer, Brigham Young University.

the workingman from the drudgery of a Hobbesian world. In sum, *The Wealth of Nations* was a declaration of economic independence.

Certain dates are turning points in the history of mankind. The year 1776 is one of them. In that prophetic year, two vital freedoms were proclaimed—political liberty and free enterprise—and the two worked together to set in motion the Industrial Revolution. It was no accident that the modern economy began in earnest shortly after 1776 (see Figure 1.1).

The Enlightenment and the Rumblings of Economic Progress

The year 1776 was significant for other reasons as well. For example, it was the year the first volume of Edward Gibbon's classic work, *History of the Decline and Fall of the Roman Empire* (1776–88), appeared. Gibbon was a principal advocate of eighteenth-century Enlightenment, which embodied unbounded faith in science, reason, and economic individualism in place of religious fanaticism, superstition, and aristocratic power.

To Smith, 1776 was also an important year for personal reasons.

His closest friend, David Hume, died. Hume, a writer and philosopher, was a great influence on Adam Smith (see "Pre-Adamites" in the appendix to this chapter). Like Smith, he was a leader of the Scottish Enlightenment and an advocate of commercial civilization and economic liberty.

For centuries, the average real wage and standard of living had stagnated, while almost a billion people struggled against the harsh realities of daily life. Suddenly, in the early 1800s, just a few years after the American Revolution and the publication of *The Wealth of Nations,* the Western world began to flourish as never before. The spinning jenny, power looms, and the steam engine were the first of many inventions that saved time and money for enterprising businessmen and the average citizen. The Industrial Revolution was beginning to unfold, real wages started climbing, and everyone's standard of living, rich and poor, began rising to unforeseen heights. It was indeed the Enlightenment, the dawning of modern times, and people of all walks of life took notice.

Advocate for the Common Man

Just as George Washington was the father of a new nation, so Adam Smith was the father of a new science, the science of wealth. The great British economist Alfred Marshall called economics the study of "the ordinary business of life." Appropriately, Adam Smith would have an ordinary name. He was named after the first man in the Bible, Adam, which means "out of many," and his last name, Smith, signifies "one who works." Smith is the most common surname in Great Britain.

The man with the pedestrian name wrote a book for the welfare of the average working man. In his magnum opus, he assured the reader that his model for economic success would result in "universal opulence which extends itself to the lowest ranks of the people" (1965 [1776], 11).[1]

---

1. All quotes from *The Wealth of Nations* are from the Modern Library edition (Random House, 1937, 1965, 1994). In this book I refer to the 1965 edition, which has an introduction by Max Lerner. There have been many editions of *The Wealth of Nations,* including the official edition issued by the University of Glasgow Press, but this edition is the most popular.

It was not a book for aristocrats and kings. In fact, Adam Smith had little regard for the men of vested interests and commercial power. His sympathies lay with the average citizens who had been abused and taken advantage of over the centuries. Now they would be liberated from sixteen-hour-a-day jobs, subsistence wages, and a forty-year life span.

Adam Smith Faces a Major Obstacle

After taking twelve long years to write his big book, Smith was convinced he had discovered the right kind of economics to create "universal opulence." He called his model the "system of natural liberty." Today economists call it the "classical model." Smith's model was inspired by Sir Isaac Newton, whose model of natural science Smith greatly admired as universal and harmonious.

Smith's biggest hurdle would be convincing others to accept his system, especially legislators. His purpose in writing *The Wealth of Nations* was not simply to educate, but to persuade. Very little progress had been achieved over the centuries in England and Europe because of the entrenched system known as mercantilism. One of Adam Smith's main objectives in writing *The Wealth of Nations* was to smash the conventional view of the economy, which allowed the mercantilists to control the commercial interests and political powers of the day, and to replace it with his view of the real source of wealth and economic growth, thus leading England and the rest of the world toward the "greatest improvement" of the common man's lot.

The Appeal of Mercantilism

Following a long-standing tradition in the West, the mercantilists (the commercial politicos of the day) believed that the world's economy was stagnant and its wealth fixed, so that one nation grew only at the expense of another. The economies of civilizations from ancient times through the Middle Ages were based on either slavery or several forms of serfdom. Under either system, wealth was largely acquired at the expense of others, or by the exploitation of man by man. As Bertrand de Jouvenel observes, "Wealth was therefore based on seizure and exploitation" (Jouvenel 1999, 100).

Consequently, European nations established government-authorized monopolies at home and supported colonialism abroad, sending agents and troops into poorer countries to seize gold and other precious commodities.

According to the established mercantilist system, wealth consisted entirely of money per se, which at the time meant gold and silver. The primary goal of every nation was always to aggressively accumulate gold and silver, and to use whatever means necessary to do so. "The great affair, we always find, is to get money," Smith declared in *The Wealth of Nations* (398).

How to get more money? The growth of nations was predatory. Nations such as Spain and Portugal sent their emissaries to faraway lands to discover gold mines and to pile up as much of the precious metal as they could. No expedition or foreign war was too expensive when it came to their thirst for bullion. Other European countries, imitating the gold seekers, frequently imposed exchange controls, forbidding, under the threat of heavy penalties, the export of gold and silver.

Second, mercantilists sought a favorable balance of trade, which meant that gold and silver would constantly fill their coffers. How? "The encouragement of exportation, and the discouragement of importation, are the two great engines by which the mercantilist system proposes to enrich every country," reported Smith (607). Smith carefully delineated the host of high tariffs, duties, quotas, and regulations that aimed at restraining trade. Ultimately, this system also restrained production and a higher standard of living. Such commercial interferences naturally led to conflict and war between nations.

Smith Denounces Trade Barriers

In a direct assault on the mercantile system, the Scottish philosopher denounced high tariffs and other restrictions on trade. Efforts to promote a favorable balance of trade were "absurd," he declared (456). He talked of the "natural advantages" one country has over another in producing goods. "By means of glasses, hotbeds, and hotwalls, very good grapes can be raised in Scotland," Smith said, but it would cost thirty times more to produce Scottish wine than to import wine from

France. "Would it be a reasonable law to prohibit the importation of all foreign wines, merely to encourage the making of claret and burgundy in Scotland?" (425).

According to Smith, mercantilist policies merely imitate real prosperity, benefiting only the producers and the monopolists. Because it did not benefit the consumer, mercantilism was antigrowth and shortsighted. "In the mercantile system, the interest of the consumer is almost always constantly sacrificed to that of the producer," he wrote (625).

Smith argued that trade barriers crippled the ability of countries to produce, and thus should be torn down. An expansion of trade between Britain and France, for example, would enable both nations to gain. "What is prudence in the conduct of every private family, can scarce be folly in that of a great kingdom," declared Smith. "If a foreign country can supply us with a commodity cheaper than we ourselves can make it, better buy it of them" (424).

Real Source of Wealth Revealed

The accumulation of gold and silver might have filled the pockets of the rich and the powerful, but what would be the origin of wealth for the whole nation and the average citizen? That was Adam Smith's paramount question. *The Wealth of Nations* was not just a tract on free trade, but a world view of prosperity.

The Scottish professor forcefully argued that the keys to the "wealth of nations" were production and exchange, not the artificial acquisition of gold and silver at the expense of other nations. He stated, "the wealth of a country consists, not of its gold and silver only, but in its lands, houses, and consumable goods of all different kinds" (418). Wealth should be measured according to how well people are lodged, clothed, and fed, not according to the number of bags of gold in the treasury. In 1763, he said, "the wealth of a state consists in the cheapness of provisions and all other necessaries and conveniences of life" (1982 [1763], 83).

Smith began his *Wealth of Nations* with a discussion of wealth. He asked, what could bring about the "greatest improvement in the productive powers of labour"? A favorable balance of trade? More gold and silver?

No, it was a superior management technique, "the division of labor." In a well-known example, Smith described in detail the workings of a pin factory, where workers were assigned eighteen distinct operations in order to maximize the output of pins (1965 [1776], 3–5). This stages-of-production approach, where management works with labor to produce goods and fulfill consumer wants, forms the basis of a harmonious and growing economy. A few pages later, Smith used another example, the woolen coat: "the assistance and co-operation of many thousands" of laborers and various machinery from around the world were required to produce this basic product used by the "day-laborer"[2] (11–12). Furthermore, expanding the market through worldwide trade would mean that specialization and division of labor could also expand. Through increased productivity, thrift, and hard work, the world's output could increase. Hence, wealth was not a fixed quantity after all, and countries could grow richer without harming or exploiting others.

Smith Discovers the Key to Prosperity

How can production and exchange be maximized and thereby encourage the "universal opulence" and the "improvement of the productive power of labor"? Adam Smith had a clear answer: Give people their economic freedom! Throughout *The Wealth of Nations,* Smith advocated the principle of "natural liberty," the freedom to do what one wishes with little interference from the state. It encouraged the free movement of labor, capital, money, and goods. Moreover, said Smith, economic freedom not only leads to a better material life, but is a fundamental human right. To quote Smith: "To prohibit a great people . . . from making all that they can of every part of their own produce, or from employing their stock and industry in the way that they judge most advantageous to themselves, is a manifest violation of the most sacred rights of mankind" (549).

Under Adam Smith's model of natural liberty, wealth creation was

---

2. This passage in the first chapter of *The Wealth of Nations* is remarkably similar to the theme developed by Leonard Read in his classic essay, "I, Pencil," which describes how a simple product like the pencil involved production processes from around the world (Read 1999 [1958]).

no longer a zero-sum game. No longer was there a conflict of interests, but a harmony of interests. According to Jouvenel, this came as an "enormous innovation" that greatly surprised European reformers. "The great new idea is that it is possible to enrich all the members of society, collectively and individually, by gradual progress in the organization of labor" (Jouvenel 1999, 102). This development could be rapid and unlimited.

Here was something that could capture the imagination and hope not only of the English worker, but of the French peasant, the German laborer, the Chinese day worker, and the American immigrant, for Smith was advocating a worldwide principle of abundance. The freedom to work could liberate everyone from the chains of daily chores.

What constitutes this new economic freedom? Natural liberty includes, according to Smith, the right to buy goods from any source, including foreign products, without the restraints of tariffs or import quotas. It includes the right to be employed in whatever occupation a person wants and wherever desired. Smith trenchantly criticized European policy in the eighteenth century wherein laborers had to obtain government permission (via certificates) to move from one town to another, even within a country (1965 [1776], 118–43).

Natural liberty also includes the right to charge whatever wage the market might bear. Smith strongly opposed the state's efforts to regulate and artificially raise wages. He wrote, "Whenever the law has attempted to regulate the wages of workmen, it has always been rather to lower them than to raise them" (131). Like every worker, Smith desired high wages, but he thought they should come about through the natural workings of the labor market, not government edict.

Finally, natural liberty includes the right to save, invest, and accumulate capital without government restraint—important keys to economic growth.

Adam Smith endorsed the virtues of thrift, capital investment, and labor-saving machinery as essential ingredients to promote rising living standards (326). In his chapter on the accumulation of capital (Chapter 3, Book II) in *The Wealth of Nations,* Smith emphasized saving and frugality as keys to economic growth, in addition to stable government policies, a competitive business environment, and sound business management.

Smith's Classic Work Receives Universal Acclaim

Adam Smith's eloquent advocacy of natural liberty fueled the minds of a rising generation. His words literally changed the course of politics, dismantling the old mercantilist doctrines of protectionism and enforced labor. Much of the worldwide movement toward free trade can be attributed to Adam Smith's work. *The Wealth of Nations* was the ideal document to usher in the Industrial Revolution and the political rights of man.

Smith's magnum opus has received almost universal acclaim. H.L. Mencken stated, "There is no more engrossing book in the English language" (in Powell 2000, 251). Historian Arnold Toynbee asserted that "*The Wealth of Nations* and the steam engine destroyed the old world and built a new one" (in Rashid 1998, 212). The English historian Henry Thomas Buckle stretched the hyperbole even further to claim that, in terms of its ultimate influence, Smith's tome "is probably the most important book that has ever been written," not excluding the Bible (in Rogge 1976, 9); and Paul A. Samuelson placed Smith "on a pinnacle" among economists (Samuelson 1962, 7).[3] Even Marxists sometimes extol the virtues of Adam Smith.

The Life of Adam Smith

Who was Adam Smith, and how did he come to write his revolutionary work on modern economics?

Seaports and commerce were an integral part of Adam Smith's life. Born in Kirkcaldy, on the east coast of Scotland near Edinburgh, in June 1723, he had the unfortunate distinction of coming into the world in the same year that his father died. It appeared that the newborn Adam Smith was destined to be a student of trade and a customs agent. His father, also named Adam Smith, was a comptroller of customs at Kirkcaldy. His guardian, named Adam Smith as well, was a customs collector in the same town, and a cousin served as customs inspector in Alloa. The cousin's name was—you guessed it—Adam Smith.

---

3. This was Samuelson's presidential address before the American Economic Association. A year later, Samuelson declared, "The first human was Adam. The first economist . . . was Adam Smith" (Samuelson 1966,1408).

The last occupation of our Adam Smith (the famous one) was, not surprisingly, customs commissioner of Scotland. But we're getting ahead of our story. In his early days in Kirkcaldy, Adam was regarded as a "delicate child." At age four, he was kidnapped by gypsies but was soon returned to his mother. "He would have made a poor gypsy," commented biographer John Rae (1895, 5). His focus of affection was always his mother, whom he cherished.

Although Smith had many female acquaintances, he never married. "He speaks harshly, with big teeth, and he's ugly as the devil," wrote Madame Riccoboni, a French novelist, upon meeting Adam Smith for the first time in Paris in May 1766. "He's a most absent-minded creature," she later wrote, "but one of the most lovable" (in Muller 1993, 16). We know pitifully little about his love interests. His biographers relate that as a young man Smith fell in love with a beautiful and accomplished young lady, but unknown circumstances prevented their marriage (Ross 1995, 402). Several French ladies pursued this unhandsome savant, but nothing came of it.

Smith occupied his spare time attending numerous clubs, such as the Poker Club, the Club of Edinburgh, the London "literati," and Johnson's Club, although David Hume frequently scolded him for being too reclusive. "His mother, his friends, his books—these were Smith's three great joys," declared John Rae (1895, 327).

At the youthful age of fourteen, Smith attended Glasgow University, then won a scholarship to Oxford, where he spent half a dozen years studying Greek and Latin classics, French and English literature, and science and philosophy. Referring to Oxford University, he wrote in *The Wealth of Nations* that "the greater part of the public professors have, for these many years, given up altogether even the pretence of teaching" (Smith 1965 [1776], 718). A few pages later, Smith made his famous denunciation of the "sham-lecture" by college professors: "If the teacher happens to be a man of sense, it must be an unpleasant thing to him to be conscious, while he is lecturing his students, that he is either speaking or reading nonsense, or what is very little better than nonsense. It must too be unpleasant to him to observe that the greater part of his students desert his lectures; or perhaps attend upon them with plain enough marks of neglect, contempt, and derision. . . . The discipline of colleges and universities is in general contrived, not for the benefit of the students, but for the interest, or more properly speaking, for the ease of the masters" (720).[4]

In terms of physical appearance, Smith was of average height and slightly overweight. He never sat for a picture, but several sketches show "rather handsome features, full forehead, prominent eyeballs, well curved eyebrows, slightly aquiline nose, and firm mouth and chin" (Rae 1895, 438). He himself exclaimed, "I am a beau in nothing but my books" (Rae 1895, 329).

After graduation, he held the position of Professor of Moral Philosophy at the University of Glasgow between 1751 and 1763. His first major work, *Theory of Moral Sentiments,* was published in 1759 and established Adam Smith as an influential Scottish thinker.

The Absent-Minded Professor

As to his personality quirks, the famous professor had a harsh, thick voice and often stuttered. He was the quintessential absent-minded professor. His life was one of ubiquitous disorganization and ambiguity. Books and papers were stacked everywhere in his study. From his childhood, he had the habit of talking to himself, "smiling in rapt conversation with invisible companions" (Rae 1895, 329). Stories of his bumbling nature abound: once he fell into a leather-tanning pit while conversing with a friend; one morning he put bread and butter into a teapot, and after tasting the tea, declared it to be the worst cup of tea he had ever had; another time he went out walking and daydreaming in his old nightgown and ended up several miles outside town.

---

4. George Stigler, whose favorite economist was Adam Smith, was known for telling his students at Chicago that he recommended all of *The Wealth of Nations* "except page 720" (Stigler 1966,168n). If students looked up this passage, found in book V, part II, article 2, they encountered Smith's attack on the teaching profession and the "sham-lecture." But if you ask me, that citation is nothing compared to what Adam Smith wrote a few pages later, in which he condemned a certain "English custom" that would cause a young person to become "more conceited, more unprincipled, more dissipated, and more incapable of any serious application either to study or to business. . . ." A father who allowed his son to engage in this "absurd practice" would soon see his son "unemployed, neglected and going to ruin before his eyes." What was this terrible practice? Youths (ages seventeen to twenty-one) traveling abroad! Smith criticized the practice of sending teenage children abroad, contending that it weakens character by removing them from the control of parents (1965 [1776], 720).

"He was the most absent man I ever knew," declared a contemporary (in West 1976, 176).

How He Wrote His Magnum Opus

In 1764, Charles Townsend, a leading British member of Parliament, offered Smith a handsome fee and lifetime pension to tutor his stepson, Henry Scott, the Duke of Buccleuch. They traveled to France, where Smith met with Voltaire, Turgot, Quesnay, and other great French thinkers. "This Smith is an excellent man!" exclaimed Voltaire. "We have nothing to compare with him" (in Muller 1993, 15).

It was in France that Smith indicated he had lost interest in his tutoring duties and began researching and writing *The Wealth of Nations.* It took him ten years to write it. When finally published by the premier English publisher, it became an instant bestseller, and the first edition of a thousand copies sold out in six months. David Hume and Thomas Jefferson, among others, praised the book, which went through several editions and foreign translations during Smith's lifetime.[5] A first printing of *The Wealth of Nations* then cost thirty-six shillings. Today a collector might well pay over $150,000 for a first edition.

The Wealth of Nations remains a classic, and various editions can be found in any major bookstore. Which edition should you read? Since the copyright expired, many publishers have put out their own editions, including the University of Glasgow, University of Chicago, Everyman's Library, and Liberty Press; there's even a Bantam paperback, unabridged! My preference is the 1937 (latest reprint, 1994) Modern Library edition, edited by Edwin Cannan.

The significance of *The Wealth of Nations* has reached such biblical proportions that a complete concordance was prepared by Fred R. Glahe (1993), economics professor at the University of Colorado. Oh, the wonders of computers! Did you know that the word "a" appears 6,691 times in *The Wealth of Nations?* A concordance is undoubtedly valuable, especially for scholars. For example, "de-

---

5. I recommend the book *Adam Smith Across Nations: Translations and Receptions of The Wealth of Nations,* edited by Cheng-chung Lai (2000), for a fascinating account of the influence of Adam Smith's book over the centuries.

mand" appears 269 times while "supply" appears only 144 times. Keynes would be pleased.

Smith Is Appointed Customs Official and Burns His Clothes

Following the publication of his classic book, Smith was appointed customs commissioner in Edinburgh, as noted earlier. He also spent time revising his published books, lived a modest life despite his pension, and over the years gave away most of his income in private acts of charity, which he took care to conceal (Rae 1895, 437). He lived in Edinburgh for the remainder of his life.

His position as a customs agent is full of irony. In *The Wealth of Nations,* Smith argued in favor of free trade. He endorsed the elimination of most tariffs and even wrote in sympathy of smuggling. Two years later, in 1778, Smith actively sought a high-level government appointment, possibly to enhance his financial condition. Smith succeeded in his quest and was named Commissioner of Customs in Scotland, despite his previous writings on free trade and the words of his friend Dr. Samuel Johnson, who said that "one of the lowest of all human beings is a Commissioner of Excise" (in Viner 1965, 64). The job was a prestigious position that paid a handsome £600 a year. In a strange paradox, the champion of free trade and laissez-faire spent the last twelve years of his life enforcing Scotland's mercantilist import laws and cracking down on smugglers.

Once in office, Smith acquainted himself with all the rules and regulations of customs law and suddenly discovered that for some time he had personally violated it: Most of the clothes he was wearing had been illegally smuggled into the country. Writing to Lord Auckland, he exclaimed, "I found, to my great astonishment, that I had scarce a stock [neck cloth], a cravat, a pair of ruffles, or a pocket handkerchief which was not prohibited to be worn or used in Great Britain. I wished to set an example and burnt them all."[6] He urged Lord Auckland and his wife to examine their clothing and do the same.

---

6. Letter to William Eden (Lord Auckland), Edinburgh, January 3, 1780, in Smith 1987, 245–46. In his letter, Smith advocated the complete abolition of all import prohibitions, to be replaced by reasonable duties.

Smith intended to write a third philosophical work on politics and jurisprudence, a sequel to his *Theory of Moral Sentiments* and *The Wealth of Nations.*[7] Yet he apparently spent a dozen years enforcing arcane customs laws instead. Such is the lure of government office and job security.

Another Burning Affair in His Final Years

A second burning incident occurred at the end of Smith's life in 1790. He dined every Sunday with his two closest friends, Joseph Black the chemist and James Hutton the geologist, at a tavern in Edinburgh. Several months before his demise, he begged his friends to destroy all his unpublished papers except for a few he deemed nearly ready for publication. (Why he didn't burn the papers himself is a mystery.) This was not a new request. Seventeen years earlier, when he traveled to London with the manuscript of *The Wealth of Nations,* he instructed David Hume, his executor, to destroy all his loose papers and eighteen thin paper folio books "without any examination," and to spare nothing but his fragment on the history of astronomy.

Smith had apparently read about a contemporary figure whose private papers had been exposed to the public in a "tell-all" biography and he feared the same might happen to him. He may have also been concerned about letters or essays written in defense of his friend Hume, who was a religious heretic during a period of intolerance. But Hume died before Smith did, and a new executor of the estate was needed.

Approaching the end of his life, Smith became extremely anxious about his personal papers and repeatedly demanded that his friends Black and Hutton destroy them. Black and Hutton always put off complying with his request, hoping that Smith would come to his senses and change his mind. But a week before he died, he expressly sent for his friends and insisted that they burn all his manuscripts, without knowing or asking what they contained, except for a few items ready for publication. Finally, the two acquiesced and burned virtually everything—sixteen volumes of manuscript, including Smith's manuscript on law.

---

7. Fortunately, extensive student notes on these lectures were discovered in 1958 and published later as *Lectures on Jurisprudence* (1982 [1763]).

After the conflagration, the old professor seemed greatly relieved. When his visitors called upon him the following Sunday evening for their regular supper, he declined to join them. "I love your company, gentlemen, but I believe I must leave you to go to another world." It was his last sentence to them. He died the following Saturday, July 17, 1790.

Adam Smith's Crown Jewel

Let us examine in depth Adam Smith's magnum opus and his revolutionary economic philosophy. An economic system that would allow men and women to pursue their own self-interest under conditions of "natural liberty" and competition would, according to Smith, lead to a self-regulating and highly prosperous economy. Eliminating restrictions on imports, labor, and prices would mean that universal prosperity could be maximized through lower prices, higher wages, and better products. It would provide stability and growth.

Smith Identifies Three Ingredients

Smith began his book with a discussion of how wealth and prosperity are created through democratic free-market order. He highlighted three characteristics of this self-regulating system or classical model:

1. Freedom: individuals have the right to produce and exchange products, labor, and capital as they see fit.

2. Competition: individuals have the right to compete in the production and exchange of goods and services.

3. Justice: the actions of individuals must be just and honest, according to the rules of society.

Note that the following statement by Adam Smith incorporates these three principles: "Every man, as long as he does not violate the laws of *justice,* is left perfectly *free* to pursue his own interest his own way, and to bring both his industry and capital into *competition* with those of any other man, or order of men" (1965 [1776], 651, emphasis added).

The Benefits of the Invisible Hand

Smith argued that these three ingredients would lead to a "natural harmony" of interests between workers, landlords, and capitalists. Recall the pin factory, where management and labor had to work together to achieve their ends, and the woolen coat that required the "joint labor" of workmen, merchants, and carriers from around the world. On a general scale, the voluntary self-interest of millions of individuals would create a stable, prosperous society without the need for central direction by the state. His doctrine of enlightened self-interest is often called "the invisible hand," based on a famous passage (paraphrased) from *The Wealth of Nations:* "By pursuing his own self interest, every individual is led by an invisible hand to promote the public interest" (423).

Adam Smith's invisible hand doctrine has become a popular metaphor for unfettered market capitalism. Although Smith uses the term only once in *The Wealth of Nations,* and sparingly elsewhere, the phrase "invisible hand" has come to symbolize the workings of the market economy as well as the workings of natural science (Ylikoski 1995). Defenders of market economics use it in a positive way, characterizing the market hand as "gentle" (Harris 1998), "wise" and "far reaching" (Joyce 2001), one that "improves the lives of people" (Bush 2002), while contrasting it with the "visible hand," "the hidden hand," "the grabbing hand," "the dead hand," and the "iron fist" of government, whose "invisible foot tramples on people's hopes and destroys their dreams" (Shleifer and Vishny 1998, 3–4; Lindsey 2002; Bush 2002). Critics use contrasting comparisons to express their hostility toward capitalism. To them, the invisible hand of the market may be a "backhand" (Brennan and Pettit 1993), "trembling" and "getting stuck" and "amputated" (Hahn 1982), "palsied" (Stiglitz 2001, 473), "bloody" (Rothschild 2001, 119), and an "iron fist of competition" (Roemer 1988, 2–3).

The invisible hand concept has received surprising praise from economists across the political spectrum. One would expect high praise from free-market advocates, of course. Milton Friedman refers to Adam Smith's symbol as a "key insight" into the cooperative, self-regulating "power of the market [to] produce our food, our clothing, our housing" (Friedman and Friedman 1980, 1). "His vision of the way in which the voluntary actions of millions of individuals can be coordinated through a price system without central direction . . . is a highly sophisticated and subtle insight" (Friedman 1978, 17; cf. Friedman 1981).

Not to be outdone are Keynesian economists. Despite its imperfections, "the invisible hand has an astonishing capacity to handle a coordination problem of truly enormous proportions," declare William Baumol and Alan Blinder (2001, 214). Frank Hahn honors the invisible hand theory as "astonishing" and an appropriate metaphor. "Whatever criticisms I shall level at the theory later, I should like to record that it is a major intellectual achievement. . . . The invisible hand works in harmony [that] leads to the growth in the output of goods which people desire" (Hahn 1982, 1, 4, 8).

The First Fundamental Theorem of Welfare Economics

The invisible hand theory of the marketplace has become known as the "first fundamental theorem of welfare economics."[8] George Stigler calls it the "crown jewel" of *The Wealth of Nations* and "the most important substantive proposition in all of economics." He adds, "Smith had one overwhelmingly important triumph: he put into the center of economics the systematic analysis of the behavior of individuals pursuing their self-interests under conditions of competition" (Stigler 1976, 1201).

Building on the general equilibrium (GE) modeling of Walras, Pareto, Edgeworth, and many other pioneers, Kenneth J. Arrow and Frank Hahn have written an entire book analyzing "an idealized, decentralized economy," and refer to Smith's "poetic expression of the most fundamental of economic balance relations, the equalization of rates of return. . . ." Hahn expects anarchic chaos, but the market creates a "different answer"—spontaneous order. In a broader perspective, Arrow and Hahn declare that Smith's vision "is surely the most important intellectual contribution that economic thought has made to the general understanding of social processes" (Arrow and Hahn 1971, v, vii, 1). Not only does welfare economics (Walras's law,

---

8. In welfare economics, "welfare" refers to the general well-being or common good of the people, not to people on welfare or government assistance.

Pareto's optimality, Edgeworth's box) confirm mathematically and graphically the validity of Adam Smith's principal thesis, but it shows how, in most cases, government-induced monopolies, subsidies, and other forms of noncompetitive behavior lead inevitably to inefficiency and waste (Ingrao and Israel 1990).

Smith's References to the Invisible Hand

Surprisingly, Adam Smith uses the expression "invisible hand" only three times in his writings. The references are so sparse that economists and political commentators seldom mentioned the invisible hand idea by name in the nineteenth century. No references were made to it during the celebrations of the centenary of *The Wealth of Nations* in 1876. In fact, in the famed edited volume by Edwin Cannan, published in 1904, the index does not include a separate entry for "invisible hand." The term only became a popular symbol in the twentieth century (Rothschild 2001, 117–18). But this historical fact should not imply that Smith's metaphor is marginal to his philosophy; it is in reality the central element to his philosophy.

The first mention of the invisible hand is found in Smith's "History of Astronomy," where he discusses superstitious peoples who ascribed unusual events to the handiwork of unseen gods:

> Among savages, as well as in the early ages of Heathen antiquity, it is the irregular events of nature only that are ascribed to the agency and power of their gods. Fire burns, and water refreshes; heavy bodies descend and lighter substances fly upwards, by the necessity of their own nature; nor was the invisible hand of Jupiter ever apprehended to be employed in those matters. (Smith 1982, 49)

A full statement of the invisible hand's economic power occurs in *The Theory of Moral Sentiments,* when Smith describes some unpleasant rich landlords who in "their natural selfishness and rapacity" pursue "their own vain and insatiable desires." And yet they employ several thousand poor workers to produce luxury products:

> The rest he [the proprietor] is obliged to distribute . . . among those . . . which are employed in the economy of greatness; all of whom

thus derive from his luxury and caprice, that share of the necessaries of life, which they would in vain have expected from his humanity or his justice. . . . [T]hey divide with the poor the produce of all their improvements. They are led by an invisible hand to, . . . without intending it, without knowing it, advance the interests of the society. (Smith 1982 [1759], 183–85)

The third mention, already quoted above, occurs in a chapter on international trade in *The Wealth of Nations,* where Smith argues against restrictions on imports, and against the merchants and manufacturers who support their mercantilist views. Here is the complete quotation:

As every individual, therefore, endeavours as much as he can both to employ his capital in the support of domestic industry, and so to direct that industry that its produce may be of the greatest value; every individual necessarily labours to render the annual revenue of the society as great as he can. He generally, indeed, neither intends to promote the public interest, nor knows how much he is promoting it. . . . [A]nd by directing that industry in such a manner as its produce may be of the greatest value, he intends only his own gain, and he is in this, as in many other cases, led by an invisible hand to promote an end which was no part of his intention. Nor is it always the worse for the society that it was no part of it. By pursuing his own interest he frequently promotes that of the society more effectually than when he really intends to promote it. I have never known much good done by those who affected to trade for the public good. (Smith 1965 [1776], 423)

A Positive or Negative Interpretation?

Most observers believe that Adam Smith uses the invisible hand in a positive way, but in her recent book, *Economic Sentiments,* Cambridge professor Emma Rothschild dissents. Using "indirect" evidence, she concludes, "What I will suggest is that Smith did not especially esteem the invisible hand." According to Rothschild, Smith views the invisible hand imagery as a "mildly ironic joke." She goes so far as to claim that it is "un-Smithian, and unimportant to his theory" (Rothschild 2001, 116, 137). She even suggests that Smith may have borrowed the expression from Shakespeare. Rothschild notes that Smith was thoroughly familiar with Act III of *Macbeth.* In the scene immediately

before the banquet and Banquo's murder, Macbeth asks his dark being
to cover up the crimes he is about to commit:

> Come, seeing night,
> Scarf up the tender eye of pitiful day,
> And with thy bloody and invisible hand
> Cancel and tear to pieces that great bond
> Which keeps me pale.

Thus we see an invisible hand that is no longer a gentle hand, but
a bloody, forceful hand. But Rothschild protests too much. Although
Smith used the "invisible hand" phrase only a few times, the idea of
a beneficial invisible hand is ubiquitous in his works. Over and over
again, he reiterated his claim that individuals acting in their own self-
interest unwittingly benefit the public weal. As Jacob Viner interprets
Smith's doctrine, "Providence favors trade among peoples in order to
promote universal brotherhood" (Viner 1972, foreword). Smith repeatedly advocated removal of trade barriers, state-granted privileges, and
employment regulations so that individuals can have the opportunity
to "better their own condition" and thus make everyone better off
(1965 [1776], 329). The idea of the invisible hand doctrine occurs
more often than Rothschild realizes. Very early in *The Theory of Moral
Sentiments,* Smith made his first statement of this doctrine:

> The ancient stoics were of the opinion, that as the world was governed
> by the all-ruling providence of a wise, powerful, and good God, every
> single event ought to be regarded as making a necessary part of the
> plan of the universe, and as tending to promote the general order and
> happiness of the whole: that the vices and follies of mankind, therefore,
> made as necessary part of this plan as their wisdom and their virtue;
> and by that eternal art which educes good from ill, were made to tend
> equally to the prosperity and perfection of the great system of nature.
> (Smith 1982 [1759], 36).

Although Smith failed to mention the invisible hand by name in
this passage, the theme is vividly portrayed. The author cited God
throughout *The Theory of Moral Sentiments,* using such names as the
Author of Nature, Engineer, Great Architect, Creator, the great Judge
of hearts, Deity, and the all-seeing Judge of the world.

How Religious Was Adam Smith?

That God is not mentioned in *The Wealth of Nations* has caused some observers to conclude that Adam Smith, like his closest friend of the Scottish Enlightenment, David Hume, was a nonbeliever. Smith did in fact share many values with Hume. Neither of them was a churchgoer or traditional believer in the Christian faith. Both Scottish philosophers opposed the Greco-Christian doctrine of antimaterialism and anticommercialism, and the Christian philosophy that carnal desires are inherently evil. Smith, like Hume, believed that a moral, prosperous society was possible in this life, and not just in the life to come, and that this civil society should be based on science and reason, not religious superstition and authoritarianism. Both advocated free trade, opposed the mercantilist system of government subsidies and regulations, and warned of the dangers of big government (Fitzgibbons 1995, 14–18).

Yet Smith explicitly opposed important aspects of Hume's philosophy, especially his hostility toward organized religion. Hume favored a noncompetitive state religion because it would sap the zeal of religious followers and maintain political order. Smith, on the other hand, opposed a state religion, which he thought would encourage intolerance and fanaticism. He thought religion was beneficial if religious beliefs and organizations were free and open. "In little religious sects, the morals of common people have been almost remarkably regular and orderly: generally much more so than in the established church" (1965 [1776], 747–48). He favored "a great multitude of religious sects" and a competitive atmosphere that would reduce zeal and fanaticism and promote tolerance, moderation, and rational religion (744–45).[9] Smith himself secretly made many charitable contributions in his lifetime, and once helped a blind young man to prepare for an intellectual career (Fitzgibbons 1995, 138).

Smith rejected Hume's amoral philosophy and both his nihilistic

---

9. Laurence Iannaccone (George Mason University), Robert Barro (Harvard), and Edwin West have tested Smith's hypothesis on religious freedom, comparing attendance at church and the degree of monopoly in various Protestant and Catholic countries, and have concluded that church attendance tends to increase in countries with religious freedom and a wide variety of religious faiths. See Iannaccone (1991), West (1990).

attitude toward informed judgment and his extreme skepticism toward traditional virtue, as found in *A Treatise on Human Nature.* Unlike Hume, Smith was a believer in a final reconciler. His faith was more in keeping with the Deist belief in a Stoic God and Stoic nature than in a personal Christian God of revelation, or rewards and punishments in a future life. His *Theory of Moral Sentiments* endured six editions during his lifetime, and the final one, written after *The Wealth of Nations,* makes frequent references to God. As Robert Heilbroner states, the theme of "the Invisible Hand . . . runs through all of the *Moral Sentiments.* . . . The Invisible Hand refers to the means by which 'the Author of nature' has assured that humankind will achieve His purposes despite the frailty of its reasoning powers" (Heilbroner 1986, 60).

Smith followed Hume in rejecting creeds and institutionalized churches, but there is little doubt that Adam Smith did believe in a Creator. As A.L. Macfie concludes, "the whole tone of his work will convince most that he was an essentially pious man" (Macfie 1967, 111).

Adam Smith's overwhelming theme throughout his works was to provide a liberal democratic society, a "system of natural liberty," where freedom is maximized economically, politically, and religiously, within a workable moral foundation of laws, customs, and values.

Faith in an Invisible God

Historian Athol Fitzgibbons has aptly called this new economic blueprint "Adam Smith's System of Liberty, Wealth, and Virtue" (1995). If this "new account of Smith" is true, the invisible hand metaphor is an entirely appropriate way to describe his system of natural liberty, since establishing a virtuous society requires a systematic understanding of right and wrong.

As indicated earlier, the invisible hand is another name Smith used to describe God. As Salim Rashid states, "perhaps the 'Invisible Hand' can be thought of as the directing hand of the Deity" (Rashid 1998, 219). Though not a traditional Christian, Smith was familiar with the Bible and Christian beliefs. In the Bible, providence is sometimes called the "Invisible God." St. Paul wrote to Timothy, "Now unto the King eternal, immortal, invisible, the only wise God, be honour and glory for ever. Amen" (1 Timothy 1:17; see also Colossians 1:15–16).

It is curious how frequently modern-day economists have invoked religious terminology in describing the invisible hand. In his famous essay, "I, Pencil," Leonard Read (a devotee of the Austrian school) characterizes the invisible hand's work in the creation of the pencil as a "mystery" and a "miracle" (Read 1999 [1958], 10–11). Milton Friedman uses similar language (Friedman and Friedman 1980, 3, 11–13). Frank Hahn notes that the invisible hand concept assumes "a lively sense of original sin [inherent in] a society of greedy and self-seeking people" (Hahn 1982, 1, 5). James Tobin talks of "true believers in the invisible hand" (Tobin 1992, 119). And this religious symbolism brings us to the four degrees of faith and how to apply it to the warring schools of economics.

Varying Degrees of Faith in Capitalism

The Bible discusses a hierarchy of individual faith in God and his works, differentiating among those who have no faith, little faith, great faith, and complete faith in the existence of a higher being. God is "invisible." Consequently, people differ widely in their religious beliefs. In today's world, a few true believers have absolute faith in God, that he lives and works miracles in their lives, and never doubt. Others have great faith in miraculous powers, though they may occasionally doubt. At the same time there are many who have little faith in God; they occasionally see his "invisible" handiwork, but seldom attend church. Finally, there are agnostics and atheists, who have no faith in God, who reject the idea of revelation or the supernatural, and who rely solely on the five senses, the natural world, and reason.

Just as people have varying levels of faith in an "invisible God," so people have differing degrees of belief in the beneficial "invisible hand" of capitalism and freedom. By faith, I mean a certain degree of confidence that, left to their own devices, individuals acting in their own self-interest will generate a positive outcome. Faith represents a level of predictability of the future: Will an unfettered economy recover on its own from a recession? Will eliminating tariffs between two countries increase trade and jobs between them? Will decontrolling oil prices eliminate the energy crisis? Will technological unemployment in one industry lead to new employment in another? Will a competitive environment eventually break down monopolistic power in a particular market? Individuals have differing levels of confidence in the marketplace to respond positively to change or crisis. Some have full faith that all will work out for the better. Others have great faith that in most cases private actions will benefit society. Still others have little faith in the free market and worry that, most of the time, private enterprise does what is best for individual people but not for society. Finally, there are a few who deny that any good thing can come from the dog-eat-dog chaotic world of Mammon, that the multinational corporate world is so corrupt and crisis-prone that nothing can improve the matter save major institutional reform or outright revolution.

In chapter 9 of my book *Vienna and Chicago, Friends or Foes?* I identify four schools of economics that fit these varying levels of belief in capitalism and free markets: the hard-core Marxists have no faith that the capitalist system can solve social problems; the Keynesians have doubts about the invisible hand; the Chicago economists have great faith that capitalism works; and the Austrians have perfect, sometimes even blind, faith in capitalism (Skousen 2005, 261–67).

Does Adam Smith Condone Egotism and Greed?

Critics worry that the Scottish blueprint for freedom would also give license to avarice and fraud, even "social strife, ecological damage, and the abuse of power" (Lux 1990). Is not *The Wealth of Nations* an unabashed endorsement of selfish greed and vanity? How could Adam Smith ignore everyday cases of rapacious capitalists deceiving, defrauding, and taking advantage of customers, thus pursuing their own self-interest at the expense of the public?

Contrary to popular belief, Smith did not condone greed, egotism, and Western-style decadence, nor did he want economic efficiency to replace morality. Self-interest does not mean ignoring the needs of others; in fact, it means just the opposite: his system assures that both buyer and seller benefit from every voluntary transaction. Most readers have misjudged Smith's famous quote, "It is not from the benevolence of the butcher, the brewer, or the baker, that we expect our dinner, but from their regard to their own interest." Here is the context of this statement:

> But man has almost constant occasion for the help of his brethren, and it is in vain for him to expect it from their benevolence only. He will be more

likely to prevail if he can interest their self-love in his favour, and shew them that it is for their own advantage to do for him what he requires of them. . . . Give me that which I want, and you shall have this which you want, is the meaning of every such offer. It is not from the benevolence of the butcher, the brewer, or the baker, that we expect our dinner, but from their regard to their own interest. We address ourselves, not to their humanity but to their self-love, and never talk to them of our own necessities but of their advantages. (Smith 1965 [1776], 14)

What Adam Smith is saying is that you can only help yourself by helping others—the Golden Rule. Businesses that focus on fulfilling the needs and desires of their customers will be the most profitable. Although capitalists are motivated by the desire for personal gain, the way that they maximize their profits is by focusing their everyday attention on meeting the needs of the public. Thus, the successful capitalist inevitably orients his everyday conduct toward the task of helping and serving others. Self-interest leads to empathy.

Smith favored self-restraint. Indeed, he firmly asserted that a free commercial society functioning within the legal restraints he outlined would moderate the passions and prevent a descent into a Hobbesian jungle, a theme he inherits from Montesquieu (see pages 40–41) and later Senior Nassau.[10] He taught that commerce encourages people to become educated, industrious, and self-disciplined, and to defer gratification. It is the fear of losing customers "which restrains his [the seller's] frauds and corrects his negligence" (1965 [1776], 129).

All legitimate exchanges must benefit both the buyer and the seller, not one at the expense of the other. Smith's invisible hand only works if businessmen have an enlightened long-term view of competition, where they recognize the value of reputation and repeat business. In short, self-interest promotes the interests of society only when the producer responds to the needs of the customer. When the customer is defrauded or deceived, an event that occurs all too frequently in the marketplace, self-interest succeeds at the expense of society's welfare.

---

10. In his inaugural address as the first Drummond Professor of Political Economy at Oxford, Senior Nassau predicted that the new science "will rank in public estimation among the first of moral sciences," and claimed that "the pursuit of wealth . . . is, to the mass of mankind, the great source of moral improvement" (Schumacher 1973, 33–34).

Smith recognized that people are motivated by self-interest. It is natural to look out for one's self and one's family above all interests, and to reject this would be to deny human nature. Yet at the same time, Smith did not condone greed or selfishness. For Adam Smith, greed and selfishness are vices. He would be uncomfortable with Ayn Rand's calling selfishness a virtue, or Walter Williams's labeling greed a good thing (Rand 1964). However, Smith accepted these as human frailties, and he contended that these base motives cannot be outlawed or prohibited, only that they might be discouraged and moderated in a commercial society with the right incentives. As Dinesh D'Souza interprets Smith, "Capitalism civilizes greed in much the same way that marriage civilizes lust. Greed, like lust, is part of our human nature; it would be futile to try to root it out. What capitalism does is to channel greed in such a way that it works to meet the wants and needs of society" (D'Souza 2005).

In fact, Smith's ideal society would be infused with virtue, mutual benevolence, and civic laws prohibiting unjust and fraudulent business practices. Smith's "impartial spectator" reflects the moral standards and judgment of the community (Smith 1982 [1759], 215 passim). His economic man is cooperative and fair without harming others. A good moral climate and legal system would benefit economic growth. Smith supported social institutions—the market, religious communities, and the law—to foster self-control, self-discipline, and benevolence (Muller 1993:2). After all, Adam Smith was not just an economist, but a professor of moral philosophy.

Das Adam Smith Problem: Sympathy Versus Self-Interest

In his 1759 work, *The Theory of Moral Sentiments,* Adam Smith wrote that "sympathy" was the driving force behind a benevolent, prosperous society. In *The Wealth of Nations,* "self-interest" became the primary motive. German philosophers called this apparent contradiction *Das Adam Smith Problem,* but Smith himself saw no conflict between the two. He took an historical perspective. In a precapitalist community described in *The Theory of Moral Sentiments,* benevolence, or love, was probably the most dominant factor within the family or in relations with colleagues and friends in a village where everyone knew each other. However, in the capitalist industrial world, cities such as

London and Paris attract thousands of strangers and the motivation changes from sympathy to self-interest in economic activity, for "it is in vain to expect it from their benevolence only" (1965 [1776], 14).

Smith combined both motives in *The Wealth of Nations,* where sympathy and self-interest were the driving motivators in a modern capitalist society. Smith believed that every man had a basic desire to be accepted by others. To obtain this sympathy, people would act in a manner that would gain respect and admiration. In economic life, this meant enlightened self-interest, wherein both seller and buyer mutually benefit in their transactions. Moreover, Smith contended that economic progress and surplus wealth were a prerequisite for sympathy and charity. In short, Smith desired to integrate economics and moral behavior (Fitzgibbons 1995, 3–4; Tvede 1997, 29).

The Scottish philosopher believed man to be motivated by both self-interest and benevolence, but in a complex market economy, where individuals move away from their closest friends and family, self-interest becomes a more powerful force. In Ronald Coase's interpretation, "The great advantage of the market is that it is able to use the strength of self-interest to offset the weakness and partiality of benevolence, so that those who are unknown, unattractive, and unimportant will have their wants served" (Coase 1976, 544).

How Monopoly Hurts the Market System

Smith said that competition was absolutely essential to turning self-interest into benevolence in a self-regulating society. He preferred the cheaper "natural price, or the price of free competition" to the high price of monopoly power and "exclusive privileges" granted certain corporations and trading companies (such as the East India Company). Smith vehemently opposed the "mean rapacity" and "wretched spirit of monopoly" (428) to which privileged businessmen were accustomed. Competition means lower prices and more money to buy other goods, which in turn means more jobs and a higher standard of living. According to Smith, monopoly power creates a political society, characterized by flattery, fawning, and deceit (Muller 1993, 135). Monopoly fosters quick and easy profits and wasteful consumption (Smith 1965 [1776], 578).

While believing in the marketplace, Smith was no apologist for merchants and special interests. In one of his more famous passages, he complained, "People of the same trade seldom meet together, even for merriment and diversion, but the conversation ends in a conspiracy against the public, or in some contrivance to raise prices" (128). His goal was to convince legislators to resist supporting the vested interests of merchants and instead to act in favor of the common good.

Adam Smith Updated

Adam Smith's model offers two hypotheses: first, that his system of natural liberty would lead to a higher standard of living; and second, that the effects of economic liberalism would benefit rich and poor alike. Since Smith wrote his book, have economists confirmed or denied these propositions? Let us examine each hypothesis.

Update 1: Free Economies Are Richer

First, has economic freedom led to higher living standards? If Adam Smith were alive today, he would undoubtedly credit a free and democratic capitalism with the widespread increase in the standard of living. An exhaustive study by James Gwartney, Robert A. Lawson, and Walter Block released in 1996 and updated subsequently each year by Gwartney and Lawson (see 2004) appears to confirm this Smithian view that economic freedom and prosperity are closely related. The authors painstakingly constructed an index measuring the level of economic freedom for more than 100 countries, based on five criteria (size of government, property rights and legal structure, sound money, trade, and regulations). Then they compared the each country's level of economic freedom with its growth rate, based on per capita income in purchasing power terms. Their conclusion is documented in the remarkable graph in Figure 1.2.

According to this study, the greater the degree of freedom, the higher the standard of living, as measured by per capita real gross domestic product (GDP) in purchasing power terms. Nations with the highest level of freedom (e.g., the United States, New Zealand, Hong Kong) grew faster than nations with moderate degrees of freedom (e.g., the United Kingdom, Canada, Germany) and substantially more

Figure 1.2   **Relationship Between Economic Freedom and per Capita GDP, 2005**

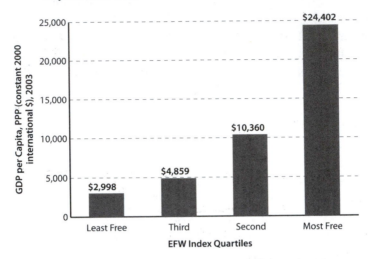

Countries with more economic freedom have substantially higher per-capita incomes.

Source: The Fraser Institute, Vancouver, B.C.

rapidly than nations with little economic freedom (e.g., Venezuela, Iran, Congo). The authors conclude, "Countries with more economic freedom attract more investment and achieve greater productivity from their resources. As a result, they grow more rapidly and achieve higher income levels" (Gwartney and Lawson 2004, 38).

What about those countries that change policies? Gwartney and Lawson state, "Countries stagnate when their institutions stifle trade and erode the incentives to engage in productive activities. . . . Countries with low initial levels of income, in particular, are able to grow rapidly and move up the income ladder when their policies are supportive of economic freedom" (2004, 38).

Update 2: The Poor Benefit from Capitalism

Second, Adam Smith argued that both rich and poor benefit from a liberal economic system. He declared, "universal opulence . . . extends itself to the lowest ranks of the people" (Smith 1965 [1776], 11). The modern-day statistical work of Stanley Lebergott and Michael Cox

Table 1.1

U.S. Living Standards, 1900–70

Percentage of households with	Among all families in 1900 (%)	Among poor families in 1970 (%)
Flush toilets	15	99
Running water	24	92
Central heating	1	58
One (or fewer) occupants per room	48	96
Electricity	3	99
Refrigeration	18	99
Automobiles	1	41

Source: Lebergott (1976, 8).
Reprinted by permission of Princeton University Press.

confirms this Smithian view and disputes the commonly held criticism that under a free market the rich get richer and the poor get poorer. The poor also get rich, according to recent studies by Lebergott (1976) and Cox and Alm (1999).

Stanley Lebergott, professor emeritus at Wesleyan University, has studied individual consumer markets in food, clothing, housing, fuel, housework, transportation, health, recreation, and religion. For example, he developed the statistics shown in Table 1.1 to show improvements in living standards from 1900 to 1970.

As Lebergott's table shows, the standard of living has risen substantially for all classes, including the lowest, in the twentieth century. He confirms the statement once made by Andrew Carnegie: "Capitalism is about turning luxuries into necessities." Through the competitive efforts of entrepreneurs, workers, and capitalists, virtually all American consumers have been able to change an uncertain and often cruel world into a more pleasant and convenient place to live and work. A typical homestead in 1900 had no central heating, electricity, refrigeration, flush toilets, or even running water. Today even a large majority of poor Americans benefit from these goods and services.

Another recent study by Michael Cox, an economist at the Federal Reserve Bank of Dallas, and Richard Alm, a business writer for the *Dallas Morning News*, concludes that the real prices of housing, food, gasoline, electricity, telephone service, home appliances, clothing, and other everyday necessities have fallen significantly during the twentieth century. The researchers also demonstrate that the poor in America have seen gradual improvements in their economic lives as well. More poor people own homes, automobiles, and other consumer products than ever before, and televisions are found in even the poorest households (Cox and Alm 1999).

Finally, Gwartney and Lawson have done studies showing that the poorest 10 percent of the world's population earn more income when the countries in which they live adopt institutions favoring economic freedom (2004, 23). Economic freedom also reduces infant mortality, the incidence of child labor, black markets, and corruption by public officials, while increasing adult literacy, life expectancy, and civil liberties (2004, 22–26).

Smith Favors a Strong But Limited Government

As a proponent of the Scottish Enlightenment and the virtues of natural liberty, Adam Smith was a firm believer in a parsimonious but strong government. He wrote of three purposes of government: "Little else is required to carry a state to the highest degree of opulence from the lowest barbarism, but peace, easy taxes, and a tolerable administration of justice" (in Danhert 1974, 218). More specifically, Smith endorsed (1) the need for a well-financed militia for national defense; (2) a legal system to protect liberty and property rights, and to enforce contracts and payment of debts; (3) public works—roads, canals, bridges, harbors, and other infrastructure projects; and (4) universal public education to counter the alienating and mentally degrading effects of specialization (division of labor) under capitalism (Smith 1965 [1776], 734–35).

In general, the Scottish professor favored a maximum degree of personal liberty in society, including a diversity of entertainment—as long as it was "without scandal or indecency" (748). Smith was no pure libertarian.

Smith Warns About the Dangers of Big Government

At the same time, he was a sharp critic of state power. Politicians are usually spendthrift hypocrites, according to Smith. Some of the following quotes from *The Wealth of Nations* could be used in political debates today:

> There is no art which one government sooner learns of another, than that of draining money from the pockets of the people. (813)
>
> It is the highest impertinence and presumption, therefore, in kings and ministers, to pretend to watch over the economy of private people, and to restrain their expense, either by sumptuary laws, or by prohibiting the importation of foreign luxuries. They are themselves always, and without exception, the greatest spendthrifts in the society. Let them look well after their own expense, and they may safely trust private people with theirs. If their own extravagance does not ruin the state, that of their subjects never will. (329)
>
> Great nations are never impoverished by private, though they sometimes are by public prodigality and misconduct. The whole, or almost the whole public revenue, is in most countries employed in maintaining unproductive hands. Such are the people who compose a numerous and splendid court, a great ecclesiastical establishment, great fleets and armies, who in time of peace produce nothing, and in time of war acquire nothing which can compensate the expense of maintaining them, even while the war lasts. Such people, as they themselves produce nothing, are all maintained by the produce of other men's labour. (325)

Smith pleaded for balanced budgets and opposed a large public debt. He advocated privatization, the sale of crown lands as a way to raise revenues and cultivate property. He favored minimal government interference in citizens' personal lives and economic activity. Smith argued that war is unnecessary and ill advised in most cases, and that ending a war will not result in massive unemployment (436–37).

He sounded as if he had just been audited by revenue agents when he expressed sympathy for taxpayers "continually exposed to the mortifying and vexatious visits of the tax-collectors" (880). After lambasting the complexity and inequality of the tax system, he prescribed tax cuts across the board, although he favored rigid usury laws and progressive taxation.

Perhaps the following statement by Smith, taken from *The Theory of Moral Sentiments,* most eloquently expresses the universal principles of individualism and liberty, and the dangers of government:

> The man of system . . . seems to imagine that he can arrange the different members of a great society with as much ease as the hand arranges the different pieces upon a chess-board. He does not consider that the pieces upon the chess-board have no other principle of motion besides that which the hand impresses upon them; but that, in the great chess-board of human society, every single piece has a principle of motion of its own, altogether different from that which the legislature might choose to impress upon it. If those two principles coincide and act in the same direction, the game of human society will go on easily and harmoniously, and is very likely to be happy and successful. If they are opposite or different, the game will go on miserably, and the society must be at all times in the highest degree of disorder. (Smith 1982 [1759], 233–34)

Smith Endorses Sound Money and the Gold Standard

Smith also worried about governments' manipulation of the monetary system. While rejecting the idea that gold and silver alone constitute a country's wealth, he favored a stable monetary system based on precious metals, and supported the doctrine of free banking. He also rejected the prevalent "quantity theory of money," which holds that the price level rises or falls in proportion to changes in the money supply. In his "Digression on Silver," Smith showed that prices have varied considerably when the supply of silver (money) increased (1965 [1776], 240).

The Essence of the Classical Model of Economics

In sum, the classical model developed by Adam Smith and endorsed by his disciples in generations to come consisted of four general principles:

1. Thrift, hard work, enlightened self-interest, and benevolence toward fellow citizens are virtues and should be encouraged.

2. Government should limit its activities to administer justice, enforce private property rights, engage in certain public works, and defend the nation against aggression.

3. The state should adopt a general policy of laissez-faire non-interventionism in economic affairs (free trade, low taxes, minimal bureaucracy, etc.).

4. The classical gold/silver standard restrains the state from depreciating the currency and provides a stable monetary environment in which the economy may flourish.

As we shall see, the classical model of Adam Smith would repeatedly come under attack over the centuries by friends and foes alike.

Adam Smith and the Age of Economists

Adam Smith was not perfect by any means. He led disciples David Ricardo and Thomas Malthus down the wrong road with his crude labor theory of value, his critique of landlords, his strange distinction between "productive" and "unproductive" labor, and his failure to recognize the fundamental principle of subjective marginal utility in price theory. But these are parenthetical deviations that were unfortunately magnified by the classical economists and distort his overwhelming positive contribution to economic science.

Adam Smith is to be congratulated for his fierce defense of free trade and free markets, his central theme of "natural liberty," and a self-regulating system of competitive free enterprise and limited government. His eloquent expression of economic liberty helped free the world from provincial mercantilism and heavy-handed intervention by the state. Without his leadership, the Industrial Revolution might have stalled for another century or more.

The Great Optimist

Adam Smith, a child of the Scottish Enlightenment, was above all an optimist about the future of the world. His principal focus throughout his economic magnum opus was the "improvement" of the individual through "frugality and good conduct," saving and investing, exchange and the division of labor, education and capital formation, and new technology. He was more interested in increasing wealth than dividing it (in sharp contrast to his disciple

David Ricardo). According to Adam Smith, even a powerful, sinister government cannot stop progress:

"The uniform, constant, and uninterrupted effort of every man to better his condition . . . is frequently powerful enough to maintain the natural progress of things toward improvement, in spite both of the extravagance of government, and of the greatest errors of administration" (1965 [1776], 326; cf. 508).

Adam Smith Makes a Famous Remark

During the American Revolution, Adam Smith was approached by a citizen who was alarmed by the defeat of the British at Saratoga in 1777. "The nation must be ruined," the man exclaimed with panic in his voice. Smith, then in his fifties, replied calmly, "Be assured, my young friend, that there is a great deal of ruin in a nation" (Rae 1895, 343; Ross 1995, 327). Smith's dictum is frequently cited by Milton Friedman, Gary Becker, and other economists in response to economic doomsayers. It suggests that a nation has built up such tremendous wealth, institutions, and goodwill over the centuries that it would take more than a major war or natural disaster to destroy it.

His life complete, Adam Smith may well have entertained the words of the psalmist, "Return unto thy rest, O my soul: for the Lord hath dealt bountifully with thee" (Psalm 116:7).

Appendix: The Pre-Adamites

Adam Smith did not create modern economics out of a vacuum, the way Athena sprang full grown and fully armed from the brow of Zeus. Instead, Smith was influenced by a wide number of economic thinkers, going all the way back to the ancient Greek philosophers.

Plato and Aristotle

A child of the Scottish Enlightenment, Smith would find little appeal in reading Plato's *Republic,* which advocated an ideal city-state ruled by collectivist philosopher-kings. He considered

Aristotle better, because of his defense of private property and his critique of Plato's communism. Private property, according to Aristotle, would give people the opportunity to practice the virtues of benevolence and philanthropy, all part of the Aristotelian "golden mean" and "good life." But Adam Smith would have no part of Aristotle's scorn of moneymaking and his denunciation of monetary trade and retail commerce as immoral and "unnatural," a philosophy that was later sanctioned by many Christian writers in the Middle Ages.

Protestants, Catholics, and the Spanish Scholastics

Adam Smith was greatly influenced by Calvinist doctrines favoring thrift and hard work while condemning excessive luxury, usury, and "unproductive" service labor. Catholics and Protestants alike debated what constituted "just price" in a market economy. The Spanish scholastics in the sixteenth century determined that the "just price" was nothing more than the common market price, and they generally supported a laissez-faire philosophy (Rothbard 1995a, 97–133). As Montesquieu later wrote, "It is competition that puts a just price on goods and establishes the true relations between them" (Montesquieu 1989 [1748], 344).

In many ways, Adam Smith aimed to replace the antimaterialist Greco-Christian doctrines of Western Europe, which were a hindrance to liberty and economic growth, with a system that combined moral living and the reasonable pursuit of material desires (Fitzgibbons 1995, v, 16).

Bernard Mandeville and *The Fable of the Bees*

Some economists contend that Adam Smith developed his "invisible hand" concept from the scandalous work *The Fable of the Bees* (1997 [1714]), by Bernard Mandeville (1670–1733), a Dutch psychiatrist and pamphleteer. In the first version, Mandeville told the story of a thriving "grumbling hive" of bees that turned "honest" and was swiftly reduced to poverty and destruction after converting to a moral community. In the second popular edition, Mandeville described a prosperous community in which all the citizens decided to abandon their luxurious spending habits and military armaments. The result was a depression and collapse in trade and housing. His conclusion: private vices of greed, avarice, and luxury lead to public benefits of abundant wealth, and "the Moment Evil ceases, the Society must be spoiled, if not totally dissolved." Clearly, under Mandeville's infamous paradox, self-interest results in social benefit.

Both Friedrich Hayek and John Maynard Keynes have written approvingly of Mandeville's fable. According to Hayek, Adam Smith gained insights into the division of labor, self-interest, economic liberty, and the idea of unintended consequences from Mandeville (Hayek 1984, 184–85). Keynes approved of Mandeville's antisaving sentiments and statist pressures to assure full employment in society (Keynes 1973a [1936], 358–61).

However, it is clear in *The Theory of Moral Sentiments* that Smith did not approve of Mandeville. Calling his book "wholly pernicious" and his thesis "erroneous," Smith disagreed that economic progress is achieved through greed, vanity, and unrestrained self-love, complaining that Mandeville seems to make no distinction between vice and virtue (Smith 1982 [1759], 308–10).

Montesquieu and *Doux Commerce*

Smith's attitude toward self-interest was more positively affected by the great French jurist and philosopher Charles de Secondat Montesquieu (1689–1755). His book *The Spirit of the Laws,* first published in 1748, encouraged James Madison and Alexander Hamilton to push for constitutional separation of powers, a concept endorsed by Smith. Montesquieu, who wrote before the Industrial Revolution, saw many virtues in *doux commerce* (gentle commerce). He expressed the novel view that the pursuit of profit making and commercial interests serve as a countervailing bridle against the violent passions of war and abusive political power. "Commerce cures destructive prejudices," Montesquieu declared, "it polishes and softens barbarous mores. . . . The natural effect of commerce is to lead to peace" (1989, 338). According to Montesquieu, Sir James Steuart, and other *philosophes* of the era, the image of the merchant and moneymaker as a peaceful, dispassionate, innocent fellow was in sharp contrast with "the looting armies and murderous pirates of the time"

(Hirschman 1997, 63). Commerce improves the political order: "The spirit of commerce brings with it the spirit of frugality, of economy, of moderation, of work, of wisdom, of tranquility, of order, and of regularity" (Hirschman 1997, 71).[11] As pointed out in this chapter, Smith endorsed this progressive view of commercial society.

In the French edition of *The General Theory*, John Maynard Keynes rated Montesquieu as France's greatest economist, primarily due to his embryonic liquidity-preference theory of interest, his opposition to hoarding, and his advocacy of a high level of money expenditure to maintain and promote economic welfare. Yet, unlike Keynes, Montesquieu was a passionate supporter of the doctrine of laissez-faire. He detested authoritarian regimes and rejected all forms of central planning, which, he said, robbed society of its natural dynamics. He defended free trade as a civilizing, educating, and cooperative force between nations. Like Adam Smith, he recognized that goods and services rather than precious metals represented the real wealth of a nation. He opposed excessive monetary inflation as ruinous, using Spain as an example. Before the Physiocrats popularized the erroneous doctrine that agriculture was the sole source of wealth, Montesquieu taught that industry and commerce were equally significant as fountains of prosperity. Entrepreneurship and frugality were essential ingredients to economic growth. And, unlike Malthus, Montesquieu regarded a large, growing population as desirable.

Dr. François Quesnay and His *Tableau Économique*

The most prominent Physiocrat encountered by Adam Smith in France was the eminent surgeon and doctor François Quesnay (1694–1774), who at one time was the personal physician of King Louis XV's favorite mistress. His famous diagram, the *tableau économique*, was

---

11. Montesquieu's propitious image of capitalism reflects the famous line by Dr. Samuel Johnson, "There are few ways in which a man can be more innocently employed than in getting money" (Boswell 1933, I, 657). It was John Maynard Keynes who wrote, "It is better that a man should tyrannize over his bank balance than over his fellow-citizens" (Keynes 1973a [1936], 374). Today we might say, "Better that a person tyrannizes over his favorite sports team (or his favorite stock) than over his fellow man."

considered by contemporaries as one of the three greatest economics inventions of mankind, after writing and money (Smith 1965 [1776], 643).

Quesnay's zigzag diagram, first published in 1758, has created considerable interest and controversy over the years. It has been hailed as a forerunner of many developments in modern economics: econometrics, Keynes's multiplier, input–output analysis, the circular flow diagram, and a Walrasian general equilibrium model. It is certainly a "macro" view of the economy, without any reference to prices, but no one is sure of its real meaning. As the principal spokesman for the Physiocrats, Quesnay endorsed the false belief in agriculture as the only "productive" expenditure and industry as "sterile."

As to Quesnay's influence, *The Wealth of Nations* proclaimed Dr. Quesnay a "very ingenious and profound author" who promoted the popular slogan "Laissez faire, laissez passer," a phrase Smith would endorse wholeheartedly, although he himself never referred to his system as laissez-faire economics. (He preferred "natural liberty" or "perfect liberty.") As a leading Physiocrat, Quesnay opposed French mercantilism, protectionism, and state interventionist policies. However, *The Wealth of Nations* denied the basic physiocratic premise that agriculture, not manufacturing and commerce, was the source of all wealth (1965 [1776], 637–52).

Richard Cantillon

The other prominent influences on the Scottish economist were Richard Cantillon, Jacques Turgot, and Etienne Bonnot de Condillac. Richard Cantillon (1680–1734) is regarded by Murray Rothbard and other economic historians as the true "father of modern economics."

An Irish merchant banker and adventurer who emigrated to Paris, Cantillon became involved in John Law's infamous Mississippi bubble in 1717–20, but shrewdly sold all of his shares before the financial storm hit. His independent status allowed him to write a short book on economics, *Essay on the Nature of Commerce in General* (published posthumously in 1755). He died mysteriously in London in 1734, apparently murdered by an irate servant who subsequently burned down his house to cover up the crime.

Cantillon's *Essay* is really quite impressive and undoubtedly influenced Adam Smith. It focuses on the automatic market mechanism of supply and demand, the vital role of entrepreneurship (downplayed in *The Wealth of Nations*), and a sophisticated "pre-Austrian" analysis of monetary inflation—how inflation not only raises prices, but changes the pattern of spending.

Jacques Turgot

Jacques Turgot (1727–81) was a leading French Physiocrat whose profound work, *Reflections on the Formation and Distribution of Wealth* (1766), also inspired Adam Smith. As a devoted free trader and advocate of laissez-faire, Turgot was an able minister of finance under Louis XVI; he dissolved all the medieval guilds, abolished all restrictions on the grain trade, and maintained a balanced budget. Turgot was so effective that he provoked the ire of the King, who dismissed him in 1776.

As a Physiocrat, Turgot defended agriculture as the most productive sector of the economy, but beyond that, his *Reflections* exhibited a profound understanding of economics, even surpassing Smith in many areas. His lucid work offers a brilliant understanding of time preference, capital and interest rates, and the role of the capitalist-entrepreneur in a competitive economy. He even described the law of diminishing returns, later popularized by Malthus and Ricardo.

Condillac

Another influential French economist and philosopher was Etienne Bonnot de Condillac (1714–80). He lived the life of a Paris intellectual in the mid-1770s and came to the defense of Turgot in the difficulties he faced in 1775 as finance minister over the grain riots. Like Turgot and Montesquieu, Condillac supported free trade. His important work *Commerce and Government* was published in 1776, only one month before *The Wealth of Nations*. Condillac's economics was amazingly advanced. He recognized that manufacturing was productive, that exchange represented unequal values, that both sides gain from commerce, and that prices are determined by utility value, not labor value (Macleod 1896).

David Hume

The great philosopher David Hume (1711–76) was a close friend of Adam Smith and was highly influential in his limited writings on trade and money. Smith identified his Scottish friend as "by far the most illustrious philosopher and historian" of his age (Fitzgibbons 1995, 9) and "nearly to the idea of a perfectly wise and virtuous man, as perhaps the nature of human frailty will permit" (Smith 1947, 248). Hume opposed ascetic self-denial and endorsed luxury and the materialistic good life.

Like Smith, Hume condemned the mercantilist restraints on international trade. Using his famous "specie-flow" mechanism, Hume proved that attempts to restrict imports and increase specie (precious metals) inflow would backfire. Import restrictions would raise domestic prices, which in turn would reduce exports, increase imports, and generate a return outflow of specie.

Hume also debunked mercantilist claims that acquiring more specie would lower interest rates and promote prosperity. Hume made the classical argument that real interest rates are determined by the supply of saving and capital, not by the money supply. An adherent to the quantity theory of money, Hume felt that an artificial expansion of the money supply would simply raise prices.

Smith's close friendship with Hume caused many observers to conclude that he endorsed Hume's antireligious rebellion and his purely secular commercial society. They point to the fact that God is not mentioned in *The Wealth of Nations*. However, as noted earlier, Smith did not abandon his religious beliefs. His *Theory of Moral Sentiments,* which he edited again after the publication of *The Wealth of Nations,* makes numerous references to God and religion.

Smith was admittedly no longer a practicing Presbyterian, rebelling against austere Calvinist behavior, but he was a believer, a Deist who adopted the Stoic belief that God works through nature. As an optimist, Smith believed in the goodness of the world and envisioned a heaven on earth.

Benjamin Franklin

Biographers John Rae and Ian Simpson Ross give credence to the story that the American founding father, Benjamin Franklin (1706–90), developed a friendship with Adam Smith and had some influence on his writing *The Wealth of Nations*. John Rae recounted how Franklin visited with Smith in Scotland and London and, according to a friend of Franklin, "Adam Smith when writing his *Wealth of Nations* was in the habit of bringing chapter after chapter as he composed it to himself [Franklin], Dr. Price, and others of the literati; then patiently hear their observations and profit by their discussions and criticisms, sometimes submitting to write whole chapters anew, and even to reverse some of his propositions" (Rae 1895, 264–65; see also Ross 1995, 255–56).

In his economic writings, Franklin wrote about the advantages of thrift, free trade, and a growing population, themes readily apparent in *The Wealth of Nations*. (However, I'm not sure Smith would agree with Franklin's case, published in 1728, for advocating a large increase of paper currency to stimulate trade in Pennsylvania.) Smith's favorable remarks toward American independence may have been due to Franklin (Smith 1965 [1776], 557–606).

2

From Smith to Marx

The Rise and Fall of Classical Economics

> That able but wrong-headed man, David Ricardo, shunted the
> car of economic science on to a wrong line—a line, however, on
> which it was further urged toward confusion by his equally able
> and wrong-headed admirer, John Stuart Mill.
> —*William Stanley Jevons (1965, li)*

The time between Adam Smith and Karl Marx was marked by the thrill
of victory and the agony of defeat. The French laissez-faire school of
Jean-Baptiste Say and Frédéric Bastiat advanced the Smithian model
to new heights, but it was not to last, as the classical model of Thomas
Robert Malthus, David Ricardo, and John Stuart Mill took economics
down into desperate straits. This chapter tells an ominous story.

Upon the publication of Adam Smith's *Wealth of Nations* in 1776,
a new era of optimism swept Europe. Social reformers were hope-
fully following the American revolution that promised "life, liberty
and the pursuit of happiness," and a French revolution that pledged
"liberté, égalité, fraternité." William Wordsworth described the early
idealism of the French Revolution when he wrote, in *The Prelude*
(Book 11, lines 108–09):

> Bliss was it in that dawn to be alive,
> But to be young was very Heaven!

Ever since Sir Thomas More wrote *Utopia*, philosophers have
dreamed of a world of universal happiness with no wars, no crime,
and no poverty. The genius of Adam Smith was his development of
an economic system of "natural liberty" that could bring about a
peaceful, equitable, and universal opulence.

Smith's model of universal prosperity was encouraged initially by disciples from a country that had for centuries been Great Britain's fierc-est enemy. The French economists Jean-Baptiste Say (1767–1832) and Frederic Bastiat (1801–50), building upon the sound principles developed by Cantillon, Montesquieu, Turgot, and Condillac, championed the boundless possibilities of open trade and a free entrepreneurial society. They improved upon the classical model of Adam Smith by rejecting the notions of a labor theory of value and the exploitation of workers under free-enterprise capitalism. Theirs was the famous school of "laissez faire, laissez passer" (leave us alone, let goods pass) and "pas trop gouverner" (not to govern too strictly). Free trade and limited government would encourage economic performance and entrepreneurial excellence.

Bastiat, a brilliant French journalist, was an indefatigable advo-cate of free trade and laissez-faire policies, a passionate opponent of socialism, and an unrelenting debater and statesman. Bastiat was unrivaled in exposing fallacies, condemning such popular cliches as "war is good for the economy" and "free trade destroys jobs." In his classic essay, *The Law* (1850), Bastiat established the proper social organization best suited for a free people, one that "defends life, lib-erty, and property . . . and prevents injustice." Under this legal system, "if everyone enjoyed the unrestricted use of his faculties and the free disposition of the fruits of his labor, social progress would be cease-less, uninterrupted, and unfailing" (Bastiat 1998 [1850], 5).

Smith was deeply influenced by Quesnay, Turgot, and Voltaire, and once *The Wealth of Nations* was published, the French were success-ful in publicizing Smith's model of free enterprise and liberalized trade throughout the Western world. They translated Smith's book, published the first encyclopedia of economics and the first history of economic thought, and wrote the first major textbook in economics, Say's *Treatise on Political Economy,* which was the principal textbook in the United States and Europe during the first half of the nineteenth century. Many of the Smithian principles were adopted by Alexis de Tocqueville in his profound study *Democracy in America,* including individualism, enlightened self-love, industry, and frugality.

"The French Adam Smith"

J.-B. Say (1767–1832) was called "The French Adam Smith." Wit-ness to both the American and French revolutions, he was a cotton manufacturer who believed that sound economics should be built upon good theory and models that could be tested by observation lest they become unrealistic and misleading. He was critical of his colleague David Ricardo's labor theory of value and his penchant to abstract model building, leading economics down a dangerous road. According to Say, economists like Ricardo who don't support their theories with facts are "but idle dreamers, whose theories, at best only gratifying literary curiosity, were wholly inapplicable in practice" (Say 1971 [1880], xxi, xxxv)

Say introduced several sound principles of economics in his *Treatise on Political Economy,* first published in 1805, particularly the essential role of the entrepreneur and Say's law of markets, which became the fundamental principle of classical macroeconomics.

In Chapter 7 of Book II, "On Distribution," Say introduced the role of the entrepreneur, the "master-agent" or "adventurer," as an economic agent separate from the landlord, worker, or even capitalist. For Say, the entrepreneur serves as a creator of new products and processes, and manager of the right combination of resources and labor. To succeed, the entrepreneur must have "judgment, perseverance, and knowledge of the world," Say noted. "He is called upon to estimate, with tolerable accuracy, the importance of the specific product, the probable amount of the demand, and the means of production: at one time he must employ a great number of hands; at another, buy or order the raw material, collect laborers, find consumers, and give at all times a rigid attention to order and the economy; in a word, he must possess the art of superintendence and administration." He must be willing to take on "a degree of risk" and there is always a "chance of failure," but when successful, "this class of producers . . . accumulates the largest fortunes" (Say 1971 [1880], 329–32).

Say's Law: The Classical Model of Macroeconomics

Say is also famous for developing the classical model of macroeconomics, known as Say's law of markets—"supply creates its own demand." It has been the source of much misunderstanding, especially by Keynes, who distorted the true meaning of Say's law (for more on this, see chapter 5 on Keynes). In chapter 15 of his textbook, Say introduced the idea that production (supply) is the source of consumption (demand). He used an example in agriculture: "The greater the crop, the larger are the purchases of the growers. A bad harvest, on the contrary, hurts the sale of commodities at large" (1971 [1880], 135). In other words, Say's law is really this: the supply (sale) of X creates the demand (purchase) for Y. To use an up-to-date example, when Microsoft created Windows software, it created a boom in jobs and consumer spending in Seattle; when Microsoft was sued by the federal government for antitrust violations and its stock fell, Seattle's economy suffered and consumption declined.

Say's law is consistent with business-cycle statistics. When a downturn starts, production is the first to decline, ahead of consumption. And when the economy begins to recover, production is the first to make a comeback, followed by consumption. Economic growth begins with an increase in productivity, a rise in new products and new markets. Hence, business spending is always a leading indicator over consumer spending. Say concluded, "Thus, it is the aim of good government to stimulate production, of bad government to encourage consumption" (1971 [1880], 139).

A corollary of Say's law is that savings is beneficial to economic growth. He denied that frugality and thrift might lead to a decline in expenditures and output. Savings is simply another form of spending, and perhaps even a better form of spending than consumption because savings is used in the production of capital goods and new processes. No doubt Say was influenced by his reading of Benjamin Franklin's defense of thrift as a virtue in the latter's *Autobiography,* and in adages such as "a penny saved is a penny earned" and "money begets money."

Steven Kates summarizes the conclusions of Say's law of markets and classical macroeconomics (Kates 1998, 29):

1. A country cannot have too much capital.

2. Saving and investment form the basis of economic growth.

3. Consumption not only provides no stimulus to wealth creation but is actually contrary to it.

4. Demand is constituted by production.

5. Demand deficiency (i.e., over-production) is never the cause of economic disturbance. Economic disturbance arises only if goods are not produced in the correct proportion to each other.

The Classical Model and the "Dismal Science"

Adam Smith's optimistic vision was never in more capable hands than those of the French devotees of laissez-faire. Short of marginal analysis, they carried the doctrine of the invisible hand and the natural harmony of the market system to its zenith. Unfortunately, though, the story of economics suddenly took an unexpected shift from the upbeat world of Adam Smith to what would be labeled "the dismal science." Remarkably, the apostasy away from Smith's masterpiece began with the writings of two of his own disciples in his own country, Thomas Malthus and David Ricardo.

The British economists Thomas Robert Malthus (1766–1834), David Ricardo (1772–1823), and John Stuart Mill (1806–73) continued the classical tradition in supporting the virtues of thrift, free trade, limited government, the gold standard, and Say's law of markets. In particular, Ricardo vigorously and effectively advocated an anti-inflation, gold-backed British pound sterling policy as well as a repeal of both the Corn Laws, England's notoriously high tariff wall on wheat and other agricultural goods, and the Poor Laws, England's modest welfare system.

The Diamond-Water Paradox

Yet there was a problem. Classical economics after Adam Smith suffered from a serious theoretical flaw that provided ammunition to Marxists, socialists, and other critics of capitalism. Smith himself supported an optimistic model favoring the harmony of interests and universal prosperity. He used the making of pins and the woolen coat to explain how laborers and capitalists work together to create usable products. But he had no real concept of how prices and the costs of productive factors were determined in the marketplace to satisfy consumer wants, a flaw that undermined his harmonic model.

The question Smith and the classical economists tried to answer was: How are goods and services, and the productive factors, valued in a growing economy to satisfy consumer wants? They tried to answer this question by resolving the famous diamond-water paradox. Why is it that an essential commodity like water is so little valued in the marketplace while impractical diamonds are so highly prized? To Smith and his disciples, this paradox was irresolvable. They were baffled by the observation that some goods were valued more in "exchange" than in "use." The failure to resolve this paradox, which remained unanswered until a generation later by the marginalist revolution (see chapter 4), led to disastrous results. Marxists and socialists used this wedge to label commercial society as unjust and immoral, a system in which profit trumps consumer satisfaction.

Furthermore, Smith's disciples, especially Malthus, Ricardo, and Mill, promoted an antagonistic model of income distribution under capitalism that gave classical economics a bad reputation, leading English critic Thomas Carlyle to label it "the dismal science." Instead of focusing on Smith's positive view of wealth creation and harmony of interests, his British disciples emphasized the distribution of wealth, the conflict of interests, and the labor theory of value.

Malthus Challenges the New Model of Prosperity

The first challenge to Smith's wonderful world came from an irreverent young parson, Thomas Robert Malthus. In 1798, at the age of thirty-two, Malthus published an anonymous work, entitled *Essay on Population*, which contended that earth's resources could not keep up with the demands of an ever-growing population. His brooding tract forever changed the landscape of economics and politics, and quickly cut short the positive outlook of Smith, Say, and other students of the Enlightenment. Malthus, along with his best friend, David Ricardo, asserted that pressures on limited resources would always keep the overwhelming majority of human beings close to the edge of subsistence. Accordingly, Malthus and Ricardo reversed the course of cheerful Smithian economics, even though, ironically, they were stringent followers of Smith's laissez-faire policies.

Malthus has had a powerful impact on modern-day thinking. He is considered the founder of demography and population studies. He is acknowledged to be the mentor of social engineers who advocate strict population control and limits to economic growth. His essay on population underlines the gloomy and fatalistic outlook of many scientists and social reformers who forecast poverty, crime, famine, war, and environmental degradation due to population pressures on resources. He even inspired Charles Darwin's theory of organic evolution, which explains how limited resources facing unlimited demands created the power of natural selection and survival of the fittest. Ultimately, the fatalistic pessimism of Malthus and Ricardo has given economics its reputation as a "dismal science."

Malthus's doomsday thesis was that "the power of population is indefinitely greater than the power of the earth to produce subsistence for man," and therefore the majority of humans were doomed to live a Hobbesian existence (1985 [1798], 71). His book identified two basic "laws of nature": first, population tends to increase geometrically (1, 2, 4, 8, 16, 32, etc.), and second, food production (resources) tends to increase only arithmetically (1, 2, 3, 4, 5, etc.). The means of supporting human life were "limited by the scarcity of land" and the "constant tendency to diminish" the use of resources, a reference to the law of diminishing returns. The result would be an inevitable crisis of "misery and vice" whereby the earth's resources would not satisfy the demands of a growing population (Malthus 1985 [1798], 67–80, 225).

Is Malthus right about the first "law of nature," that human population grows geometrically? Indeed, since Malthus wrote his essay, the world's population has skyrocketed from fewer than 1 billion people to over 6 billion. However, in looking more deeply at the sharp rise in world population since 1800, we see that the cause is not Malthusian in nature. The increase has been due to two factors unforeseen by Malthus. First, there has been a sharp drop in the infant mortality rate due to the elimination of many life-threatening diseases and illnesses through medical technology. Second, there has been a steady rise in the average human life span due to higher living standards; medical breakthroughs; improvements in sanitation, health care, and nutrition; and a decline in the accident rate. As a result, more people are living to adulthood, and more adults are living longer.

At the same time, there is a good chance that world population will soon top out, due especially to the sharp slowdown in the birthrate over the past fifty years in both industrial and developing countries. This is largely due to the wealth effect: wealthier people tend to have fewer children (contrary to what Malthus predicted). Over the past fifty years, the birthrate in developed countries has fallen from 2.8 to 1.9 children per family, and in developing countries from 6.2 to 3.9. The trend is unmistakable: women are having fewer children, and in some more developed countries, especially in Europe, the birthrate is far below replacement.

Malthus's Sins of Omission

What about Malthus's second "law of nature," which says that resources are limited and restricted by the law of diminishing returns? Here again, history has not supported Malthus. The law of diminishing returns only applies if we assume "all other things equal," that technology and the quantity of other resources are fixed. But no input is fixed in the long run—neither land, nor labor, nor capital. The economic importance of land has in fact dwindled in the modern world, due to intensive farming techniques and the green revolution. Malthus ignored the technological advances in agriculture, the constant discovery of new minerals and other resources in the earth, and the role of prices in determining how fast or slow resources are used up. In short, he failed to recognize human ingenuity.[1]

Malthus proved to be spectacularly wrong about food production, the advent of farming technology, the use of fertilizers, and the vast expansion of irrigation. The amount of cultivated land and the volume of food production have both risen dramatically. In fact, most famines have been blamed on ill-advised government policies, not nature.

The story of Thomas Malthus is instructive in developing an understanding of the dynamics of a growing economy and a rising population. Granted, Malthus recognized that government intervention is typically counterproductive in alleviating poverty and controlling population growth, and thus he joined Adam Smith in adopting a laissez-faire policy (he was vilified by critics for opposing poverty programs, birth control, and even vaccines). But he ultimately abandoned his mentor by disavowing faith in Mother Earth and the free market's ability to match the supply of resources with the growing demands of a rising population. Essentially, he failed to comprehend the role of prices and property rights as an incentive to ration scarce

---

1. For an alternative view to Malthusianism, see Julian L. Simon, ed., *The State of Humanity* (1995) and *The Ultimate Resource 2* (1996).

resources and as a problem-solving mechanism. Worse, he misunderstood the dynamics of a growing entrepreneurial economy—how a larger population creates its own seeds of prosperity through the creation of new ideas and new technology.

Although Adam Smith did hint at the idea of a subsistence wage, he firmly believed that wage earners could rise above subsistence through the adoption of machinery, tools, and equipment. Free-market capitalism was the escape mechanism from poverty. Malthus, on the other hand, was gloomy and even fatalistic about man's ability to break away from misery and vice. For him, mankind was destined to be chained to the iron law of wages.

David Ricardo, for Good or Bad

The eminent British economist David Ricardo fell into the same trap as his friend Malthus. A financial economist who made a fortune in government securities, Ricardo made many positive contributions to economic science, especially the law of comparative advantage and the quantity theory of money. He promoted free trade and hard money, and his writings influenced the repeal of the Corn Laws, England's notorious high tariff wall on agricultural goods in 1846, and England's return to the gold standard in 1844. Yet David Ricardo had a dark side. His analytical modeling is a two-edged sword. It gave us the quantity theory of money and the law of comparative advantage, but it also gave us the labor theory of value, the iron law of subsistence wages, and something economists call the "Ricardian vice," defined as either the excessive use of abstract model building or the use of false and misleading assumptions to "prove" the results one desires (such as his labor theory of value). Some of the worst ideas picked up by Karl Marx and the socialists come directly from reading Ricardo's textbook *On Principles of Political Economy and Taxation* (1951 [1817]). Marx hailed Ricardo as his intellectual mentor. A school of "neo-Ricardian" socialists has developed under the influence of Piero Sraffa, Ricardo's official biographer.[2]

---

2. For a critical examination of Sraffian economics, see Mark Blaug, *Economics Through the Looking Glass: The Distorted Perspective of the New Palgrave Dictionary of Economics* (1988).

Essentially, Ricardo, for all his love of Smith, took economics down a very dangerous road, apart from his policy recommendations. He created a new economic way of thinking, away from the harmonious "growth" model of Adam Smith and toward an antagonistic "distribution" model, where workers, landlords, and capitalists fought over the economy's desserts. Marx and the socialists exploited Ricardo's hostile system to the fullest. Smith's model focuses on how to make the economy grow, while Ricardo's model stresses how the economy is divided up among various groups or classes. Ricardo emphasized class conflict rather than Smith's "natural harmony" of interests.

The Ricardian Device or Vice?

Ricardo is considered the founder of economics as a rigorous science involving mathematical precision. The financial economist had a remarkable gift of abstract reasoning, developing a simple analytical tool involving only a few variables that yielded, after a series of manipulations, powerful conclusions. This model-building approach has been adopted by many prominent economists, including John Maynard Keynes, Paul Samuelson, and Milton Friedman, and has led to the popularity of econometrics. Mark Blaug comments, "If economics is essentially an engine of analysis, a method of thinking rather than a body of substantial results, Ricardo literally invented the technique of economics" (Blaug 1978, 140).

But "blackboard economics," as Ronald Coase calls it, has its drawbacks. It uses unrealistic and sometimes even false assumptions. Without reference to history, sociology, philosophy, or institutional framework, Ricardo's device becomes a Ricardian vice, stripping economics of its soul. Purely deductive reasoning and high mathematical formulas divorce theory from history. Take a look at Paul Samuelson's *Foundations of Economic Analysis* (1947) or neo-Ricardian Piero Sraffa's *Production of Commodities by Means of Commodities* (1960). Samuelson's book is virtually nothing but differential equations and assumptions far removed from reality. Sraffa's work hardly contains a single sentence that refers to the real world. They are both very much in the tradition of Ricardo.

"The origin of the misapprehension upon which the whole of economic theory is based must be traced to David Ricardo," writes

Elton Mayo, a business professor at Harvard (1945, 38). Mayo blames Ricardo's unrealistic theorizing on his background as a stockbroker,[3] far removed from the realities of the producing economy (1945, 39).

Adam Smith's *Wealth of Nations* abounded with theoretical propositions, but his theories were followed by numerous historical illustrations. Not so with Ricardo. "His ingenious mind," writes one historian, "essentially that of a brilliant theoretician, never displayed any significant interest in the past" (Snooks 1993, 23). It was this kind of abstract theorizing that caused J.-B. Say to label economists "idle dreamers" (1971 [1880], xxxv). Even Paul Samuelson (himself an abstract thinker) confessed once, "It has sometimes been suggested that our most advanced students know everything except common sense" (1960, 1652). Indeed, studies by Arjo Klamer and David Colander suggest a certain disillusionment with the highly abstract mathematical modeling that pervades Ph.D. programs in economics. After surveying the graduate programs at six Ivy League schools, Klamer and Colander conclude that "economic research was becoming separate from the real world" (1990, xv). Formalism has an iron grip on the discipline.

Heuristic model building can be useful in generating best estimates and decent results, but modeling can easily distort reality and lead to damaging results. In his classic work, *On the Principles of Political Economy and Taxation,* Ricardo carried his theorizing to extreme levels, whereby he made all kinds of limiting and dubious assumptions in order to get the results he was looking for. Ricardo's *Principles* was tedious and abstract, full of Euclidian-like deductions with no historical case studies. Students often called it "Ricardo's book of headaches" (St. Clair 1965, xxiii).

Economists are seldom indifferent about Ricardo. They either love or hate him, and sometimes both. Perhaps John Maynard Keynes best sums up this attitude: "Ricardo's mind was the greatest that ever addressed itself to economics," Keynes said, and then complained that "the complete domination of Ricardo's [economics] for a period of

---

3. A highly successful speculator who made a fortune as a stockjobber and government loan contractor during the Napoleon wars. See my article, "How Ricardo Became the Richest Economist in History," *The Making of Modern Economics* (2001, 96–97).

a hundred years has been a disaster to the progress of economics" (Keynes 1951 [1931], 117).

Ricardo Focuses on Distribution, Not Growth

How did Ricardo shift away from his mentor, Adam Smith? Smith recognized that economic freedom and limited government would create "universal opulence," but the founder of classical economics struggled to develop a sound theoretical framework (other than the division of labor) with which to explain how consumers and producers work through the profit-and-loss system to achieve this "universal opulence." Ricardo and the British disciples took Smith's parenthetical statements (such as his labor theory of value in a crude economy, and his criticism of landlords) and created a model of class struggle rather than one of harmony of interests—the iron law of subsistence wages instead of universal economic growth. They viewed the economy as if it were a large cake, where a larger dessert for capitalists and landlords could only mean a smaller piece for workers.

In a letter to Malthus, Ricardo explained his primary difference: "Political economy, you think, is an enquiry into the nature and causes of wealth [Adam Smith's view]; I think it should rather be called an enquiry into the laws which determine the division of the produce of industry among the classes who concur in its formulation" (in Rothbard 1995b, 82).

The difference between Adam Smith and Ricardo on this macro model of the economy can best be illustrated in terms of a pie chart (see Figure 2.1). For Ricardo's "class conflict" model, the focal point is how the fruits of the economy (the pie) should be divided between workers, landlords, and capitalists. Clearly, if landlords and capitalists get more of the pie, workers get less. And vice versa. For Adam Smith's "harmony of interests" model, the focal point is on making the economy grow, to make the pie bigger. In this way, there need not be a conflict of interests. If the pie gets bigger, everyone—the workers, landlords, and capitalists—gets more.

Ricardo's antagonistic system was tragic for everyone except the landlords. In his "corn model," as it is called, Ricardo's workers were machinelike units earning only subsistence wages over the long run. If wages rose, workers would have more children, which would in

Figure 2.1 **Two Models of the Economy**

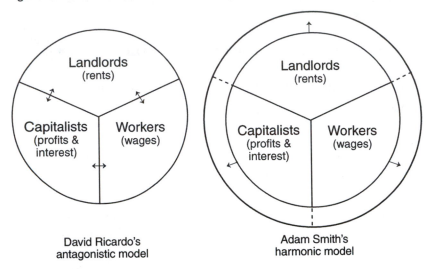

David Ricardo's
antagonistic model

Adam Smith's
harmonic model

turn increase the supply of laborers and force wages back down. Thus, Ricardo's "iron law of wages" presented a bleak outlook for workers.

Capitalists fared better, but were hardly animated. In Ricardo's model, they were a uniform, boring lot mechanically saving and accumulating capital. Moreover, profits could increase only at the expense of lower wages, and vice versa. In his *Principles,* Ricardo called this inverse relationship between wages and profits the "fundamental theorem of distribution." He repeatedly stated, "In proportion then as wages rose, would profits fall" (Ricardo 1951, I, 111) and "profits depend on wages" (1951, I, 143, 35).

Worse, profits were also inclined to fall in the long run due to the "law of diminishing returns." Under Ricardo's myopic worldview, higher wages would stimulate population growth, which in turn meant farming more land to feed more mouths, and that meant using less productive land. The price of grain would rise, benefiting landlords' rents, but profits would fall because capitalists would have to pay workers more to keep them from starving (due to higher food prices).

The only beneficiaries in Ricardo's picture were the landlords. They earned higher rents as grain prices rose. The tenant farmers did not benefit from higher grain prices because they had to pay higher rents. Ricardo vindicated the words of Adam Smith: "landlords love to reap where they never sowed" (Smith 1965 [1776], 49).

According to Ricardo's fatalistic system, wages tend toward subsistence levels, profits decline long term, and landlords keep adding to their share of unjust returns. As Oswald St. Clair comments, landlords, "though contributing nothing in the way of work or personal sacrifice, will nevertheless receive an ever-increasing portion of the wealth annually created by the community" (St. Clair 1965, 3).

What was the flaw in Ricardo's thinking? His corn model ignored the benefits that workers accrue from technological advances that make them more productive. Their wages would tend to rise as companies became more profitable. (Empirical studies demonstrate that industries with high profit margins tend to pay workers more.) He failed to see landlord rents as price signals determining the highest value or opportunity cost of land. Yet most economists would not recognize these insights for another generation. Meanwhile, Marx and the socialists picked up on Ricardo's attack on the idle landlords and the exploitive capitalists. In addition, Ricardo's critique encouraged Henry George's land nationalization and single tax movement in the late nineteenth century.

Ricardo Searches in Vain for Intrinsic Value in Labor

Finally, Ricardo was determined to find an "invariable measure of value." Instead of gold, the ultimate unit of account, he focused on quantity of labor units (not wages!) as the *numeraire*. In classical tradition, Ricardo fixed upon a cost-of-production theory of value, arguing that price was generally determined by costs (supply) rather than utility (demand). He was aware of exceptions to this cost theory, such as "rare statues and pictures, scarce books and coins, wines of a peculiar quantity" (Ricardo 1951, 12), and the impact of machinery. But machinery and capital were nothing more than "accumulated labour" (1951, 410). He later wrote, "my proposition that with few exceptions the quantity of labour employed on commodities determines the rate at which they will exchange for each other . . . is not rigidly true, but I say that it is the nearest approximation to truth, as a rule for measuring relative value, of any I have ever heard" (Vivo 1987, 193).

He struggled with the labor theory of value until the very last days of his life. About a month before his death he wrote a fellow economist, "I cannot get over the difficulty of the wine which is kept in a cellar for 3 or 4 years, or that of the oak tree, which perhaps had not 2/- expended on it in the way of labour, and yet comes to be worth £100" (Vivo 1987, 193). Even Thomas Malthus disagreed with his friend, writing, "neither labour nor any other commodity can be an accurate measure of real value in exchange" (Ricardo 1951, 416).

Economists over the years have had difficulty understanding Ricardo's "corn model" and his *Principles* textbook, especially the twisted assumptions he required to prove his theories. Ricardo once remarked that only twenty-five people in the entire country could understand it. A century later, Chicago economist Frank H. Knight remarked, "there is much [here] I cannot follow" (1959, 365). Joseph Schumpeter lambasted Ricardo for making most of the economic players "frozen and given," piling "one simplified assumption upon another," and developing a theory "that can never be refuted and lacks nothing save sense" (Schumpeter 1954, 472–73). Just the kind of theory Marx needed!

Perhaps Keynes had Ricardo in mind when he wrote, "It is astonishing what foolish things one can temporarily believe if one thinks too long alone, particularly in economics" (Keynes 1973a [1936], xxiii).

A Defective Classical Model Solidifies Under John Stuart Mill

Yet David Ricardo was able to convince practically all his contemporaries of his labor theory of value and his laissez-faire doctrines. "Ricardo conquered England as completely as the Holy Inquisition conquered Spain," said Keynes (1973a [1936], 32). It was principally through John Stuart Mill that the next generation adopted this classical model that was more in line with Ricardo's system of "class conflict" than Adam Smith's upbeat "harmony of interests" model.

The year 1848 was especially significant in this regard. It was a year of rebellion and mass protest in continental Europe. Karl Marx and Friedrich Engels wrote their revolutionary tract, *The Communist Manifesto*. A specter was indeed haunting Europe—not just communism, but a whole string of isms—Fourierism, Owenism, Saint-Simonism, and transcendentalism. They all fell under the new expression "socialism." There was utopian socialism, revolutionary socialism, and national socialism. All grew out of a reaction to the rapid transformation from a rural economy to an industrial world. The first half of the nineteenth century was an era of discontent—the Industrial Revolution, the Napoleonic wars, and democratic revolts throughout Europe. The growth model of Adam Smith was already undermined by the discouraging works of Malthus and Ricardo. The revolt of the masses in 1848 reflected the practical difficulties of adjusting to a new industrial era.

The year 1848 was also significant for John Stuart Mill and his influence in the world: it was the year of publication of Mill's textbook, *Principles of Political Economy,* a work that would dominate the Western world for half a century, going through thirty-two editions, until Alfred Marshall's landmark textbook took over in 1890.

It was Mill's textbook that declared that the laws of production were objectively determined but the laws of distribution were variable. "The Distribution of Wealth is a matter of human institution solely. They can place them [goods] at the disposal of whomsoever they please, and on whatever terms" (Mill 1884 [1848], 155). He added, "If the choice were to be made between Communism with all its chances and the present state of society with all its sufferings and injustices, all the difficulties, great or small, of Communism, would be but as dust in the balance" (1884 [1851], 159). His book also questioned the veracity of private property.

Mill was a reflection of his times, enigmatic and lost in an age of turmoil. In many ways, he was the embodiment of a Greek tragic hero, a dashing protagonist who ended his career in bewildered misfortune, including the early death of his beloved wife, Harriet. Here was a great intellect, a classical liberal, and the last major proponent of the classical school of economics. Like Ricardo, Mill espoused personal liberty in his classic libertarian tract *On Liberty* (1989 [1859]). He vigorously defended Say's law of markets, the foundation of classical macroeconomics, and opposed irredeemable paper money. He objected to coercive morality, intolerance, and a state religion. And he was an abolitionist who supported a woman's right to vote.

Yet Mill was famous for his inconsistencies and contradictions. He defended free enterprise but insisted he was a socialist. He flirted with socialism throughout his career, favored revolutionary change in Victorian culture, railed against overpopulation, and advocated

Ricardo's distribution theory, separating production entirely from distribution.[4] His love of Benthamite utilitarianism blinded him to frequent government intervention in the economy. He saw nothing wrong with heavy taxation of inheritances and nationalization of land, and questioned the justice of private property. According to Friedrich Hayek, it was this kind of thinking that led intellectuals to support all kinds of attacks on property and wealth, and grandiose tax and confiscation schemes aimed at redistributing wealth and income, thinking that such radical schemes can be accomplished without hurting economic growth. Hayek observed, "I am personally convinced that the reason which led the intellectuals to socialism was a man who is regarded as a great hero of classical liberalism, John Stuart Mill" (Boaz 1997, 50).

Mill influenced intellectuals from H.G. Wells to Sidney and Beatrice Webb toward socialist thinking, so much so that Sir William Harcourt, chancellor of the exchequer, could say in 1884, "we are all socialists now" (Stafford 1998, 18). It would be years later before economists, educated in marginal analysis, would counter the radical redistributionists, who argued that the theory of distribution cannot be separated from the theory of production. According to the marginalist revolution, the producers of goods and services are paid according to the fruits of their labor, based on their discounted marginal product, and heavy taxation can only distort their incentive to produce. Socialist measures to redistribute wealth and income do indeed affect economic activity. As Hayek states, "if we did do with that product whatever we pleased, people would never produce those things again" (Boaz 1997, 50).

Mill was critical of revolutionary socialism, but expressed considerably sympathy with utopian communitarianism, which operated with a social conscience and without coercion. It was this kind of socialism that he identified with. Thus, Mill set the stage "on a downward slope leading from the eighteenth-century sanity and conservatism of David Hume to the Fabian socialism and collectivism of Beatrice Webb" (Stafford 1998, 19).

---

4. Some critics blame his long love affair and marriage to Harriet Taylor for his socialist tendencies. See Skousen (2001, 118–19).

John Stuart Mill longed for the bliss of a voluntary communitarian village, but all such communities have suffered from one defect: they never lasted. New Harmony, Modern Times, United Order—they all had high-minded names, yet they all eventually disintegrated as a result of laziness, debt, or fraud.

A Dismal Science?

It was Thomas Carlyle (1795–1881), the English critic, who lashed out at the classical economics of Malthus, Ricardo, and Mill and labeled it "the dismal science," because he thought free competition and utilitarian democracy would lead to "anarchy plus the constable." Behold the pessimism of the iron law of subsistence wages and a miserly Mother Nature: Carlyle saw a more sinister view of the ubiquitous marketplace. A romantic conservative and Victorian moralist, Carlyle complained that supply and demand puts a price on everything, and "reduces the duty of human governors to that of letting men alone," leading to "a dreary, desolate, and indeed quite abject and distressing . . . dismal science" (Carlyle 1904, IV, 353–54).

Classical economics, as characterized by Carlyle, left the West in intellectual disequilibrium. Not long after Mill's time, a new form of socialism came onto the horizon, the violent revolutionary kind. If fellow citizens could not be persuaded to cooperate and escape the ills of raw anarchy and barbaric competition, then they must be forced to obey through the iron fist and the bayonet. Gradually the eyes of reformers all turned toward one authority, the second of the "big three" in economics. Karl Marx is the subject of our next chapter.

3

Karl Marx Leads a Revolt
Against Capitalism

> Jenny! If we can but weld our souls together, then with
> contempt shall I fling my glove in the world's face, then
> shall I stride through the wreckage a creator!
> —*Karl Marx to his fiancée (Wilson 1940)*

> Karl Marx was possessed of demonic genius that was to
> transform the modern world.
> —*Saul K. Padover (1978)*

If the work of Adam Smith is the Genesis of modern economics, that of
Karl Marx is its Exodus. If the Scottish philosopher is the great creator
of laissez-faire, the German revolutionary is its great destroyer. Marxist
John E. Roemer admits as much. According to him, the "main difference" between Smith and Marx is as follows: "Smith argued that the
individual's pursuit of self-interest would lead to an outcome beneficial
to all, whereas Marx argued that the pursuit of self-interest would lead
to anarchy, crisis, and the dissolution of the private property–based

system itself. . . . Smith spoke of the invisible hand guiding individual, self-interested agents to perform those actions that would be, despite their lack of concern for such an outcome, socially optimal; for Marxism the simile is the iron fist of competition, pulverizing the workers and making them worse off than they would be in another feasible system, namely, one based on the social or public ownership of property" (Roemer 1988, 2–3).

For all the horrors committed in Marx's name, the German philosopher has for more than a century struck an inspirational chord among workers and intellectuals disenfranchised by global capitalism. Malthus and Ricardo may have sown the seeds of dissension, but Karl Marx (1818–83) broke the bonds of capitalism and tore asunder the foundations of Adam Smith's system of natural liberty. No longer could the commercial system be viewed as "innocent" (Montesquieu), "mutually beneficial" (Smith), or "naturally harmonious" (Say and Bastiat). Now, under Marx, it was pictured as alien, exploitative, and self-destructive. In Marx's mind, emancipation came as people moved away from the Adam Smith model.

His mark on the world is indelible and the evidence of a brilliant if not disturbed mind. That Marx was a genius is not in dispute—he had a genuine doctorate in Greek philosophy; spoke French, German, and English fluently; could talk intelligently about science, literature, art, mathematics, and philosophy; and wrote a classic book that created a powerful new model of economic thinking. Never mind that he couldn't balance a checkbook or keep a job. A non-Marxist biographer called him a "towering, learned, and extraordinarily gifted man" (Padover 1978: xvi). Martin Bronfenbrenner deemed Marx "the greatest social scientist of all times" (1967: 624).[1]

Marx and Communism

Yet, like Cain in the Bible, Marx is cursed with a black mark in history. His name will forever be associated with the dark side of communism. A specter is haunting Karl Marx—the history of Lenin, Stalin, Mao, and Pol Pot, and the millions who died and suffered under the "evil empire," as Ronald Reagan called it. Apologists say Marx cannot be held accountable

---

1. I think German sociologist Max Weber deserves this honor. See Skousen (2001), chapter 10.

for his communist followers' atrocities and even assert that Marx would have been one of the first to be executed or sent to the Gulag. Perhaps. For one thing, he vehemently opposed press censorship throughout his career. Yet, without Marx, could there have been such a violent revolution and repression? Did not Marx support a "reign of terror" on the bourgeoisie? As one bitter critic put it, "In the name of human progress, Marx has probably caused more death, misery, degradation and despair than any man who ever lived" (Downs 1983, 299).

Marx Engenders Youthful Fanaticism

Among schools of thought, no other economist or philosopher engenders so much passion and religious fever as Marx. Above all, Marx was a visionary and a revolutionary idol, not just an economist. In reading *The Communist Manifesto*, written over 150 years ago, one cannot help feeling the passionate power, the pungent style, and the astonishing simplicity of Marx and Engels's words (1964 [1848]).

Youthful followers become true believers, and it usually takes them years to grow out of their Marxist addiction. It happened to Robert Heilbroner, Mark Blaug, Whittaker Chambers, and David Horowitz. I even saw it among my students at Rollins College, a decade after Soviet communism had collapsed and Marxism was supposedly dead. In my class, "Survey of Great Economists," I require students to read a book authored by an economist. One student chose *The Communist Manifesto*. After reading it, he came to me and exclaimed with some emotion, "This is incredible! I must do my book report on this!" pointing to his well-marked copy. It was eerie. In my lectures, I did my best to counter Marxian doctrine, but it didn't matter. He was converted.

I can easily see how a young revolutionary could be swayed by these unforgettable lines from the polemical *Communist Manifesto*:

> A specter is haunting Europe—the specter of Communism. . . . The history of all hitherto existing society is the history of class struggles. . . . The bourgeoisie has pitilessly torn asunder the motley feudal ties that bound man to his 'natural superiors,' and has left remaining no other nexus between man and man than naked self-interest, than callous 'cash payment.' . . . Veiled by political and religious illusions, it has substituted

naked, shameless, direct, brutal exploitation. . . . Let the ruling classes tremble at the communistic revolution. The proletarians have nothing to lose but their chains. They have a world to win. WORKING MEN OF ALL COUNTRIES, UNITE! (1964 [1848])

Marshall Berman, a longtime Marxist living in New York City, recounts how he, as a youth, encountered another book by Marx, *Economic and Philosophical Manuscripts of 1844*. This book generated the same kind of fanatic enthusiasm. "Suddenly I was in a sweat, melting, shedding clothes and tears, flashing hot and cold" (Berman 1999, 7)—not from staring at *Playboy* magazine or trading a penny stock for the first time, but from reading Marx!

In many ways, Marxism has become a quasi-religion, with its slogans, symbols, red banners, hymns, party fellowship, apostles, martyrs, bible, and definitive truth. "Marx had the self-assurance of a prophet who had talked to God. . . . He was a poet, prophet, and moralist speaking as a philosopher and economist; his doctrine is not to be tested against mere facts but to be received as ethical-religious truth. . . . Marx was to lead the Chosen People out of slavery to the New Jerusalem. . . . Becoming a Marxist or a Communist is like falling in love, an essentially emotional commitment" (Wesson 1976, 29–30, 158). A guidebook for youth was published in 1935 entitled *Teachings of Marx for Girls and Boys*, authored by protestant minister William Montgomery Brown, highlighted by pictures on the cover of Marx's "greatest pupils," Lenin and Stalin.

Marx's Contributions to Economics

Few economists break out into other disciplines as did Karl Marx. There's Marx the philosopher, Marx the historian, Marx the political scientist, Marx the sociologist, and Marx the literary critic. He was prolific and wrote unendingly about nearly everything. Even today a compilation of the complete works of Marx and his colleague Friedrich Engels has not been finished. The commentaries on Marx and related subjects are so vast that it would take volumes to tell it all. (On the Internet, Amazon.com lists over 4,000 entries on Marx and communism, second only to Jesus and Christianity.) Thus, our chapter on Marx must of necessity be limited largely to his economic contributions. Even then, Marx the economist is not an easy subject.

Marx was probably the first major economist to establish his own school of thought, with its own methodology and specialized language. In creating his own school in his classic work, *Capital* (1976 [1867]), he contrasted his system with that of laissez-faire—as espoused by Adam Smith, J.-B. Say, and David Ricardo, among others. It was Marx who dubbed laissez-faire the "classical school." In developing a Marxist approach to economics, he created his own vocabulary: surplus value, reproduction, bourgeoisie and proletarians, historical materialism, vulgar economy, monopoly capitalism, and so on. He invented the term "capitalism."[2] Since Marx, economics has never been the same. Today, there is no universally acceptable macro model of the economy as there is in physics or mathematics—there are only warring schools of economics.

Early Training: Marx's Internal Contradictions

Who was this German philosopher? Who could have brought about such passion, such devotion, such a powerful new model of economics that would challenge the classical model of Adam Smith?

Karl Heinrich Marx was born on May 5, 1818, in an elegant townhouse in Trier in the Rhine province of Prussia. Trier is the oldest town in Germany. From crib to coffin, Marx was full of contradictions. He railed against the petty bourgeois, yet grew up in a bourgeois family. He lived years of his adult life in desperate poverty despite his relatively well-to-do origins. He exalted capitalism's technology and material advances, yet damned the capitalist society. He felt deeply for the working man, yet never held a steady job or visited a factory during his adult life. His mother complained, "If only Karl had made capital instead of writing about it!" (Padover 1978, 344).

Marx shouted anti-Semitic epithets at his opponents, yet was Jewish from both sides of his family. In an essay published in 1843, "On the Jewish Question," Marx expressed anti-Jewish sentiments that were common in Europe at the time. His language was vindictive: "What is the worldly cult of the Jew? Schacher. What is his worldly God? Money! . . . Money is the jealous god of Israel before whom no other

---

2. Frank H. Knight and other market-oriented economists prefer "free enterprise" to "capitalism" as a description of the market economy. See Knight (1982 [1947], 448).

god may exist. Money degrades all the gods of mankind—and converts them into commodities. . . . What is contained abstractly in the Jewish religion—contempt for theory, for art, for history" (Padover 1978, 169). Marx's racial slander never let up. He never retracted his 1843 defamation of the Jews. "On the contrary," wrote biographer Saul Padover, "he harbored a lifelong hostility toward them. . . . His letters are replete with anti-Semitic remarks, caricatures, and crude epithets: 'Levy's Jewish nose,' 'usurers,' 'Jew-boy,' 'nigger-Jew,' etc. For reasons perhaps explainable by the German concept Selbsthass [self-hate], Marx's hatred of Jews was a canker which neither time nor experience ever eradicated from his soul" (Padover 1978, 171).

Prominent Marxists have denied Marx's anti-Semitism, however. *A Dictionary of Marxian Thought* states, "Although we know that Marx was not averse to using offensive vulgarisms about some Jews, there is no basis for regarding him as having been anti-Semitic" (Bottomore 1991, 275). Gareth Stedman Jones writes, "Marx's alleged anti-Semitism . . . cannot be understood except in the context of his hatred of all forms of national and ethnic particularism" (Blumenberg 1998 [1962], x).

Marx suffered contradictions throughout his life. He cherished his children, yet saw them die prematurely from malnutrition and illness or drove them to suicide. Marx protested the evils of exploitation in the capitalist system, and yet, according to one biographer, he "exploited everyone around him—his wife, his children, his mistress and his friends—with a ruthlessness which was all the more terrible because it was deliberate and calculating" (Payne 1968, 12). Paul Samuelson adds, "Marx was a gentle father and husband; he was also a prickly, brusque, egotistical boor" (Samuelson 1967b, 616). In sum, Marx ranted about the inner contradictions of capitalism, yet he himself was constantly beset by inner dissension.

Marx's Christian Faith

The most surprising irony is that Karl Marx—considered one of the most vicious opponents of religion—was brought up a Christian though many of his ancestors were rabbis.

His father, Heinrich Marx, overcame insuperable obstacles to become a well-to-do Jewish lawyer. When he was faced with a new Prussian law in 1816 prohibiting Jews from practicing law, he switched from Judaism to the Lutheran faith. His mother, Henrietta Pressborch, was the daughter of a rabbi, yet she also saw the social value in converting to Christianity.

Karl, the oldest surviving son in a family of nine children, was baptized a Christian and wrote several essays on Christian living while attending gymnasium (high school). As a senior in high school, Karl wrote an essay entitled "The Union of the Faithful with Christ," which spoke of alienation, a fear of rejection by God. He was mesmerized by the story of a peaceful paradise in Genesis and the coming of a dreadful apocalypse in The Revelation of St. John. Later, these first and last books of the Bible would help formulate Marx's doctrines of alienation, class struggle, a revolutionary overthrow of bourgeois society, and the glories of a stateless, classless millennial-type era of peace and prosperity. His vision of a proletarian victory may have come from this early training in Christian messianism. He was first and foremost a millennial communist.

Many of Marx's dogmas were not original. They came from the Bible, which he twisted and changed to suit his purposes. As biographer Robert Payne notes, "when he [Marx] turned against Christianity he brought to his ideas of social justice the same passion for atonement and the same horror of alienation" (1968, 42).

Marx Becomes a College Radical

Marx's faith was challenged almost immediately upon attending the University of Bonn, where he, like many college freshmen, spent more time drinking and carousing than studying. He piled up bills, joined a secret revolutionary group, and was wounded in a duel. Later he was arrested for carrying a pistol, and jailed for rowdiness.

His father hoped to reform his eldest son by transferring him to the renowned University of Berlin, where Marx spent the next five years. But his undisciplined lifestyle continued. He read voraciously and lived the life of a bohemian. He fancied himself a poet, translated Greek plays, and filled his notebooks with dark tragedies and romantic poetry. He joined the Doctor's Club (Doktorklub), a small society of radical Young Hegelians.

Fellow students described him as having a brilliant mind and being ruthlessly opinionated, his dark excitable eyes staring in defiance.

His black beard and thick mane of hair, his shrill voice and violent temper, stood out. He was so exceptionally swarthy that his family and friends called him "Mohr" or "Moor." During his college years, he was described colorfully in a short poem (Payne 1968, 81; Padover 1978, 116).

> Who comes rushing in, impetuous and wild—
> Dark fellow from Trier, in fury raging?
> Nor walks nor skips, but leaps upon his prey
> In tearing rage, as one who leaps to grasp
> Broad spaces in the sky and drags them down to earth,
> Stretching his arms wide open to the heavens.
> His evil fist is clenched, he roars interminably
> As though ten thousand devils had him by the hair.

The Influence of Radical German Philosophers

Two radical philosophers greatly influenced Marx during these college years and soon after: G.W.F. Hegel (1770–1831) and a contemporary, Ludwig Feuerbach (1804–72). From Hegel, Marx developed the driving force of his "dialectical materialism"—that all progress was achieved through conflict. From Feuerbach's *The Essence of Christianity* (1841), Marx rationalized his mythical view of religion and his rejection of Christianity. God did not create man; man created God! Engels described the liberating impact of Feuerbach's book: "In one blow it . . . placed materialism back upon the throne. . . . The spell was broken . . . . The enthusiasm was universal: We were all for the moment Feuerbachians" (Padover 1978, 136).

Marx's parents were worried sick about their prodigal son who wanted to become a writer and a critic instead of a lawyer. His letters reveal the often harsh correspondence between him and his parents. His father, Heinrich, was a classic liberal and a defender of bourgeois culture, so one can imagine his despair over his son. His letters charged Karl with being "a slovenly barbarian, an anti-social person, a wretched son, an indifferent brother, a selfish lover, an irresponsible student, and a reckless spendthrift," all accurate accusations that haunted Marx throughout his adult life. Heinrich Marx railed, "God help us! Disorderliness, stupefying dabbling in all the sciences, stupefying brooding at the gloomy oil lamp; barbarism in a scholar's dressing-gown and unkempt hair" (Padover 1978, 106–07). In another letter, he accused Karl of being possessed by a "demonic spirit" that "estranges your heart from finer feelings" (Berman 1999, 25). This letter of Karl's father would not be the only time Marx would be accused of devilish behavior, however.

Marx's Satanic Verses

One of the nightmarish aspects of Marx's life was his fascination with Goethe's Faust, the story of a young man who is at war with himself over good and evil and makes a pact with Satan. Faust exchanges his soul (through his intermediary Mephistopheles) for a life of pleasure and for the right ultimately to control the world through massive organized labor. Goethe's Faust was Marx's bible throughout his life. He memorized whole speeches of Mephistopheles, and could recite long passages to his children. (He equally loved Shakespeare, whom he also quoted regularly.)

While he was a student at Berlin University in 1837, Marx wrote romantic verses dedicated to his fiancée, Jenny von Westphalen. One of these poems, "The Player," was published in a German literary magazine, *Athenaeum*, in 1841 (reprinted in Payne 1971, 59). It describes a violinist who summons up the powers of darkness. The player, either Lucifer or Mephistopheles, boldly declares,

> Look now, my blood-dark sword shall stab
> Unerringly within thy soul.
> God neither knows nor honors art.
> The hellish vapors rise and fill the brain.
>
> Til I go mad and my heart is utterly changed.
> See this sword—the Prince of Darkness sold it to me.
> For me he beats the time and gives the signs.
> Ever more boldly I play the dance of death.

Marx Writes a Greek Tragedy

A pact with the devil was the central theme of *Oulanem*, a poetic play Marx wrote in 1839. He completed only the first act, but it reveals a number of violent and eccentric characters. The main character, Oulanem, is an anagram for Manuelo, meaning Immanuel or God (Payne 1971, 57–97). In a Hamlet-like soliloquy, Oulanem asks himself if he must destroy the world. He begins,

> Ruined! Ruined! My time has clean run out!
> The clock has stopped, the pygmy house has crumbled,
> Soon I shall embrace eternity to my breast, and soon
> I shall howl gigantic curses at mankind.

And ends,

> And we are chained, shattered, empty, frightened,
> Eternally chained to this marble block of Being,
> Chained, eternally chained, eternally.
> And the worlds drag us with them on their rounds,
> Howling their songs of death, and we—
> We are the apes of a cold God.

Marx's fixation with self-destructive behavior was prevalent through most of his life. He even composed and published an entire book on suicide while living in exile in Belgium in 1835. And he translated the work of Jacques Peuchet detailing the accounts of four suicides, three by young women. The focus is on the industrial system that would encourage suicidal behavior (Plaut and Anderson 1999).

Marx Marries and Moves to Paris

Marx finally left Berlin on grounds that the university administration had been taken over by anti-Hegelians. Fearing his Ph.D. dissertation on Greek philosophy might be rejected, he submitted it to the University of Jena, which accepted it without any attendance requirements. In 1842, he worked briefly as editor of a German newspaper, fearlessly defending free speech. He resigned when the censors made it impossible for him to continue.

In 1843, Marx married his teenage sweetheart and neighbor, Jenny von Westphalen, over objections from both families. Jenny, four years older than Marx, was the daughter of Baron Johann Ludwig von Westphalen, a wealthy aristocrat who represented the Prussian government in the city council. After the baron died, the Marxes lived off the baroness's largess. Jenny was deeply devoted to Karl and his revolutionary ideas. For the rest of their lives, they were inseparable through poverty, illness, and failure. Their love was deep and lasting, though not without heartache and trouble. They exchanged numerous love letters. They had six children, although only two daughters survived them.

In less than a year, Karl and his new wife moved to Paris, where he became editor of a monthly German magazine. Karl and Jenny Marx loved Paris and French culture. Here Marx had little interest in associating with Bastiat and the French laissez-faire school—he later labeled Bastiat the most "superficial" apologist of the "vulgar economy" (Padover 1978, 369)—but fell in among the radical French socialists, including Pierre Proudhon and Louis Blanc. He plunged into oceans of books and would often go three to four days without sleep (Padover 1978, 189). Seeing the class struggle firsthand, he wrote eloquently of alienation and labor suffering under capitalism in *The Economic and Philosophical Manuscripts of 1844*, a compilation of articles not published until 1932.

Marx Meets Friedrich Engels

It was in Paris that Marx met his lifelong colleague in arms, Friedrich Engels (1820–95). Five-and-a-half feet tall, blond, Teutonic-looking with cold blue eyes, Engels had a critical eye for detail. Together Marx and Engels started working on a book attacking their socialist rivals. It would be a close collaboration that would last another forty years, until Marx died in 1883.

Engels, the son of a wealthy German industrialist, hated his tyrannical father and his "boring, dirty, and abominable" business, even as he himself achieved financial success running a textile operation in Manchester (though there is no evidence he improved the condition of his workers). Engels was as fascinating as Marx: a gifted cartoonist, an expert on military history, and a master of nearly two dozen languages. When excited, he could "stutter in twenty languages"! He was also a notorious womanizer.

Engels's influence on Marx was twofold: His vast financial resources allowed him to subsidize Marx for decades, and he played a critical role in directing Marx's thinking toward political economy.

Engels's own work, *The Condition of the Working Class in England in 1844,* had a profound impact on Marx, and it was Engels who converted Marx to revolutionary communism, not the other way around. He coauthored *The Communist Manifesto* but, in every other way, lived in the shadow of the great philosopher.

Engels outlived Marx by a decade, corresponding with revolutionaries, editing and publishing Marx's books, and keeping the Marxist flame ablaze.

The World's Greatest Critic

The spiteful nature of Marx and Engels's style was clear in the title of their first collaboration: *Critique of Critical Critique*! (A more palatable title, *The Holy Family*, was superimposed on the cover while the book was being printed.) This emphasis on fault-finding reflected Marx's harsh hostility and his hot-blooded anger against his enemies. "He denounced everyone who dared to oppose his opinions" (Barzun 1958 [1941], 173). He initiated the practice of "party purges," which would be perfected a generation later by Lenin and Stalin (Wesson 1976, 34). In 1847, responding to fellow socialist Proudhon's *The Philosophy of Poverty*, Marx wrote a caustic rejoinder, *The Poverty of Philosophy*. If the *Guinness Book of World Records* listed the World's Most Critical Man, Marx would have easily won the award. Almost every one of his book titles contained the word "critique." He wrote sparingly about the happy world of utopian communism, prodigiously about the flaws of capitalism.

Marx Writes a Powerful Polemic

Marx's life in Paris did not last long. He was expelled for inciting revolution in Germany. He left for Brussels, the first stage of a life of permanent exile. It was in Belgium that Marx and Engels were commissioned by the London-based League of the Just, later renamed the Communist League, to write their famous pamphlet, *The Communist Manifesto.*

The Communist Manifesto, the final version written by Marx, was a forceful call to arms, a powerful reflection of the new machine age and new hardships as men, women, and children moved to enormous chaotic cities, worked sixteen hours a day in factories, and often lived in desperate squalor. "The bourgeoisie, wherever it has got the upper hand, has put an end to all feudal patriarchal, idyllic relations. . . . It has left remaining no other bond between man and man than naked self-interest, than callous 'cash-payment.'" Consequently, "the bourgeoisie has stripped of its halo every occupation hitherto honored and looked up to with reverent awe. It has converted the physician, the lawyer, the priest, the poet, the man of science into its paid wage-laborers." Further, "all that is solid melts into air, all that is holy is profane." Capitalism "has substituted naked, shameless, direct, brutal exploitation" (Marx and Engels 1964 [1848], 5–7).

When the *Manifesto* was published in German in February 1848, the timing could not have been better. By the summer, worker revolts spread throughout Europe—in France, Germany, Austria, and Italy. Images of the French Revolution a generation earlier dominated the spirit of the times. However, the European revolts were quickly quelled and Marx was arrested by Belgian police for spending his inheritance from his father (6,000 gold francs) on arming Belgian workers with rifles. He was released from jail in 1849 and moved to Cologne, Germany, where he edited another journal. The last issue was printed in red ink, the revolutionary color.

Hungry Years in London

Marx was constantly getting into trouble and continually on the run. After being expelled from Germany in August 1849, and deeply depressed by the failure of worker revolutions, he moved to London with his wife and their three children. This would turn out to be his final move. For the next thirty years, he would live, research, and write in the largest bourgeois city in the world.

The first six years in London were trying times for the Marx family, which suffered from serious illness, premature death, and desperate poverty. Marx pawned everything to keep his family alive—the family silver, linens, even the children's clothing (Padover 1978, 56). While the family was living in a small apartment in Soho, a Prussian police spy came by in 1853 and made a detailed report:

> Marx is of medium height, 34 years old; despite his relative youth, his hair is already turning gray; his figure is powerful. . . . His large, piercing

fiery eyes have something uncannily demonic about them. At first glance one sees in him a man of genius and energy. . . .

In private life he is a highly disorganized, cynical person, a poor host; he leads a real gypsy existence. Washing, grooming, and changing underwear are rarities with him; he gets drunk readily. Often he loafs all day long, but if he has work to do, he works day and night . . . very often he stays up all night. . . .

Marx lives in one of the worst, and thus cheapest, quarters in London . . . everything is broken, ragged and tattered; everything is covered with finger-thick dust; everywhere the greatest disorder. When one enters Marx's room, the eyes get so dimmed by coal smoke and tobacco fumes that for the first moments one gropes. . . . Everything is dirty, everything full of dust. . . . But all this causes no embarrassment to Marx and his wife. (In Padover 1978: 291–93)

Marx, living in squalor and sorrow, was constantly broke and took few work opportunities. What work he did was mainly as a part-time journalist for the *New York Daily Tribune* and other newspapers. He stubbornly refused to be "practical," and at times Engels had to ghostwrite his articles. Three of Marx's young children died of malnutrition and illness. Such was the life of this demonic genius and his long-suffering wife.

Marx's Personality Quirks

Keynes was fascinated by people's hands, Marx by people's skulls. Wilhelm Liebknecht, one of Marx's disciples, wrote that when he met his leader for the first time at a summer picnic for communist workers near London in the 1850s, Marx "began at once to subject me to a rigid examination, looked straight into my eyes and inspected my head rather minutely." Liebknecht was relieved to have passed the examination (Liebknecht 1968 [1901], 52–53).

Not everyone survived Marx's skullduggery. Ferdinand Lassalle, a German social democrat and labor organizer, was viciously attacked by Marx, who called him "the Jewish Nigger" and a "greasy Jew." "It is now perfectly clear to me," Marx wrote Engels in 1862, "that, as the shape of his head and the growth of his hair indicates, he is descended from the Negroes who joined in Moses' flight from Egypt (unless his mother or grandmother on the father's side was crossed with a nigger).

This union of Jew and German on a Negro base was bound to produce an extraordinary hybrid" (Marx and Engels 41, 388–90).

Marx was apparently taken in by the pseudoscience of phrenology, the practice of examining a person's skull to determine his or her character, developed during the early 1800s by two German physicians. Marx was not the only person who believed in phrenology. Queen Victoria in Great Britain and the American poets Walt Whitman and Edgar Allan Poe did as well.

Why Did Marx Grow Such a Long Beard?

Revolutionary followers often played on Marx's vanity by comparing him to the Greek gods. He was much pleased by an 1843 political cartoon portraying him as Prometheus when his newspaper, *Rheinische Zeitung*, was banned. Marx is shown chained to his printing press, while an eagle representing the king of Prussia tears at his liver. The editor looks defiant, hoping someday to free himself and pursue his revolutionary causes.

While working on *Das Kapital* in the 1860s, Marx received a larger-than-life statue of Zeus as a Christmas present. It became one of his prized possessions, which he kept in his London study. From then on, Marx sought to imitate the statue of Zeus. He stopped cutting his hair and let his beard grow out until it assumed the shape and size of Zeus's bearded head. He pictured himself as the god of the universe, casting his thunderbolts upon the earth. One of the last photographs of Marx shows his white hair flowing everywhere in magnificent splendor, reminding us of these lines in Homer's *Iliad* (Book I, line 528):

> Zeus spoke, and nodded with his darkish brows,
> and immortal locks fell forward from the lord's deathless head,
> and he made great Olympus tremble.

Cover-up: Marx Fathers an Illegitimate Son

In 1850–51, Marx had an affair with his wife's unpaid but devoted maidservant Helene Demuth, known as Lenchen, and fathered an illegitimate son. The affair was hushed up by Marx, who begged Engels to pretend to be the father. Engels agreed, even though the boy, named Freddy, looked like Marx. "If Jenny had known the truth, it might have killed her, or at the very least destroyed her marriage" (Padover 1978, 507). Jenny may in fact have known; she and Karl allegedly did not sleep together for years afterward.

Marx completely disowned this son. Finally, Engels declared the child to be Marx's on his deathbed in 1895. He was speaking to Marx's daughter Eleanor, who took the news hard (she later committed suicide). The facts became public only in the next century in Werner Blumenberg's 1962 biography of Marx (Blumenberg 1998 [1962], 111–113). They proved to be an embarrassment to Marxist apologists who had always maintained that Marx was a good family man despite the premature deaths of three children and the suicides of two daughters in adulthood. For decades, Robert Heilbroner declared Marx a "devoted husband and father" in his best-seller, *The Worldly Philosophers* (1961, 124), only later to admit Marx's indiscretion. Yet Heilbroner defended Marx, arguing that the infidelity "could not undo a relationship of great passion" (1999, 149).

Marx: Rich or Poor?

Things finally started looking up for Marx in 1856. Money from Engels and a legacy from Jenny's mother's estate allowed the Marx family to move from Soho to a nice home in fashionable Hampstead. Suddenly Marx started living the life of a bourgeois gentleman, wearing a frock coat, top hat, and monacle. The Marxes gave parties and balls, and traveled to seaside resorts. Marx even played the stock market. He speculated in American shares and English joint-stock shares, realizing sufficient gains to write Engels in 1864, "The time has now come when with wit and very little money one can really make a killing in London." Details of his speculations are lost, however (Payne 1968, 354; North 1993, 91–103).[3]

---

3. Marx's stock market speculations were all the more ironic given that one of the first acts in a communist takeover was to abolish the stock exchange as a case of "vulgar economy."

Sympathetic historians have always noted the poor conditions under which Marx lived, but during most of his life it was not for lack of money. Historian Gary North investigated Marx's income and spending habits, and concluded that except for his self-imposed poverty of 1848–63, Marx begged, borrowed, inherited, and spent lavishly. In 1868, Engels offered to pay off all the Marxes' debts and provide Marx with an annuity of £350 a year, a remarkable sum at the time. North concludes: "He was poor during only fifteen years of his sixty-five-year career, in large part due to his unwillingness to use his doctorate and go out to get a job. . . . The philosopher-economist of class revolution—the 'Red Doctor of Soho' who spent only six years in that run-down neighborhood—was one of England's wealthier citizens during the last two decades of his life. But he could not make ends meet. . . . After 1869, Marx's regular annual pension placed him in the upper two percent of the British population in terms of income" (North 1993, 103).

Marx Writes *Das Buch* and Changes the Course of History

Basically, Marx did not want to waste his time doing routine work to support his young family. He preferred to spend long hours, months, and years at the British Library in London researching and writing. He would come home and tell Jenny he had made the colossal discovery of economic determinism, that all society's actions were determined by economic forces. His work culminated in his classic *Das Kapital*, published in German in 1867. *Capital* (the English title) introduced economic determinism and a new "exploitive" theory of capitalism based on universal "scientific" laws discovered by Marx.

Marx considered his work the "bible of the working class," and even expected laborers to read his heavy pedantic tome. He saw himself as "engaged in the most bitter conflict in the world," and hoped his book would "deliver the bourgeoisie a theoretical blow from which it will never recover" (Padover 1978, 346). Marx viewed himself as the "Darwin of society," and in 1880 he sent Charles Darwin a copy of *Capital*. Darwin courteously replied, begging ignorance of the subject.

Only a thousand copies were printed and it sold slowly, primarily because "Das Buch" was theoretically abstract and scholastically dense, with over 1,500 sources cited. The reviews of *Capital* were almost universally poor, but through the efforts of Engels and other die-hard supporters, the work was translated into Russian in 1872 and French in 1875. The Russian edition was a momentous publishing event, luckily passing czarist censors as "nonthreatening" high theory. It was studied heavily by Russian intellectuals, and eventually a copy fell into the hands of Vladimir Ilich Ulyanov—V.I. Lenin. It was Lenin, Marx's most powerful disciple, who brought Marx to light. "Without Marx there would have been no Lenin, without Lenin no communist Russia" (Schwartzchild 1947, vii).

The English edition did not appear until 1887. In 1890, an American edition became a best-seller and the print run of 5,000 sold out quickly because *Capital* was promoted as a book informing readers "how to accumulate capital"—a course on making money! (Padover 1978, 375).

Most economists wonder how such a "long, verbose, abstract, tedious, badly written, difficult labyrinth of a book [could] become the Talmud and Koran for half the world" (Gordon 1967, 641). Marxists respond, "That's the beauty of it!" *Capital* has survived and blossomed as a classic in part because of its intellectual appeal. According to an eminent socialist, the prestige of *Capital* owes much to "its indigestible length, its hermetic style, its ostentatious erudition, and its algebraical mysticism" (Wesson 1976, 27).

Marx Dies in Obscurity

Marx was only forty-nine years old when he published *Capital*, but he refused to finish any more full-length books and instead read, researched, and took notes on huge quantities of books and articles on such wide topics as mathematics, chemistry, and foreign languages. "He delved into such problems as the chemistry of nitrogen fertilizers, agriculture, physics, and mathematics. . . . Marx immediately wrote a treatise on differential calculus and various other mathematical manuscripts; he learned Danish; he learned Russian" (Raddatz 1978, 236).

Marx had a hard time completing anything in his later years, especially with regard to economics. He never finished the next two volumes of *Capital*, which exasperated Engels, who finally edited and published them himself.

Marx was a sick man most of his life, constantly beset with chronic illnesses—asthma attacks, prolonged headaches, strep throat, influenza, rheumatism, bronchitis, toothaches, liver pains, eye inflammations, laryngitis, and insomnia. His boils and carbuncles were so severe that by the end of his life, his entire body was covered with scars. His "eternally beloved" Jenny died of cancer in 1881; Marx was so ill he couldn't attend her funeral. His daughter, also named Jenny, died of the same disease two years later. That same year, on March 17, 1883, Marx passed away sitting in his easy chair. Not surprisingly, there was no will or estate.

Marx was buried at Highgate Cemetery in London along with his wife Jenny, his housemaid Lenchen (in 1890), and other family members. A twelve-foot monument with a bust of Marx was erected in the 1950s by the Communist Party. The famous phrase "Workers of all lands, unite!" is emblazoned on the monument in gold. At the bottom are printed the words of Marx, "The philosophers have only interpreted the world in various ways; the point, however, is to change it."

Engels conducted the service at Marx's burial. He spoke eloquently of Marx's position in history, proclaiming him the Darwin of the social sciences.[4] "His name will live on through the centuries, and so will his work."

Indeed. In *The 100 Most Influential Books Ever Written*, by Martin Seymour-Smith (1998), seven economists are listed: Adam Smith, Thomas Robert Malthus, John Stuart Mill, Herbert Spencer, John Maynard Keynes, Friedrich von Hayek . . . and Karl Marx.

The Living Marx: A Dismal Failure

Engels would have to wait until the twentieth century before Marx's influence would be felt. In 1883, it was merely a delusion of gran-

---

4. There is a long-persistent myth that Marx wrote Darwin to ask if he could dedicate a volume of *Capital* to Darwin. In fact, no such letter was written. See Colb (1982: 461–81).

deur. At the time of his death, Marx was practically a forgotten man. Fewer than twenty people showed up for his funeral. He was not mourned by his fellow workers in the Siberian mines, as Engels had suggested, and few remembered even *The Communist Manifesto*, let alone *Capital*. John Stuart Mill never heard of him. At the end of his life, Marx could recall with agreement the words of the Bible, "For a testament is of force after men are dead: otherwise it is of no strength at all while the testator liveth" (Heb. 9:17).

The fate of his family is sad to contemplate. It was a nightmare. Marx was survived by only two daughters and his illegitimate son. In 1898, his daughter Eleanor Marx, known as Tussy and a strong-willed revolutionary like her father, committed suicide after learning that Freddy was the illegitimate son of her father and that her cynical Irish revolutionary husband was a bigamist. In 1911, Marx's surviving daughter, Laura, an eloquent speaker and a striking beauty, consummated a suicide pact with her husband, a French socialist. In sum, there was little joy in the last years of Karl and Jenny Marx and their descendants. Engels, known as the "General," died of cancer in 1895.

Marx's Exploitation Model of Capitalism

Let us now review Marx's major contributions to economics and determine what has had a lasting impact and what has been discarded.

In *Capital,* published in 1867, Karl Marx attempted to introduce an alternative model to the classical economics of Adam Smith. This system aimed to demonstrate through immutable "scientific" laws that the capitalist system was fatally flawed, that it inherently benefited capitalists and big business, that it exploited workers, that labor had been reduced to a mere commodity with a price but no soul, and that it was so crisis-prone that it would inevitably destroy itself. In many ways, the Marxist model rationalized its creator's belief that the capitalist system must be overthrown and replaced by communism.

The Labor Theory of Value

Marx found the Ricardian system well suited for his exploitation model. In many ways, David Ricardo was his mentor in economics.

As noted in chapter 2, Ricardo focused on production and how it was distributed between large classes—landlords, workers, and capitalists. Ricardo and his successor, John Stuart Mill, attempted to analyze the economy in terms of classes rather than the actions of individuals.

Say and the French laissez-faire school (chapter 2) did focus on the subjective utility of individuals, but Marx rejected Say and followed Ricardo by concentrating on the production of a single homogeneous "commodity" and the distribution of income from commodity production into classes.

In Ricardo's class system, labor played a critical role in determining value. First Ricardo and then Marx claimed that labor is the sole producer of value. The value of a "commodity" should be equal to the average quantity of labor-hours used in creating the commodity.

The Theory of Surplus Value

If indeed labor is the sole determinant of value, then where does that leave profits and interest? Marx labeled profits and interest "surplus value." It was only a short logical step to conclude, therefore, that capitalists and landlords were exploiters of labor. If indeed all value was the product of labor, then all profit obtained by capitalists and interest obtained by landlords must be "surplus value," unjustly extracted from the true earnings of the working class.

Marx developed a mathematical formula for his theory of surplus value. The rate of profit (p) or exploitation is equal to the surplus value (s) divided by the value of the final product (r). Thus,

$$p = s/r$$

For example, suppose a clothing manufacturer hires workers to make dresses. The capitalist sells the dresses for $100 apiece, but labor costs are $70 per dress. Therefore the rate of profit or exploitation is

$$p = \$30/\$100 = 0.3, \text{ or } 30\%$$

Marx divided the value of the final product into two forms of capital, constant capital (C) and variable capital (V). Constant capital represents factories and equipment. Variable capital is the cost of labor. Thus, the equation for the rate of profit becomes

$$p = s/[v + c]$$

Marx contended that profits and exploitation are increased by extending the workday for employees, and by hiring women and children at lower wages than men. Moreover, machinery and technological advances benefit the capitalist, but not the worker, Marx declared. Machinery, for example, allows capitalists to hire women and children to run the machines. The result can only be more exploitation.

Critics countered that capital is productive and deserves a reasonable return, but Marx offered the rebuttal that capital was nothing more than "frozen" labor and that, consequently, wages should absorb the entire proceeds from production. The classical economists had no answer to Marx, at least initially. And thus Marx won the day by "proving" through impeccable logic that capitalism inherently created a monstrous "class struggle" between workers, capitalists, and landlords—and the capitalists and landlords had an unfair advantage. Murray Rothbard observes, "As the nineteenth century passed its mid-mark, the deficiencies of Ricardian economics became ever more glaring. Economics itself had come to a dead end" (Rothbard 1980, 237). It was not until the work of Philip Wicksteed, the British clergyman, and Eugen von Böhm-Bawerk, the influential Austrian economist, that Marx was answered effectively, with a focus on the risk-taking and the entrepreneurial benefits the capitalists provide. But this topic must wait until chapter 4.

Falling Profits and the Accumulation of Capital

Marx had a perverse view of machinery and technology. The accumulation of capital was constantly growing in order to meet competition and keep the costs of labor down. "Accumulate, accumulate! That is Moses and the prophets! . . . Therefore, save, save, i.e., reconvert the greatest possible portion of surplus-value, or surplus-product into capital!" pronounced Marx in *Capital* (1976 [1867], 742).

Yet this leads to trouble, a crisis in capitalism, all according to the "law of the falling rate of profit." For, according to Marx's formula for the profit rate, $s/[v + c]$, we can see that adding machinery increases c and therefore drives down profits. Big business becomes more concentrated as the larger firms produce more cheaply, which "always ends in the ruin of many small capitalists." Meanwhile, workers become all the more miserable, having less and less with which to buy consumer goods. More and more workers are thrown out of work, becoming increasingly unemployed in an "industrial reserve army" earning a subsistence wage.

The Crisis of Capitalism

Lowering costs, falling profits, monopolistic power, underconsumption, massive unemployment of the proletarian class—all these conditions lead to "more extensive and more destructive crises" and depressions for the capitalistic system (Marx and Engels 1964 [1848], 13). And all this is derived from the labor theory of value!

Marx rejected Say's law of markets, which he labeled "childish babble . . . claptrap . . . humbug" (Buchholz 1999, 133). There was no stability in capitalism, no tendency toward equilibrium and full employment. Marx emphasized both the boom and the bust nature of the capitalist system, and that its ultimate demise was inevitable.

The Imperialism of Monopoly Capitalism

Marx was greatly impressed with the ability of capitalists to accumulate more capital and create new markets, both domestically and abroad. *The Communist Manifesto* described this phenomenon in a famous passage: "The bourgeoisie, during its rule of scarce one hundred years, has created more massive and more colossal productive forces than have all preceding generations together." The capitalists are engaged pell-mell "by the conquest of new markets, and by the more thorough exploitation of the old ones" (Marx and Engels 1964 [1848], 12–13).

Marxists ever after have characterized capitalism and big business as inherently "imperialistic," exploiting foreign workers and foreign resources. The theory of imperialism and colonialism was developed largely by J.A. Hobson and V.I. Lenin. Much of the developing world's anti-American and antiforeign attitudes during the twentieth century came from Marxist origins, and the results of this anticapitalist attitude have been devastating, resulting in retarded and even negative growth in many parts of Asia, Africa, and Latin America.

Historical Materialism

So where was capitalism headed? Marx was heavily influenced by George Wilhelm Hegel in developing his process of economic determinism. Hegel's basic thesis was "Contradiction (in nature) is the root of all motion and of all life." Hegel described this contradiction in terms of the dialectic, opposing forces that would eventually bring about a new force. An established "thesis" would cause an "antithesis" to develop in opposition, which in turn would eventually create a new "synthesis." This new synthesis then becomes the "thesis" and the process starts all over again as civilization progresses.

The diagram in Figure 3.1 reflects this Hegelian dialectic. Marx applied Hegel's dialectic to his deterministic view of history. Thus, the course of history could be described by using Hegelian concepts—from slavery to capitalism to communism.

Figure 3.1 **The Hegelian Dialectic Used to Describe the Course of History**

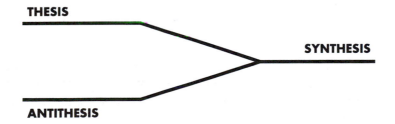

According to this theory, slavery was viewed as the principal means of production or thesis during Greco-Roman times. Feudalism became its main antithesis in the Middle Ages. The synthesis became capitalism, which became the new thesis after the Enlightenment. But capitalism faced its own antithesis—the growing threat of socialism. Eventually, this struggle would result in the ultimate system of production, communism. In this way, Marx was an eternal optimist. He firmly believed that all history pointed to higher forms of society, culminating in communism.

Marx's Solution: Revolutionary Socialism

But while communism was supposedly inevitable, Marx felt that revolution was necessary to bring it about. First and foremost, Marx was a leading proponent of the violent ("forceful") overthrow of government and the establishment of revolutionary socialism. He delighted in violence. Marx promoted revolutionary causes in *The Communist Manifesto* in 1848, the First International in 1860, and the Paris Commune in 1871. Although the German revolutionary failed to reveal his plans in detail, *The Communist Manifesto* did include a ten-point program (Marx and Engels 1964 [1848], 40):

1. Abolition of property in land and applications of all rents of land to public purposes.

2. A heavy progressive or graduated income tax.

3. Abolition of all right of inheritance.

4. Confiscation of the property of all emigrants and rebels.

5. Centralization of credit in the hands of the state by means of a national bank with state capital and an exclusive monopoly.

6. Centralization of the means of communication and transport in the hands of the state.

7. Extension of factories and instruments of production owned by the state; the bringing into cultivation of waste lands, and the improvement of the soil generally in accordance with a common plan.

8. Equal obligation of all to work. Establishment of industrial armies, especially for agriculture.

9. Combination of agriculture with manufacturing industries; gradual abolition of the distinction between town and country, by a more equitable distribution of the population over the country.

10. Free education for all children in public schools. Abolition of child factory labor in its present form. Combination of education with industrial production, and so on.

It is difficult to imagine instigating some of these measures without violence. But this was not all. Marx also advocated an authoritarian "dictatorship of the proletariat." He favored a complete abolition of private property, based on his theory that private property was the cause of strife, class struggle, and a form of slavery (1964 [1848], 27). He agreed with Proudhon that "property is theft." Without private property, there was no need for exchange, no buying and selling, and therefore Marx and Engels advocated the elimination of money (30). Production and consumption could continue and even thrive through central planning without exchange or currency.

Marx and Engels also demanded the abolition of the traditional family in an effort to "stop the exploitation of children by their parents" and to "introduce a community of women." The founders of communism supported a program of youth education that would "destroy the most hallowed of relations" and "replace home education by social" (33–35).

What about religion? Marx noted that "religion is the opium of the people." "Communism abolishes eternal truths, it abolishes all religion, and all morality, instead of constituting them on a new basis; it therefore acts in contradiction to all past historical experience" (38).

Marx anticipated that revolutionary socialism would for the first time allow the full expression of human existence and happiness. The goal of "universal opulence" that Adam Smith sought would finally be achieved under true communism. Marx was a millennialist at heart. Heaven could be achieved on earth. Eventually the dictatorship of the proletariat would be replaced by a classless, stateless society. Homo Marxist would be a new man!

Marx's Predictions Fail to Materialize

But all this was not to be. Marx's predictions went awry, though not all right away. As late as 1937, Wassily Leontief, the Russian émigré who later won the Nobel Prize for his input–output analysis, proclaimed that Marx's record was "impressive" and "correct" (Leontief 1938, 5, 8). But Leontief's praise was premature. Since then, as Leszek Kolakowski, former leader of the Polish Communist Party, declared, "All of Marx's important prophecies turned out to be false" (Denby 1996, 339). To review:

1. Under capitalism, the rate of profit has failed to decline, even while more and more capital has been accumulated over the centuries.

2. The working class has not fallen into greater and greater misery. Wages have risen substantially above the subsistence level. The industrial nations have seen a dramatic rise in the standard of living of the average worker. The middle class has not disappeared, but expanded. As Paul Samuelson concludes, "The immiserization of the working class . . . simply never took place. As a prophet Marx was colossally unlucky and his system colossally useless" (1967, 622).

3. There is little evidence of increased concentration of industries in advanced capitalist societies, especially with global competition.

4. Socialist utopian societies have not flourished, nor has the proletarian revolution inevitably occurred.

5. Despite business cycles and even an occasional great depression, capitalism appears to be flourishing as never before.

Update: Marxists as Modern-Day Doomsdayers

In *The Communist Manifesto*, Marx and Engels warned, "It is enough to mention the commercial crises that by their periodical return put on its trial, each time more threatening, the existence of the entire bourgeois society" (1964 [1848], 11–12).

Following their leader's footsteps, modern-day Marxists are constantly predicting the collapse of capitalism, only to be rebuffed time and again. In 1976, in the midst of the energy crisis and inflationary recession, socialist Michael Harrington published a book entitled *The Twilight of Capitalism*, which he dedicated to Karl Marx. He predicted that the crisis of the 1970s would be the end of capitalism.

In the same year, Marxist Ernest Mandel wrote an introduction to *Capital*, forcefully declaring, "It is most unlikely that capitalism will survive another half-century of the crises (military, political, social, monetary, cultural) which have occurred uninterruptedly since 1914" (Mandel 1976 [1867], 86).

Paul M. Sweezy, the Marxist professor at Harvard, was a longtime pessimist. Since the 1930s, he forecasted that capitalism was on the decline and that socialism, promoting higher standards of living, would advance "by leaps and bounds" (Sweezy 1942, 362). He coauthored a book entitled *The End of Prosperity* in 1977.

Yet, entering a new century, capitalism is even more dynamic than ever before. The modern-day Marxists, always the pessimists, have been proved wrong again.

The Curious Case of Nikolai Kondratieff

One famous Russian economist to contradict the official Marxist prediction of capitalism's inevitable demise was Nikolai Kondratieff (1892–1938). In 1926, he delivered a paper before the prestigious Economic Institute in Moscow, making the case for a fifty- to sixty-year business cycle. Based on price and output trends since the 1780s, Kondratieff described two-and-a-half upswing and downswing "long wave" cycles of prosperity and depression. Kondratieff found no evidence of an irreversible collapse in capitalism; rather, a strong recovery always succeeded depression.

In 1928, Kondratieff was removed from his position as head of Moscow's Business Conditions Institute and his thesis was denounced in the official Soviet encyclopedia (Solomou 1987, 60). He was soon arrested as the alleged leader of the nonexistent Working Peasants Party and deported to Siberia in 1930. On September 17, 1938, during Stalin's great purge, he was subjected to a second trial and condemned to ten years without the right to correspond with the outside world; however, Kondratieff was executed by firing squad on the same day this decree was issued. He was forty-six at the time of his murder.[5]

---

5. Just because Kondratieff was persecuted by the Soviets should not imply that his theory that capitalism automatically goes through fifty-to-sixty-year cycles is correct. Belief in the so-called Kondratieff long-wave cycle still survives on among some economists, historians, and financial analysts who regularly predict another depression and economic crisis. However, it has now been nearly eighty years since the last worldwide depression. As Victor Zarnowitz concluded recently, "There is much disagreement about the very existence of some of the long waves even among the supporters of the concept, and more disagreement yet about the timing of the waves and their phases" (Zarnowitz 1992, 238).

Criticisms of Marx

Why was Marx so terribly wrong after establishing what he insisted were "scientific" laws of economics?

First and foremost, his labor theory of value was defective. In rejecting Say's law of markets, he also denied Say's sound theory of value. Say correctly noted that the value of goods and services is ultimately determined by utility. If individuals do not demand or need a product, it doesn't matter how much labor or effort is put into producing it; it won't command value.

As historian Jacques Barzun noted, "Pearls are not valuable because men dive for them; men dive for them because pearls are valuable" (Barzun 1958, 152). And Philip Wicksteed, writing the first scientific criticism of Marx's labor theory in 1884, noted, "A coat is not worth eight times as much as a hat to the community because it takes eight times as long to make it. . . . The community is willing to devote eight times as long to the making of a coat because it will be worth eight times as much to it" (Wicksteed 1933, vii).[6]

And what about all those valuable things that keep increasing in value even though they require little or no labor, such as art or land? Marx recognized these were exceptions to his theory, but considered them of minor importance to the fundamental issue of labor power.

The Transformation Problem

Marx also faced a dilemma that became known as the "transformation problem," known as the profit rate and value problem. A conflict arises under Marx's system because some industries are labor intensive and others are capital intensive. (In Marxist language, they have a higher organic composition of capital.) In volume 1 of *Capital*, Marx insisted that prices varied directly with labor time, concluding therefore that capital-intensive industries should be less profitable than labor-intensive industries. Yet the evidence seems to

---

6. It was precisely this article, appearing in the socialist monthly *Today* in October 1884, that convinced George Bernard Shaw and Sidney Webb that the labor theory of value was untenable and thereby brought the whole Marxist edifice down in ruins (Lichtheim 1970, 192–93).

indicate similar profitability across all industries over the long run, since capital and investment could migrate from less to more profitable industries. Marx never could resolve this thorny issue, which Rothbard called "the most glaring single hole in the Marxian model" (Rothbard 1995b, 413).

Marx wrestled with this transformation problem his entire life, promising to have an answer in future volumes of *Capital*. In the introduction to volume 2 of *Capital*, Engels offered a prize essay contest on how Marx would solve the dilemma. For the next nine years, a large number of economists tried to solve it, but upon the publication of volume 3 of *Capital*, Engels announced that no one had succeeded[7] (Rothbard 1995b, 413). Eugen Böhm-Bawerk jumped on this singular failure in Marxian economics; in the words of Paul Samuelson, "make no mistake about it, Böhm-Bawerk is perfectly right in insisting that volume III of *Capital* never does make good the promise to reconcile the fabricated contradictions" (Samuelson 1967, 620).

The Vital Role of Capitalists and Entrepreneurs

Second, Marx blundered in failing to value the knowledge and work of capitalists and entrepreneurs. As we shall see in the next chapter, Böhm-Bawerk, Alfred Marshall and other great economists recognized the huge contribution capitalists and entrepreneurs make in taking on risk and providing the necessary capital (saving) and management skills necessary to operate a profitable enterprise.

The Worker-Capitalist Phenomenon

One of the biggest problems facing Marxism today is the gradual disintegration of economic classes. No longer is there is a clear division between capitalist and worker. Fewer and fewer workers are simply employees or wage earners. They are often shareholders and part owners of the companies they work for—through profit-sharing and pension plans, where they own shares in the companies they work for. Many workers are self-employed and are part-time capitalists.

---

7. A complete summary of the transformation debate among Marxists can be found in Howard and King (1989, 21–59).

Today, over half of American families own stock in publicly traded companies. Main Street has teamed up with Wall Street to create a new mass of worker-capitalists, which has greatly diminished revolutionary zeal within the labor markets.

Finally, Marx's view of machinery and capital goods is perverse and one-sided. Time-saving and labor-saving machinery does not simply lay off workers or reduce wages. It frequently makes the job easier to perform and allows workers to engage in other productive tasks. Machinery and technology have done an amazing job in reducing or eliminating the "worker alienation" Marx complained about so bitterly. By cutting costs, machinery and technological advances create new demands and new opportunities to produce other products. They create other jobs, often at better pay, for workers who are displaced. As Ludwig von Mises stated a century later, "there is only one means to raise wage rates permanently and for the benefit of all those eager to earn wages—namely, to accelerate the increase in capital available as against population" (Mises 1972, 89). The evidence is overwhelming that increasing labor productivity (output per man-hour) leads to higher wages.

To sum up Marxist economics, Paul Samuelson years ago concluded that almost nothing in the economics of classical Marxism survives analysis (Samuelson 1957). And Jonathan Wolff, a British professor sympathetic to Marxist ideas, recently concluded that while "Marx remains the most profound and acute critic of capitalism, even as it exists today, we may have no confidence in his solutions. . . . Marx's grandest theories are not substantiated" (Wolff 2002, 125–26).

Marx, the Anti-economist?

Michael Harrington claimed that Marx was the ultimate anti-economist (1976, 104–148). Indeed, he may be right. Marx was a naive idealist who failed profoundly to comprehend the role of capital, markets, prices, and money in advancing the material abundance of mankind.

The irony is that it is capitalism, not socialism or Marxism, that has liberated the worker from the chains of poverty, monopoly, war, and oppression, and has better achieved Marx's vision of a millennium of hope, peace, abundance, leisure, and aesthetic expression for the "full" human being.

Could Marxist socialism create the abundance and variety of goods and services, breakthrough technologies, new job opportunities, and leisure time of today? Hardly. Marx was incredibly ingenuous in thinking that his brand of utopian socialism could achieve a rapid rise in the workers' living standards. He wrote in the 1840s, "in communist society . . . nobody has one exclusive sphere of activity but each can become accomplished in any branch he wishes, . . . thus making it possible for me to do one thing today and another tomorrow, to hunt in the morning, fish in the afternoon, rear cattle in the evening, criticize after dinner, in accordance with my inclination, without becoming hunter, fisherman, shepherd or critic" (Marx 2000, 185). This is sheer ivory-tower naiveté, a characteristic of the early Marx. Marx's idealism would take us back to a primitive, if not barbaric, age of barter and tribal living, without the benefit of exchange and division of labor.

Thus, as we enter the twenty-first century, Adam Smith—the father of capitalism—is moving back in front of Karl Marx—the father of socialism. In the first edition of *The 100: The 100 Most Influential People in the World* (1978), author Michael Hart placed Marx ahead of Smith. But in the second edition, written in 1992 after the collapse of Soviet communism, Smith moved ahead of Marx.

Did Marx Recant?

Marx is said to have said, "I am not Marxist," in the late 1870s, but apparently it has been taken out of context. At times he was so despairing over his son-in-law Lafargue's socialist "theoretical gibberish," that Marx declared, "If that is Marxist, I am no Marxist." Biographer Fritz J. Raddatz concludes, "It is certainly not to be taken as a recantation or deviation from his own doctrine but, on the contrary, as a defense of that doctrine against those who would distort it" (Raddatz 1978, 130). But while Marx may not have relinquished his taste for violent revolution and his own theories, Engels appears to have revised his views in later years. He conceded that workers may earn more than subsistence wages, that other noneconomic factors could play a role in society, and that legal political means might achieve reform. "The one-time would-be dashing general of revolution had almost become a Social-Democratic reformer," writes Robert Wesson (1976, 37–38).

What's Left of Marxism?

If Marx's economic theories and predictions have proved to be inaccurate, is there anything salvageable from *Capital* and the rest of Marx's economic writings? Indeed, there is.

First and foremost is the issue of economic determinism. What moves society—ideas or vested interests? In his "law" of historical materialism, Marx countered the traditional view that religion or any other institutional philosophy determined the culture of a community. Instead, Marx contended the opposite, that the material or economic forces of society determined the legal, political, religious, and commercial "superstructure" of national culture. In *The Poverty of Philosophy*, Marx explained, "the handmill gives you society with the feudal lord, the steam-mill gives you society with the industrial capitalist" (Marx 1995, 219–20). Today most sociologists recognize the important role economic forces play in society.

Second is the issue of classes in society. Marx's theory of class consciousness and class conflict has engaged historians and sociologists. To what extent are behavior and thought reflections of bourgeois or proletarian values? To what point does the ruling class protect and advance its interests through the political process? Does the group that owns or controls property and the means of production dominate? Is it true that "law and politics are in the service of industrial capital"? If so, asks Wolff, "why are trade unions allowed? Why do universities have Arts Faculties as well as Engineering (indeed, why allow the teaching of Marxism)? Why don't the multinationals win every one of their court cases?" (Wolff 2002, 59) If the state is under the thumb of the capitalist interests, why did the Great Depression occur, since it severely harmed them? Karl Popper ridiculed the all-knowing Marxist position: "A Marxist could not open a newspaper without finding on every page confirming evidence for his interpretation of history; not only in the news, but also in its presentation—which revealed the class bias of the paper—and especially of course in what the paper did not say" (Popper 1972, 35).

Third, Marxists stress several contemporary issues that Marx raised:

- The problem of alienation and monotonous work in the workplace.

- The problems of greed, fraud, and materialism under a money-seeking capitalist society.

- The concerns over inequality of wealth, income, and opportunity.

- Conflicts over race, feminism, discrimination, and the environment.

David Denby, an essayist who read Marx as an adult in a college classic literature course, discusses several modern-day issues frequently raised by today's Marxists. First, alienation. Denby states: "Alienation is a loss of self: We work for others, to fulfill other people's goals, and often we confront what we produce with an indifference bordering on disgust" (1996, 349). How do we deal with boredom and meaninglessness in today's business world? Yet what is the alternative? Is a communal or socialist society any less boring or meaningless? A capitalist society that gradually improves the quantity, quality, and variety of goods and services offers less boredom and a greater chance of fulfillment, often by providing shorter workdays that allow workers to find fulfillment in avocations outside their work.

What about greed? Does the market system reduce human activity to a complete focus on material things? Marx complained that the capitalism of Adam Smith causes society to be a "commercial enterprise," where "everyone of its members is a salesman. . . . The less you eat, drink, and buy books, go to the theater or the balls, or to the public-house, and the less you think, love, theorize, sing, paint, fence, etc., the more you will be able to save and the greater will become your treasure which neither moth nor rust will corrupt—your capital. The less you are, the less you express your life, the greater is your alienated life and the greater is the saving of your alienated being" (Fromm 1966, 144).

Modern-day Marxists complain about today's materialistic society. "We go to work to earn money, and then go to shops to spend it. We are people with tunnel vision," contends Wolff. In her book, *The Overworked American* (1991), Harvard economist Juliet Schor contends that modern capitalism, especially since World War II, has forced Americans to become workaholics.[8] Denby writes, "Capitalism created envy and the desire to define oneself through goods. Capitalism itself, in its American version, bears part of the responsibility for low morals" (1996, 349). According to this view, capitalism crushes the human spirit's potential by forcing us to think always of work. Thus, according to Marx, the marketplace becomes a monster, the "universal whore" (Marx 2000, 118).

This argument is popular, but is countered by the thesis of Adam Smith and Montesquieu, among others, that the business culture gradually restrains fraud and greed (see chapter 1). Smith noted that man is not simply a work machine: "It is in the interest of every man to live as much at his ease as he can" (Smith 1965[1776], 718). Capitalism also produces wealthy individuals who spend much time and effort on spiritual, artistic, nonmaterial, nongreedy initiatives, providing many benefits to society. It even allows individuals to drop out of the material world, and engage in spiritual interests. Private surplus wealth goes toward many good causes, including the arts, charities, foundations, and programs to help the needy.

Denby's college professor posed another Marxist criticism: "In bourgeois society the relations between human beings imitate the relations between commodities. . . . If cash is the only thing connecting us, what keeps society together?" The yearning for community in a highly individualistic market economy is a major concern. Do we measure people solely by their income and net worth? Does the chasing of the almighty dollar cause the tearing down of historic homes and the building of high-rise apartments? Does capitalism pressure us to work so long and hard that we don't have time to develop relationships outside the office? Denby warns, "In America, there seemed less and less holding us together" (1996, 344–351).

There is no question that the fast-paced market economy makes us live more independently from the community. The exchange of goods

---

8. Other economists dispute Schor's contention that Americans are overworked. See "New Study Suggests Americans Aren't Overworked After All," *Wall Street Journal*, September 15, 2005, p. D2. It states, "The Bureau of Labor Statistics found Americans over the age of 15 on average sleep 8.6 hours a day and full-time workers on average clock in 8.1 hours on the job. That's more work than occurs in many European countries, but still leaves time for other activities."

and services often becomes anonymous and unfriendly. Undoubtedly in a communitarian society, we would all know our neighbors and local businesspeople better. But what are we giving up?

The Money Nexus

Beyond the issues of economic determinism, class consciousness, and contemporary social issues, I find Marx's commentary on the evolutionary role of capitalism valuable in my own work as a financial economist. In chapter 3 of *Capital*, he begins with a discussion of the barter of two commodities, C and C'. The exchange takes place as follows:

$$C - C'$$

When money is introduced, the relationship changes to:

$$C - M - C'$$

Here, money represents the medium of exchange of two commodities. Normally in the production process from raw commodities to the final product, money is exchanged several times. The focus of the capitalist system is on the production of useful goods and services, and money simply serves as a medium of exchange—a means to an end.

However, Marx pointed out that it is very easy for the money capitalist to start viewing the world differently and more narrowly in terms of "making money" rather than "making useful goods and services." Marx represents this new business way of thinking as follows:

$$M - C - M'$$

In other words, the businessman uses his money (capital) to produce a commodity, C, which, in turn, is sold for more money, M'. By focusing on money as the beginning and end of their activities, it is very easy for capitalists to lose sight of the ultimate purpose of economic activity—to produce and exchange goods. The goal is no longer C, but M.

Finally, the market system advances one step further to the point where commodities (goods and services) do not enter the picture at all. The exchange process becomes:

$$M - M'$$

This final stage reflects the capital or financial markets, such as money markets and securities (stocks and bonds). By now, it is easier for commodity capitalism to become pure financial capitalism, further removed from its roots of commodity production. In this environment, businesspeople often forget the whole purpose of the economic system—to produce useful goods and services—and concentrate solely on "making money," whether through gambling, short-term trading techniques, or simply earning money in a bank account or from T-bills. Ultimately the goal of making money is best achieved by providing useful goods and services, but it is a lesson that must be learned over and over again in the commercial world.

Thus, we can see how a capitalistic culture can lead to the loss of both ultimate purpose and a sense of community. This tendency to move away from the true purpose of economic activity constantly challenges business leaders, investors, and citizens to get back to the basics.

In sum, Karl Marx cannot be entirely dismissed. His economic theory may have been defective, his revolutionary socialism may have been destructive, and Marx himself may have been irascible, but his philosophical analysis of market capitalism has elements of merit and deserves our attention.

Update: Marxists Keep Their Hero Alive and Kicking

Marxism has never made much of an inroad into economics, which emphasizes high theory and econometric model-building. The few Marxists on campus have included Maurice Dobb at Cambridge, Paul Baran at Stanford, and Paul Sweezy at Harvard. Sweezy (1910–2004) was the most fascinating, being the only economist I know who went from laissez-faire to Marxism. (Whittaker Chambers, Mark Blaug, and Thomas Sowell all went in the opposite direction.) Born in New York City in 1910 to a Morgan banker, Paul Sweezy graduated with honors from the best private schools, Exeter, and Harvard. Brilliant, handsome, and witty, Sweezy left Harvard in 1932 as a classical economist, went to the London School of Economics for graduate work, became an ardent Hayekian, then briefly fell under the spell of Harold Laski and John Maynard Keynes, and finally converted to

Marxism! From then on, the debonair Sweezy made every effort to make Marxism respectable on college campuses.

Returning to Harvard as an instructor during the golden era of the Keynesian revolution, he befriended John Kenneth Galbraith, tutored Robert Heilbroner, and collaborated with Joseph Schumpeter on his forthcoming *Capitalism, Socialism and Democracy*. Sweezy wrote his most famous article on the "kinked" demand curve, helped organize the Harvard Teachers' Union, and published *The Theory of Capitalist Development* (1942), an extremely coherent and compelling exposition of Marxism (although the author overly committed himself to citing Stalin). Like Schumpeter, Sweezy predicted at the end of his book that capitalism would inevitably collapse and socialism would "demonstrate its superiority on a large scale" (1942, 352–63).

His teaching at Harvard was interrupted when he joined the Office of Strategic Services (the predecessor of the Central Intelligence Agency) in 1942. After the war, Sweezy came up for tenure at Harvard, but despite vigorous backing by Schumpeter, was rejected, never to have a permanent academic position again. In 1949, he co-founded *Monthly Review*, "an independent socialist magazine," whose first issue made a major splash by publishing "Why Socialism?" by Albert Einstein. (Einstein's essay is remarkably Marxist in tone.) Sweezy has been associated with *Monthly Review* ever since, in addition to collaborating with Paul Baran on writing *Monopoly Capital* (1966). Yet throughout his career, Sweezy was known for taking "far-fetched and unreal" positions (his words), such as his arch defense of Fidel Castro's Cuba (a nation currently ranked by the UN as the world's worst human rights violator) and his constant anticipation of capitalism's imminent collapse (1942, 363). In 1954, during the McCarthy era, he was jailed for refusing on principle to answer questions about "subversive activities" in New Hampshire; in 1957 the Supreme Court overturned the verdict.

Other Radical Trends

Other radical journals and organizations emerged during the Vietnam War: the journals *Dissent* and *New Left Review*, and the Union of Radical Political Economists, or URPE for short. They all reached their heyday in the protest days of the 1960s and the crisis-prone 1970s. It was 1968 when several Marxists met at the University of Michigan to establish the Union of Radical Political Economists and chose the acerbic-sounding acronym URPE. The purpose of URPE is to develop a "critique of the capitalist system and all forms of exploitation and oppression while helping to construct a progressive social policy and create socialist alternatives" (URPE website).

By 1976, Paul Samuelson reported that at least 10 percent of the profession consisted of Marxist-style economists. Although Marxism has had a far greater influence in sociology, political science, and literary theory, some economics departments are known for their radicalism, including the University of Massachusetts at Amherst, the New School of Social Research in New York City, the University of California at Riverside, and the University of Utah.

Since the collapse of the Soviet Union and the central-planning socialist paradigm, the lure of Marxism has faded, at least in economics. Attendance at URPE sessions at the annual American Economic Association meetings is down, and URPE membership has fallen to around 800.

Marx and his followers have traditionally taken a dim view of the future of capitalism. In the twentieth century, Marxists frequently wrote of the "twilight of capitalism," a favorite book title (William Z. Foster in 1949, Michael Harrington in 1977, and Boris Kagarlitsky in 2000). They all predicted the imminent collapse of the capitalist system. However, Lord Meghnad Desai, an economist at the London School of Economics, recently proposed the startling thesis that Marx would have supported the resurgence of capitalism around the world. *The Communist Manifesto* spoke eloquently about the "ever growing ... constantly expanding ... rapid" advance of vigorous and vital capitalist forces, reaching beyond natural borders to a world market (1964 [1848], 4). The old Marxists were premature in their dire predictions. But what happens after global capitalism runs its course? Desai asks, "Will there ever be Socialism beyond Capitalism?" (Desai 2004, 315). Some Marxists, such as David Schweickart, suggest some form of "economic democracy" will develop after the "current late decadent" stage of capitalism plays itself out (Schweickart 2002).

The Rise and Fall of Liberation Theology

In the late 1960s and early 1970s, a Marxist-driven ideology developed in Latin America, especially among Catholic priests who worked in the *barrios* and *favelas*, known as "liberation theology." While reject-ing the Marxist extremes of atheism and materialism, these political activists sought to liberate the poor by combining Marxist doctrines of exploitation, class struggle, and imperialism with the Christian theology of compassion for the poor and underprivileged. Popular books carried the titles *Communism and the Bible* and *Theology of Liberation*, both published in English by Orbis Books, a subsidiary of the Catholic ministry Maryknoll Fathers and Sisters. "Christ led me to Marx," declared Ernesto Cardenal, the Nicaraguan priest, to Pope John Paul II in 1983. "I'm a Marxist who believes in God, follows Christ and is a revolutionary for the sake of his kingdom" (Novak 1991, 13).

The father of liberation theology, Gustavo Gutiérrez, is a short, mild-mannered professor of theology who wrote about his work with the poor in his native city of Lima, Peru, in *Theology of Liberation* (1973). Gutiérrez explained his "liberation theology" in Marxist terms (McGovern 1980, 181–82):

> I discovered three things. I discovered that poverty was a destructive thing, something to be fought against and destroyed, not merely something which was the object of our charity. Secondly, I discovered that poverty was not accidental. The fact that these people are poor and not rich is not just a matter of chance, but the result of a structure. It was a structural question. Third, I discovered that poverty was something to be fought against.....[I]t became critically clear that in order to serve the poor, one had to move into political action.

Marxist theologists blamed capitalism, and especially the "imperial-istic" United States and its multinational corporations, for this oppres-sive atmosphere in Latin America. They expressed a radical hostility to private property, markets, and profits as an "exploitive" process in favor of the rich at the expense of the poor. And if the choice was be-tween revolution and democracy, revolution, even violent revolt, was preferable. Their policies included nationalization, aversion to foreign investment, and imposition of price controls and trade barriers.

Critics of liberation theology contend that these statist policies have only made poverty and inequality worse in Latin countries. Michael Novak sees the Latin American system differently from the Marx-ists: "The present order is not free but statist, not market-centered but privilege-centered, not open to the poor but protective of the rich.

Large majorities of the poor are propertyless. The poor are prevented by law from founding and incorporating their own enterprises. They are denied access to credit. They are held back by an ancient legal structure, designed to protect the ancient privileges of a pre-capitalist elite" (Novak 1991, 5).

What is the Adam Smith solution to poverty and inequality in Latin America? The challenge, according to Novak, is to create genuine private-sector jobs, the real solution to poverty. "Revolutionaries," he states, "seem mostly to create huge armies. Economic activists create jobs." To truly liberate Latin America, he and other disciples of Adam Smith advocate open markets, foreign investment, low taxes, opportunities for business creation and ownership of property by all citizens, and political stability under the rule of law—a "liberal, pluralistic, communitarian, public-spirited, dynamic, inventive" nation not unlike the Asian tigers adopted in the recent past (Novak 1991, 32).[9]

Since the fall of Soviet communism and the socialist central-planning model, liberation theology has lost its steam and most Latin American countries have adopted a more open economy. Consequently, Latin nations have grown rapidly and the percentage of poor has declined. Orbis Books and the Maryknoll Fathers and Sisters ministry no longer publish books on liberation theology.

The Next Revolution

Only a few years after Marx's masterpiece, *Capital*, was published, a new breed of European economists came on the scene. These economists corrected the errors of Marx and the classical economists, and brought about a permanent revolution. As noted earlier, the cost-of-production approach to price theory had put economics in a box, a box containing a bombshell that could annihilate the classical system of natural liberty. It would take a revolutionary breakthrough in economic theory to rejuvenate the dismal science and restore the foundations of Adam Smith's model. That is the subject of chapter 4.

---

9. Peruvian economist Hernando de Soto has written several popular books on the need for legal and economic reforms in Latin America and developing countries in general. See Soto (2002, 2003).

Scottish economist Adam Smith (1723–90) was a professor of moral philosophy at Glasgow University between 1751 and 1763. "I am a beau in nothing but my books."

In 1776, Adam Smith published the "crown jewel" of economics, *The Wealth of Nations.* "It contains the most important substantive proposition in all economics: the pursuit of self-interest under conditions of competition."

Three writers who influenced Adam Smith's "system of natural liberty"…

| Charles Louis de Montesquieu (1689–1755) France | David Hume (1711–76) Scotland | Benjamin Franklin (1706–90) United States |

The French advanced Smith's laissez faire model . . .

Jean-Baptiste Say
(1767–1832)

Frédéric Bastiat
(1801–50)

Alexis de Tocqueville
(1805–59)

. . . while the British classical economists took it down a dangerous road.

Thomas Robert Malthus
(1766–1834)

David Ricardo
(1772–1823)

John Stuart Mill
(1806–73)

German Philosopher G.W.F. Hegel (1770–1831): His theory of recurring rhythm of destruction and re-creation formed the basis of Marx's dialectical materialism.

Marx and Engels among socialists in Paris, the late summer of 1844. They released *The Communist Manifesto* in 1848.

Das Kapital,

Kritik der politischen Oekonomie.

Von

Karl Marx.

Erster Band.
Buch I: Der Produktionsprozess des Kapitals.

Das Recht der Uebersetzung wird vorbehalten.

Hamburg
Verlag von Otto Meissner.
1867.
New-York: L. W. Schmidt, 24 Barclay-Street.

German philosopher and economist Karl Marx (1818–83) published the first volume of *Das Kapital*, his magnum opus, in 1867. "The most powerful attack on capitalism ever written."

Marx and Engels with Marx's daughters Laura and Eleanor, 1864

Author views Karl Marx's tomb in Highgate Cemetery in London: "Workers of the World, Unite!"

Marx grew his beard in order to imitate a statue of Zeus given by his friends in the 1860s.

Chinese banners honoring the founders of Communism: Marx and Engels, Lenin and Stalin, Mao Zedong (1960s)

Austrian Eugen Böhm-Bawerk (1851–1914) was the first economist to critique Marxist theory of capitalism.

Columbia professor John Bates Clark (1847–1938) countered Marx's exploitation theory of labor with his marginal productivity theory.

Cambridge professor Alfred Marshall (1842-1924) helped transform economics into a formal, rigorous science following the marginalist revolution.

Yale Professor Irving Fisher (1867–1947) created the first price indexes and developed the quantity theory of money, but failed to predict the 1929–33 economic crisis.

THE
GENERAL THEORY
OF
EMPLOYMENT INTEREST
AND MONEY

BY

JOHN MAYNARD KEYNES
FELLOW OF KING'S COLLEGE, CAMBRIDGE

MACMILLAN AND CO., LIMITED
ST. MARTIN'S STREET, LONDON
1936

John Maynard Keynes (1883–1946), British economist and statesman, published his influential *General Theory* in 1936: "I believe myself to be writing a book which will largely revolutionise the way the world thinks about economic problems."

Keynes was a financial wizard who made trading decisions while still in bed in the morning (1940).

Keynes shocked his Bloomsbury friends when he married Russian ballet dancer Lydia Lopokova in 1925.

Keynes, meeting Harry Dexter White at Bretton Woods, New Hampshire, in 1944, helped frame the post-war international economic system based on fixed exchange rates and the creation of the International Monetary Fund and the World Bank.

MIT Professor Paul Anthony Samuelson (1915-) and his popular textbook, *Economics* (1948), made Keynesianism the standard theory in the post-war period. Samuelson was the first American to win the Nobel prize in Economics in 1970.

In the 1970s, Austrian economist Friedrich von Hayek (1899–1992) and Chicago professor Milton Friedman (1912–2006) led a free-market counterrevolution. "Half a century later, it is Keynes who has been toppled and Hayek and Friedman, the fierce advocates of free markets, who are preeminent."

4

From Marx to Keynes

Scientific Economics Comes of Age

> The success of the marginal revolution is intimately associated
> with the professionalization of economics in the
> last quarter of the nineteenth century.
> —*Mark Blaug (in Black, Coats, and Goodwin 1973)*

The period between Karl Marx and the next big-three economist, John Maynard Keynes, witnessed a gigantic leap in economics as a powerful new engine of analysis that achieved unparalleled success among the social sciences.

In the previous chapter, we ended with Karl Marx and his damning indictment of the Adam Smith model. How did Adam Smith and his system of natural liberty make a comeback after being left for dead by the socialist critics? The first step to recovery came as a result of powerful economic forces. The colossal might of the Industrial Revolution catapulted the Western world into a new age of prosperity of the sort never before witnessed in history. The commercial power of capitalism spread from Britain to Germany to the United States during the nineteenth century and throughout the world in the twentieth. While Marx anticipated the expansionary growth of capitalism, he overlooked a significant event: all economic classes—capitalists, landlords, and workers—experienced improvement in their material living conditions, and the proportion of the population living in dire poverty fell sharply. By the time Karl Marx died in 1883, evidence was mounting that the Malthus-Ricardo-Marx "subsistence wage" thesis was terribly wrong. Adam Smith's upbeat system of universal prosperity was gaining credence.

Yet, while the industrial economy was making progress, economic theory was at a dead end. Adam Smith recognized that economic freedom and limited government would unleash wealth and ubiquitous prosperity, but he had only a limited theoretical framework with which to explain how consumers and producers worked through the price system to achieve a higher standard of living. Ricardo, Mill and the classical school developed a cost-of-production rationale for prices of goods, commodities, and labor; but in doing so, they ignored consumer demand and became hostage to Marxian polemics. Having no understanding of price theory and marginal analysis, the classical economists created a false dichotomy between "production for profits" and "production for use." Under this defective model, capitalists could make money without necessarily fulfilling consumer needs. "Exchange" value was unrelated to "use" value. Moreover, the Ricardian system was antagonistic. If profits or rents increased, they did so only at the expense of the workers' wages. As class struggle appeared inevitable, the Smithian world of universal prosperity and harmony of interests disintegrated. The classical economists tragically separated the questions of "production" and "distribution," which, as we have noted, gave ammunition to the socialist causes of redistribution, nationalization, and state central planning.

Economics as a science stagnated in England. John Stuart Mill had arrogantly declared in his popular *Principles* textbook, "Happily, there is nothing in the laws of value which remains for the present or any future writer to clear up; the theory of the subject is complete" (Black, Coats, and Goodwin 1973, 181). Classical economics was out of favor in France. The profession had reached such a low point that professors in Germany, Marx's homeland, rejected the idea that there was any such thing as economic theory. "Under the onslaughts of the Historical School," Friedrich Hayek confessed, "not only were the classical doctrines completely abandoned—but any attempt at theoretical analysis came to be regarded with deep distrust" (Hayek 1976, 13).

If capitalism was to survive and prosper, it would require a new epistemology, a breakthrough in economic theory. Economics desperately needed a new impetus, a general theory that could explain how all classes gain—landlords, capitalists, and workers—and all consumers benefit. But where would it come from?

Three Economists Make a Remarkable Discovery

We have noted how certain years stand out in the history of economics, how a cluster of events occurs at the same time, such as

1776, the year of the Declaration of Independence and the *Wealth of Nations,* and 1848, the year of *The Communist Manifesto* and Mill's *Principles* textbook. The early 1870s—and especially the year 1871—was a similar time, marking the period in which three economists independently discovered the principle of marginal subjective utility and ushered in the "neoclassical" marginalist revolution. The idea that prices and costs are determined by final consumer demand and their relative marginal utility, was the last major piece missing from the evolution of modern economics. Its discovery resolved the paradox of value that had frustrated the classical economists from Adam Smith to John Stuart Mill, and was also the undoing of Marxian economics.

Who were these economists? From Austria came Carl Menger (1840–1921); from France, Leon Walrus (1834–1910); and from Britain, William Stanley Jevons (1835–1882). While it is true that a few forerunners, such as Hermann Gossen, Samuel Longfield, Antoine Cournot, and Jules Dupuit, had earlier employed the principles of marginal utility, it was not until these three came together that the marginality principle became widely recognized and adopted in the profession. Swedish economist Knut Wicksell, an eyewitness to the marginalist revolution, described it as a "bolt from the blue" (Wicksell 1958, 186).

The Meaning of the Marginalist Revolution

Both Menger and Jevons published their new theories in 1871, although Jevons gave a lecture on his fundamental ideas in 1862. Menger published his *Grundsätze der Volkswirtschaftslehre,* later translated as *Principles of Economics* (1976 [1871]), and Jevons issued *The Theory of Political Economy.* A few years later, in 1874 and 1877, Walras published his two-part *Elements of Pure Economics.* Together, these economists developed what has come to be called the "neoclassical" school of economics. It combines the original work of Adam Smith's model of free competition with the marginal theory of subjective value. By the next generation, the marginalist revolution had swept through the economics profession and, to a large extent, replaced the Ricardian framework with a new orthodoxy. Though not as rapid as the Keynesian revolution in the late 1930s, the marginalist revolution of the 1870s conquered the profession with equal unanimity and force over the next generation.

The triumvirate of the marginalist revolution—Menger, Jevons, and Walras—rejected the objective cost-of-production theories of value and focused instead upon the subjective principle of utility and consumer demand as the keystone of a new approach to economics. They noted that individuals make choices on the basis of preferences and values in the real world. Like J.-B. Say, they recognized that no amount of labor or production confers value on a product. There is no such thing as "intrinsic value," as Ricardo alleged. Value consists of the subjective valuations of individual users. In short, customers have to be willing to pay a certain amount before producers will employ productive resources to produce a product, enough to make a reasonable profit.

As noted earlier, Adam Smith made a strategic error in distinguishing between value in "use" and value in "exchange." This gave ammunition to the socialists and Marxists, who complained about the difference in the marketplace between "production for profit" and "production for use." They blamed capitalists for being more interested in "making profits" than in "providing a useful service," as if profitable exchange is unrelated to consumer use.

Now the marginal revolution resolved the paradox of value and, in doing so, undercut the socialists' argument. Resolving the diamond-water paradox, the marginalists demonstrated that the difference in value between water and diamonds is due to the relative abundance of water and the relative scarcity of diamonds (given the demand for each). Since the supply of water is abundant, the demand for each additional unit (marginal utility) is low. Since the supply of diamonds is extremely limited, the demand for each additional diamond is high. Hence, there is no longer a contradiction between value in use and value in exchange.[1] They are equalized at the margin.

---

1. Here's a strange twist in the history of economics: Adam Smith actually had the correct answer to the diamond-water paradox a decade prior to writing *The Wealth of Nations*. Smith's lectures on jurisprudence, delivered in 1763, reveal that he recognized that price was determined by scarcity. Smith said, "It is only on account of the plenty of water that it is so cheap as to be got for the lifting, and on account of the scarcity of diamonds. . . . that they are so dear." The Scottish professor added that when supply conditions change, the value of a product changes

Under the new microeconomics, profits and use are directly connected. Prices of goods and supplies (costs) are determined by subjective demands and their best marginal or alternative use (known as "opportunity cost"). Price–cost margins determine profit and loss, the driving force behind what is produced, at what price, and in what amount, all according to what customers are willing to pay and demand. Prices reflect consumer demands, and profit-driven production seeks to meet those demands. If producers do not provide a useful service, their business will be unprofitable.

Under this advance in economic thinking, a new generation of economists found that production and distribution could once again be linked together. The demands of consumers ultimately determine the final prices of consumer goods, which in turn set the direction for productive activity. Final demand establishes the prices of the cooperative factors of production—wages, rents, and profits—according to the value they add to the production process. In short, income was not distributed, it was earned, according to the value added by each participant in the production process. In the case of labor, the idea that wages are determined by the marginal productivity of labor evolved out of this marginal principle of value and was more fully perfected by John Bates Clark, an American economist at Columbia University, at the turn of the century. According to Clark, under

---

also. Smith noted that a rich merchant lost in the Arabian desert would value water very highly. If the quantity of diamonds could "by industry . . . be multiplied," the price of diamonds would drop (Smith 1982 [1763], 33, 3, 358). Oddly, his cogent explanation of the diamond-water paradox disappeared when he was writing Chapter 4, Book I, of *The Wealth of Nations*. Was Smith suffering from absent-mindedness? Economist Roger Garrison doesn't think so. He blames the change on Smith's Calvinist background, which emphasized the benefits of hard work, useful production, and frugality. In his mind, diamonds and jewels were vain luxury items and relatively "useless" compared to water and other "useful" goods. Garrison points to Smith's odd dichotomy between "productive" and "unproductive" labor; see the third chapter of Book II in *The Wealth of Nations,* where Smith refers to professions such as minister, physician, musician, orator, actor, and other producers of services as "frivolous" occupations (1965 [1776], 315). Farmers and manufacturers, on the other hand, are "productive." Why? Because Smith's preference for Presbyterian conscience argues against consumption in favor of saving and work. As Garrison states, "The basis for the distinction in not Physiocratic fallacies but Presbyterian values. Productive labor is future oriented; unproductive labor is present oriented" (Garrison 1985, 290; Rothbard 1995a, 444–50).

competitive conditions, each factor of production—land, labor, and capital—received fair compensation for its added value.

Böhm-Bawerk Makes Two Devastating Arguments Against Marx

Another Austrian economist, Eugen Böhm-Bawerk (1851–1914), was the first major economist to contest Marx's critique of capitalism, and his blistering attack on Marx's theories was so devastating that Marxism has never really taken hold in the economics profession as it has done in sociology, anthropology, history, literary theory, and other disciplines.

Böhm-Bawerk introduced his critique of Karl Marx in his classic work, *Capital and Interest* (1959 [1884]), in which he first fully reviewed the history of interest theories from ancient times. The last half of this section deals with the exploitation theories of Rodbertus, Proudhon, Marx, and other socialists. Yet Böhm-Bawerk was not simply a bitter critic of Marx. He built upon the work of Menger and made original contributions in the areas of saving and investing, capital and interest, and economic growth. Even today, no work on economic growth theory is complete without a discussion of Böhm-Bawerk's contributions.

Recall from chapter 3 that Marx's theory of surplus value argued that workers deserve the full value of the products they produce. Landlords who receive rents and capitalists who earn profits and interest exploit the workers and take from them the fruits of their labors. In response, Böhm-Bawerk made two points of rebuttal.

First, Böhm-Bawerk's "waiting" argument. Here, he relied on the abstinence theory of interest, a concept earlier developed by Nassau Senior. Capitalists abstain from current consumption and use their savings to expand and improve goods and services. Interest income reflects this waiting factor in all economic life, and is therefore justified as a legitimate compensation to capitalists and investors. Capital-goods producers must wait for their goods to be manufactured and sold to their customers (further down the road toward consumption) before they can be paid. Investors in bonds and real estate must wait before they fully earn back their investment.

In short, businesspeople, capitalists, investors, and landlords all have to wait to be paid. But what about hired workers? They do not have to wait. They agree to perform a certain amount of labor for a wage or salary, and they are paid every month or every two weeks, regardless of whether the products they produce are sold or not. They do not have to worry about accounts receivable or accounts payable, about investment debt or changing markets. They get paid like clockwork, assuming their employers are honest and solvent. In fact, the capitalist-owner is constantly advancing the funds to pay the workers' wages, prior to receipt of payment for the products to be sold, which may mean waiting months and sometimes years, depending on how quickly the products can be sold and the money received. As Böhm-Bawerk concluded, "the workers cannot wait. . . . [T]hey continue to be dependent on those who already possess a finished store of the so-called intermediate products, in a word, on the capitalists" (1959 [1884], 83).

Capitalists as Risk Takers

Böhm-Bawerk made another important point. Business capitalists take risks that workers do not. They combine the right amount of land, labor, and capital to create a product that competes in the marketplace, a product on which they may or may not make a profit. The capitalist-entrepreneur takes that risk while hired workers do not. Workers get paid regularly and, if the business goes under, the most they will lose is a paycheck; they only need to search for another job. But the business entrepreneur may face financial ruin, heavy debts, and bankruptcy. In short, the workers' risk level is substantially less than the capitalist-entrepreneurs'.

How does the market reward this additional risk? By compensating the capitalist-entrepreneur with a significant portion of the product's value, via profits and interest. In sum, the hired workers are justifiably not paid the full product of their labor, but only that part commensurate with their immediate satisfaction in wages and the lower degree of risk involved in working in the business.

After Böhm-Bawerk's attack on Marxist doctrines of surplus value, few mainstream economists accepted the labor theory of value, Marx's exploitation theory, or his theory of surplus value. Marxists ever after have been on the defensive when it comes to theoretical rigor.

Böhm-Bawerk Introduces a Non-Marxist
Capitalist Theory

After demolishing the socialist arguments against capitalism, Böhm-Bawerk created a whole new chapter in economic theory by focusing on his "positive" theory of capital development. In fact, his 1884 book was aptly titled in English, *The Positive Theory of Capital*. Like Marx, Böhm-Bawerk focused on capital in all its forms—saving, investing, technology, capital goods, productivity, knowledge, education, research and development—as the key to fulfilling Adam Smith's worldview of universal prosperity.

Böhm-Bawerk, like Adam Smith, was a strident defender of saving and investment as a critical element in economic growth. Simple labor and hard work are not enough to achieve a higher standard of living. "It is simply not true that the man is 'merely industrious.' He is both industrious and thrifty" (Böhm-Bawerk 1959 [1884], 116).

In justifying the need for saving and investment, he began his theory with a discussion of the function of capital as a tool of production. According to Böhm-Bawerk, an economy grows through the adoption of new "roundabout" production processes. It takes time and money to adopt a new technology or invention, but once it is finished, new products and production processes expand at a faster pace. An increase in savings may mean a temporary reduction in the production of current consumer goods, but investment goods would increase. "For an economically advanced nation does not engage in hoarding, but invests its savings. It buys securities, it deposits its money at interest in savings banks or commercial banks, puts it out on loan, etc. . . . . In other words, there is an increase in capital, which rebounds to the benefit of an enhanced enjoyment of consumption goods in the future" (Böhm-Bawerk 1959 [1884], 113).

Alfred Marshall and the Cambridge School Advance
Economic Science

As a result of the marginalist revolution, the discipline of economics was never the same. It left Marxism behind and rapidly became a grown-up science, with its own box of tools, systematic laws, and quantitative analysis. Economists hoped that political economy, once the domain of theology, philosophy, and law, could become a new science that would match the logic and precision of mathematics and physics. It was time to unburden the world of what Carlyle had caustically labeled the "dismal science" and replace it with a more formal, rigorous discipline.

The principal economist to lead this revolutionary shift was Alfred Marshall (1842–1924), a famed Cambridge professor. Marshall made a singular change that reflected this transformation. By calling his textbook *Principles of Economics* (Marshall 1920 [1890]), he altered the name of the discipline from "political economy" to "economics," sending a signal that economics is as much a formal science as physics, mathematics, or any other precise body of knowledge. Moreover, this change acknowledged that the economy is governed by natural law rather than political policy. Marshall's path-breaking 1890 textbook introduced graphs of supply and demand, mathematical formulas, quantitative measurements of "elasticity" of demand, and other terms borrowed from physics, engineering, and biology. Economics would soon become a social science second to none in rigor and professional status. (That economics qualifies as a Nobel Prize category is proof enough that it is the "queen of the social sciences.")

The period surrounding Marshall's textbook was a time of new beginnings in economic science. Official associations were established, such as the American Economic Association in 1885 and the British Economic Association in 1890 (renamed the Royal Economic Society in 1902). Journals were published—the *Quarterly Journal of Economics* at Harvard in 1887, the *Economic Journal* at Cambridge in 1891, and the *Journal of Political Economy* at Chicago in 1892 (although the *Journal des Economistes* in France has been published since December 1841). By the turn of the century, major universities had finally established their own departments of economics, separate from law, mathematics, and political science, and had begun granting degrees in their own field. This was one of Marshall's most cherished ambitions. In 1895, the London School of Economics (LSE) was established, devoted almost entirely to economic studies.

In sum, Adam Smith had talked about his "Newtonian" method in his study of the wealth of nations, but not for another century did economics truly become established as a science and a separate discipline.

The Role of Jevons

Alfred Marshall was at the forefront of the movement to establish economics as a science, but his story cannot be told without recounting the tremendous influence of several other colleagues on both sides of the ocean. William Stanley Jevons was older than Marshall and one of the founders of the marginalist revolution. Jevons's most important contribution was his mathematical and graphical demonstration of the principle of marginal utility. His purpose was to overthrow "the noxious influence of authority" of David Ricardo and John Stuart Mill. "Our English Economists," he wrote, "have been living in a fool's paradise" (Jevons 1965 [1871], xiv). His aim was to cast free "from the Wage-Fund theory, the Cost of Production doctrine of Value, the Natural Rate of Wages, and other misleading or false Ricardian doctrines" (Jevons 1965 [1871], xlv–xlvi).

Jevons challenged the classical model that cost determines value. He came to the same conclusion as Menger, though independently: "Repeated reflection and inquiry have led me to the somewhat novel opinion that *value depends entirely upon utility*" (Jevons 1965 [1871], 2). Furthermore, he asserted, the Ricardian doctrine that value is determined by labor or costs of production "cannot stand for a moment." Jevons noted that labor (or capital) once spent has no influence on the future value of an article; bygones are forever bygones (1965 [1871], 157, 159).

Jevons developed a theory of consumer behavior and designed a graphic display of declining marginal utility. Yet he never developed the downward-sloping demand curve, nor a complete supply-and-demand diagram. That work was left for Marshall to accomplish. Keynes summed it up well: "In truth, Jevons's *Theory of Political Economy* is a brilliant but hasty, inaccurate, and incomplete brochure, as far removed as possible from the painstaking, complete, ultra-conscientious methods of Marshall. It brings out unforgettably the notions of final utility and of the balance between the disutility of labor and utility of the product. But it lives merely in the tenuous world of bright ideas when we compare it with the great working machine evolved by the patient, persistent toil and scientific genius of Marshall" (Keynes 1963, 15).

What did Marshall accomplish? Unlike Jevons, Marshall founded his own school, the so-called British or Cambridge school, with student prodigies such as A.C. Piguo and John Maynard Keynes. He was a synthesizer, combining the classical economics of cost (supply) and the marginalist economics of utility (demand). He often compared supply and demand to the combination of the blades of scissors; each is necessary to determine price. He took supply and demand far beyond a written expression: He developed the graphics for supply and demand, the mathematics of elasticity, and new concepts such as consumer's surplus. His formulas now serve as the foundation for any course in microeconomics.

In short, Marshall advanced Smith's model into a more precise quantitative science. Adam Smith provided the fundamental philosophy of economic growth—universal prosperity, the system of natural liberty, and the symbol of the invisible hand. Alfred Marshall provided the engine to advance Smith's system.

What is this engine? It consists of the principles of supply and demand, marginal analysis, the determination of price, the costs of production, and equilibrium in the short run and the long run. All these tools are found in today's microeconomics, the theory of individual consumers and producers. It is the toolbox economists employ today to analyze and illustrate a theory of consumer and firm behavior.

The European Wizards of Economics: Walras, Pareto, and Edgeworth

Marshall's work was followed up by the work of others in Europe and America who helped professionalize economics. Leon Walras (1834–1910) from France, Vilfredo Pareto (1848–1923) from Italy, and Francis Edgeworth (1845–1926) from Ireland introduced sophisticated mathematical methods and attempted to validate Adam Smith's invisible hand doctrine in mathematical form. The invisible hand idea, that laissez-faire leads to the common good, has become known as the first fundamental theorem of welfare economics (as noted in chapter 1). Welfare economics deals with the issues of efficiency, justice, economic waste, and the political process in the economy. Since the late 1930s, when welfare economics was popularized by John Hicks, Kenneth Arrow, Paul Samuelson, and Ronald Coase (all of whom became Nobel Prize winners), the technique of welfare economics has been extended to issues of monopoly and government policies. In most cases, the welfare economists have demonstrated that government-imposed monopoly and subsidies lead to inefficiency and waste.

Walras, Pareto, and Edgeworth were the first economists to use advanced mathematical formulas and graphic devices to prove certain hypotheses in welfare economics. Walras, whom Schumpeter ranked as "the greatest of all economists" in terms of pure theoretical contribution, introduced the notion of a "general equilibrium" theory. As one of the founders of the marginalist revolution, he sought to demonstrate mathematically the merits of laissez-faire on grounds of efficiency and justice. Using a two-party, two-commodity barter system, he was able to show that a "freely competitive" market would maximize the social utility of the two parties through a series of exchanges. In *Elements of Pure Economics* (1954 [1874, 1877]), Walras extended his analysis to multiparty, multicommodity exchanges under the assumptions of free competition, perfect mobility of factors of production, and price flexibility. By simulating a market auctioneering process, Walras showed that prices change according to supply and demand, and grope toward equilibrium. Thus, he was able to demonstrate that, without central authority, a trial-and-error market system could still achieve maximum social satisfaction or general equilibrium (GE).

Pareto is best known for the concept of Pareto optimality. Like Walras, he attempted to show that a perfectly competitive economy achieves an optimal level of economic justice, where the allocation of resources cannot be changed to make anyone better off without hurting someone else. Edgeworth, like Marshall, was a toolmaker, and developed indifference curves, utility functions, and fundamentals of the Edgeworth box, a way of expressing various trading relationships between two individuals or countries. (It is named after Edgeworth, but was actually drawn first by Pareto!)

The works of Walras, Pareto and Edgeworth initially upheld Adam Smith's vision of a beneficial capitalism, but their unrealistic assumptions made it difficult to sustain a free-market defense. Both Walras and Pareto, after years of laying the foundation of welfare economics, found themselves moving away from the Smithian vision. For example, the problem with Pareto optimality is that it ignores the omnipresent trade-offs in economic life. Seldom is one policy undertaken that improves some people's lives without injuring others in the short run. Opening trade, eliminating subsidies, and deregulating industries could help some groups and hurt others. Eliminating tariffs between the United States and Mexico will create many new jobs, but it will also destroy many traditional jobs. This is an inevitable feature of the mixed economy. The net effect is undoubtedly beneficial, but the transition might not fit Pareto optimality.

Americans Solve the Distribution Problem in Economics

The European schools of economics—followers of Menger, Marshall, and Walras, among others—had made a major breakthrough with the discovery of the subjective marginality principle. The principle explained how prices are determined and value is created in a market economy to improve the lives of all participants. But what about the distribution problem? What determines rents, wages, profits, and interest income? Does the marginality principle apply to income earned by landlords, workers, and capitalists?

Capitalism has always been hailed as a powerful producer of goods and services, an unsurpassed engine of economic growth, but it was heavily criticized by Karl Marx as well as John Stuart Mill for its disturbing inequality of wealth and income. Is this criticism valid?

It fell upon the shoulders of American economists, especially John Bates Clark, to address the fundamental questions of income distribution. As the United States became the largest economic powerhouse in the world at the turn of the twentieth century, so also did the American economics profession begin to gain prominence. The most prominent scholars in this era were John Bates Clark at Columbia University, Frank A. Fetter at Cornell and Princeton, Richard T. Ely at the University of Wisconsin, and Thorstein Veblen, who established the institutional school of economics.

It would be fair to say that the Americans were more remodelers than architects of a new building. Using the marginality principle developed in Europe, they were able to solve a mystery that had remained unsolved for many years, the so-called distribution problem in economics.

John Bates Clark (1847–1938) was instrumental in this discovery. He was the first American economist to gain international fame as an original theorist, and his principal claim to fame was his contribution to wage theory, what he called "the law of competitive distribution." Clark was by inclination a social reformer, but he gradually shifted ground and became a conservative defender of the capitalist system. What changed his mind? Largely it was his marginal productivity theory of labor, land, and capital.

Clark developed his marginal productivity thesis while seeking to resolve a troublesome problem in microeconomics: How are two or more cooperating inputs compensated from the total product they jointly produce? This joint-input problem had long been viewed as unsolvable, like deciding whether the father or the mother were responsible for the birth of a child. Indeed, Sir William Petty called labor the father of production and land the mother. Marx resolved the riddle by proclaiming that labor deserved the entire product, but this proved naïve, unproductive, and unsatisfactory to the rest of the profession.

Building on the marginality concept of the Austrian economists, Clark pioneered the concept that each input contributes its marginal product. Essentially, he argued that under competitive conditions, each factor of production—land, labor, and capital—is paid according to the "value added" to the total revenue of the product, or its marginal product. In his vital work, *The Distribution of Wealth,* Clark called his theory of competitive distribution a "natural law" that was "just" (Clark 1965 [1899], v). "In other words, free competition tends to give labor what labor creates, to capitalists what capital creates, and to entrepreneurs what the coordinating function creates" (1965 [1899], 3).

Following Jevons, Clark created a diagram showing a downward-sloping demand curve for labor, and illustrating how wages are equal to the marginal product of the last worker added to the labor force. Thus, if workers become more productive and add greater value to the company's long-term profitability, their wages will tend to rise. If wages rise in one industry, competition will force other employers to raise their wages, and thus, "wages tend to equal the product of marginal labor," or what the last worker is paid (Clark 1965 [1899], 106).

Clark used his marginal productivity theory to justify the wage rates in the United States and criticized labor unions for trying to raise rates above this "natural law." For example, although he supported the Knights of Labor, Clark advocated compulsory arbitration to end long labor disputes, believing that striking workers should be paid wages prevailing in comparable labor markets elsewhere (Dewey 1987, 430). On the other hand, Clark opposed the power of monopolies and big business that attempted to exploit workers by forcing wages below labor's marginal product. According to Clark, a competitive environment in both labor and industry is essential to a legitimate wage and social justice. He wrote a book on the subject entitled *Social Justice Without Socialism* (1914).

Clark's prescriptive economics was heavily criticized by fellow economists, who made the allegation that "neoclassical economics was essentially an apologetic for the existing economic order" (Stigler 1941, 297). Thorstein Veblen, in particular, used Clark as a foil in his diatribes against the prevailing economic system. Yet Clark's application of the marginality principle to labor had its impact. Even Marxists felt compelled to alter their extreme views of exploitation based on the labor theory of value. No longer could they demand that workers be paid "the whole product of their labor." Now employees were seen to be exploited only if they received wages less than the value of their marginal product of labor (Sweezy 1942, 6).

Henry George and the Land Tax

Clark also was a vociferous critic of Henry George (1839–97), the social reformer who blamed the monopolistic power of landlords for poverty and injustice in the world. According to George, who drew heavily upon Ricardian rent theory, the solution to poverty and inequality was a single tax on unimproved land. Although George was popular, Clark condemned his single tax idea in *The Distribution of Wealth*. Clark began his critique by rejecting the Ricardian view that land is fixed. "The idea that land is fixed in amount," he wrote, "is really based on an error which one encounters in economic discussions with wearisome frequency" (1965 [1899], 338). While the amount of land existing on earth does indeed remain constant, the supply of land *available for sale* varies with the price, as any other commodity. And land prices, like wages and capital goods, are determined by their marginal productivity—"at the margin"—allocated according to its most "productive" use (346–48). According to Clark, taxing away the value of land, even if unimproved, will drive capital out of land into housing, and misallocate capital in favor of housing. Rent and land prices help investors to allocate a scarce resource (land) to its most valued use in society. Rent controls and confiscatory land taxes can only create distortions in land use.[2]

Finally, Clark applied his marginal productivity theory to capital and interest. He differed strenuously with the Austrians on the structure of the capital markets, arguing that investment capital was a "permanent fund," like a big reservoir, where "the water that at this moment flows into one end of the pond causes an overflow from the other end" (Clark 1965 [1899], 313). On the other hand, the Austrians viewed the capital structure as an array of capital goods, from early stages to final stages of production, and believed that this structure was influenced by interest rates, which were determined by time preference. Progress is achieved, according to Böhm-Bawerk in Europe and Frank Fetter in America, by capitalists investing their savings in more "roundabout" production processes. Despite these differences, Clark recognized that investment would increase if society saved more, interest rates would decline, and the size of the capital stock would increase—all leading to higher economic performance.

Two Critics Debate the Meaning of the Neoclassical Model

By the turn of the twentieth century, a whole new model of the capitalist economy had been fashioned, thanks to the marginalist revolution in Europe and the United States. Adam Smith and the classical economists had provided the foundation, but it took another generation of economists to finish the job. It was now time to stand back and take a look at this brand-new model of modern capitalism.

Critics such as Thomas Carlyle and Karl Marx had assaulted the house that Adam Smith built, but that was before the marginalist revolution. It was time to take a second look, and it fell upon the shoulders of two social economists (today they would be known as sociologists) to examine in detail the meaning of the new structure.

---

2. Oddly enough, while Henry George was largely an advocate of laissez-faire, his land tax scheme encouraged many of his listeners, including George Bernard Shaw and Sydney Webb, to become socialists. See Skousen (2001, 229–30).

They are the American Thorstein Veblen (1857–1929) and the German Max Weber (1864–1920).

Thorstein Veblen: The Voice of Dissent

Veblen was the principal faultfinder and censor of the new theoretical capitalism. Having taught at ten institutions, including the University of Chicago and Stanford, he had little use for the rational-abstract-deductive approach of the neoclassical model. Above all, he was a critic, not a creator of a new worldview. In his best-known work, *The Theory of the Leisure Class,* Veblen applied a Darwinian view to modern economics. He saw industrial capitalism as a form of early "barbaric" evolution, like the ape. Imitating Proudhon's famous statement, "property is theft," Veblen stated that private property was nothing less than "booty held as trophies of the successful raid" (Veblen 1994 [1899], 27). Capitalists' pursuit of wealth, leisure, and the acquisition of goods in competition with their neighbors was part of the "predatory instinct" (29). A life of leisure had "much in common with the trophies of exploit" (44). Gambling and risk-taking reflected a "barbarian temperament" (276, 295–96). Women were, like slaves, treated as property, to be dominated by the prowess of the owner (53). Patriotism and war were badges of "predatory, not of productive, employment" (40).

Progress meant that primitive capitalism needed to be advanced toward a higher social plane. War must be rejected (Veblen was a pacifist). Capitalism must be replaced by a form of workers' socialism and technocracy, a "soviet of technicians." But he rejected Marxism as a philosophy. Marxist doctrines, according to Veblen, failed the evolutionary test. Many nations had collapsed without any class struggle, he said. "The doctrine that progressive misery must effect a socialistic revolution [is] dubious," he declared. "The facts are not bearing . . . out [Marx's theories] on certain critical points" (Jorgensen and Jorgensen 1999, 90).

Veblen envisioned a different kind of class conflict than Marx. Rather than dividing the world into capitalists and proletariats, the haves and the have-nots, Veblen emphasized the alliance of the technicians and the engineers, and the opposing businessmen, lawyers, clergymen, military, and gentlemen of leisure. He saw conflict between industry and finance, between the blue-collar manual laborers and the white-collar workers, and between the leisure class and the working class.

In chapter 4 of *The Theory of the Leisure Class,* Veblen cynically described in great detail the "conspicuous consumption" of the wealthy class. "High-bred manners and ways of living are items of conformity to the norm of conspicuous leisure and conspicuous consumption," he wrote (1994 [1899], 75). Veblen condemned the wealthy for purposely engaging in "wasteful" spending and ostentatious behavior, withdrawn from the industrial class. Moreover, "the leisure class is more favorable to a warlike attitude and animus than the industrial classes" (271).

In highlighting the excesses of the "vulgar" class, Veblen expressed hostility to business culture, which he characterized as "waste, futility, and ferocity" (1994 [1899], 351). As Robert Lakachman wrote in the introduction to *The Theory of the Leisure Class,* Veblen dismissed commercial society as "a profoundly anti-evolutionary barrier to the full fruition of man's life-giving instinct of workmanship," clearly in opposition to Adam Smith's view of a benevolent commercial society. Where Adam Smith saw order, harmony, benevolence, and rational self-interest, Veblen saw chaos, struggle, and greed. "Veblen was able to contradict flatly almost every premise and assumption upon which the ideology of capitalism rested" (Diggins 1999, 13).

Veblen ignored the benefits of wealth creation—the expansion of capital, the investment in new technology, the funding of higher education, and the philanthropic generosity of the business community. Amazingly, he claimed absolutely no improvement in the standard of living of the common man during his lifetime (Dorfman 1934, 414). He cited approvingly a view first expressed by John Stuart Mill, who wrote in his *Principles of Political Economy* textbook, "Hitherto it is questionable if all the mechanical inventions yet made have lightened the day's toil of any human being" (Mill 1884 [1848], 516). This same quote is found in Marx's *Capital* (1976 [1867], 492).

We can forgive Mill and Marx for making such uninformed statements in the mid-nineteenth century, but for Veblen it demonstrates astonishing ignorance of consumer statistics. By 1918, when Veblen made this statement, millions of American consumers were beginning to enjoy refrigeration, electricity, the telephone, running water, indoor toilets, and automobiles. No wonder Veblen left this life in a depressed state—his gloomy view of capitalism transpired during the Roaring Twenties, when American consumers were making tremendous advances.

Max Weber: A Spirited Defense of "Rational" Capitalism

Fortunately, Thorstein Veblen was not the only social commentator on capitalism at the turn of the century. His chief antagonist came from across the Atlantic—the German sociologist and economist Max Weber, author of the famous book *The Protestant Ethic and the Spirit of Capitalism*. Weber's views on capitalism were more in the spirit of Adam Smith than Veblen. As John Patrick Diggins states, "No two social theorists could be more intellectually and temperamentally opposed than Thorstein Veblen and Max Weber" (1999, 111).

Both Veblen and Weber were obsessed with the meaning of contemporary industrial society—the issues of power, management, and surplus wealth. Both published their best-selling works near the turn of the century. And both were highly critical of the Marxist interpretation of history. Yet Weber came to far different conclusions than Veblen or Marx. He rejected both Veblen's description of modern capitalism as a form of barbaric evolution and Marx's theory of exploitation and surplus value. Rather, the development of modern society ("the heroic age of capitalism") came about because of strenuous moral discipline and joyless devotion to hard work, leading to long-term investments and advanced corporate management. What was the powerful source of Western economic development? Unlike Veblen and Marx, Weber saw the source as being religion, specifically the Protestant Reformation and its doctrines of frugality and a moral duty to work, and its concept of the "calling."

Weber's *Protestant Ethic and the Spirit of Capitalism* countered the popular intellectual views of Karl Marx and Friedrich Nietzsche that religion was a delusion, a crutch, or worse, an irrational neurosis. Weber praised Christianity as a "social bond of world-encompassing brotherhood" (Diggins 1996, 95). He disapproved of Marx, contending that capitalism had its origins in religious ideals rather than historical materialism.

According to Weber, it was not unbridled avarice and the unfettered pursuit of gain that brought about the age of capitalism. Such an impulse has existed in all societies of the past. That "greed" is the driving force beyond capitalism is a "naïve idea" that "should be taught in the kindergarten of cultural history." Echoing Montesquieu and Adam Smith, Weber exclaimed, "Unlimited greed for gain is not in the least identical with capitalism, and is still less its spirit. Capitalism may even be identical with the restraint, or at least a rational tempering, of this irrational impulse" (Weber 1930 [1904/5], 17).

So what did cause the historical development of modern capitalism, especially in the West—"the most fateful force in our modern life" (Weber 1930 [1904/5], 17)? Weber's thesis is that religion, which had a firm grip on people's minds for centuries, kept capitalism back until the Protestant reformation of the seventeenth century. Until then, the making of money was frowned upon by almost all religions, including Christianity. All that changed, according to Weber, with the Lutheran doctrine of the "calling," the Calvinist and Puritan doctrine of labor to promote the glory of God, and the Methodist admonition against idleness. Only among the Protestants could the devout Christian hear John Wesley's sermon on wealth: "Earn all you can, save all you can, give all you can" (Weber 1930 [1904/5], 175–76).

Protestantism not only promoted industry; it also stressed a critical element in economic growth, the virtue of thrift. As Weber explained, Christianity proclaimed self-denial and abstinence while warning against materialism and pride. Protestant preachers disapproved of "conspicuous consumption," and so capitalists and workers saved and saved and saved. Weber saw in the American founding father Benjamin Franklin the epitome of the Protestant ethic. His book cites quotation after quotation from Franklin's virtuous sayings, such as "Remember, time is money," and "A penny saved is a penny earned."

Historians have disagreed with Weber's thesis, pointing out that capitalism first flourished in Italian city-states, which were Catholic. Catholic Antwerp in the sixteenth century was a flourishing financial and commercial center. The Spanish scholastics, mainly Jesuits and Dominicans in the mid-sixteenth and seventeenth centuries, advocated economic freedom. Yet, despite these criticisms, Weber's thesis went a long way toward dispelling the negative cultural notions of modern capitalism and religious faith expressed by Veblen. Weber stressed spiritual rather than material factors in the development of capitalism. While Veblen the anthropologist viewed modern capitalism as an example of barbarian exploitation, Weber the sociologist saw capitalist ethics and moral discipline as a decisive break from the predatory behavior of men. While Veblen depicted the capitalist as a predator and status-seeker, Weber emphasized individual conscience and Christian exhortations against idleness and wastefulness.

Irving Fisher and the Mystery of Money

The neoclassical model of modern economics, having been remodeled and scrutinized many times over, was now facing one more challenge as it entered the twentieth century. There was a key element missing in the capitalist model of prosperity: a fundamental understanding of money. The financial and economic crises of the nineteenth century raised serious questions about the role of money and credit: What is the ideal monetary standard? What constitutes a sound money banking system? Was Adam Smith's system of natural liberty inherently unstable? Comprehending the role of money and credit, the lifeblood of the economy, was the unresolved issue of twentieth-century macroeconomics; this lingering mystery posed the greatest challenge to the defenders of the neoclassical model, and ultimately led to the Keynesian revolution.

The man who spent his entire career seeking an answer to the mystery of money was Irving Fisher (1867–1947), the eminent Yale professor and founder of the "monetarist" school. From James Tobin to Milton Friedman, top economists have hailed Fisher as the forefather of monetary macroeconomics and one of the great theorists in their field. Mark Blaug calls him "one of the greatest and certainly one of the most colorful American economists who has ever lived" (Blaug 1986, 77). Fisher's entire career, both professional and personal, was devoted to the issue of money and credit. He invented the famed Quantity Theory of Money, and created the first price indexes. He became a crusader for many causes, from healthy living to price stability. He wrote over thirty books. He was a wealthy inventor (of today's Rolodex, or card catalog system) who became the Oracle on Wall Street, but was destroyed financially by the 1929–33 stock market crash.

Fisher's failure as a monetarist to anticipate the greatest economic collapse in the twentieth century must lie squarely with his incomplete monetary model of the economy, and it was this defective model that led directly to the development of Keynesian economics, the subject of our next chapter.

Fisher's Quantity Theory of Money

The problem is with Fisher's interpretation of his famed Quantity Theory of Money. The main theme of his Quantity Theory, published in *The Purchasing Power of Money* (1963 [1911]), is that inflation (the general rise in prices) is caused primarily by the expansion of money and credit, and that there is a direct connection between changes in the general price level and changes in the money supply. If the money supply doubles, prices will double.

This monetarist concept was not new. Many economists had held to this theory prior to Fisher, including David Hume and John Stuart Mill. But Fisher went further by developing a mathematical equation for the quantity theory. He started with an "equation of exchange" between money and goods formulated by Simon Newcomb in 1885:

$$MV = PT,$$

where
   M = quantity of money in circulation
   V = velocity of money, or the annual turnover of money
   P = general price level
   T = total number of transactions of goods and services during the year.

The equation of exchange is really nothing more than an accounting identity. The right-hand side of the equation represents the transfer of money, the left-hand side represents the transfer of goods. The value of the goods must be equal to the money transferred in any exchange. Similarly, the total amount of money in circulation multiplied by the average number of times money changes hands in a year must equal the dollar amount of goods and services produced and sold during the year. Hence, by definition, MV must be equal to PT.

However, Fisher turned the equation of exchange into a theory. He assumed that both V (velocity) and T (transactions) remained relatively stable, and therefore changes in the price level must be directly related to changes in the money supply. As Fisher stated, "The level of prices varies in direct proportion with the quantity of money in circulation, provided that the velocity of money and the volume of trade which it is obliged to perform are not changed" (1963 [1911], 14). He called this the Quantity Theory of Money.

Fisher firmly believed in the long-term neutrality of money; that is, an increase in the money supply would result in a proportional increase in prices without causing any long-term ill effects. While he referred to "maladjustments" and "overinvestments" (terms used by the Austrians) that might occur in specific lines of production, Fisher regarded them as points of short-term disequilibria that would eventually work themselves out (Fisher 1963 [1911], 184–85).

Thus, in the mid-1920s, he suggested that the business cycle no longer existed. He believed in a "new era" of permanent prosperity, in both industrial production and stock market performance. This naïve conviction led to his undoing. He favored the gradual expansion of credit by the Federal Reserve and, as long as prices remained relatively stable, he felt there should be no crisis. Fisher, a New Era economist, had a great deal of faith in America's new central bank and expected the Federal Reserve to intervene if a crisis arose.

Fisher Is Deceived by Price Stability

According to Fisher, the key variable to monitor in the monetary equation was P, the general price level. If prices were relatively stable, there could be no major crisis or depression. Price stabilization was Fisher's principal monetary goal in the 1920s. He also felt that the international gold standard could not achieve price stability on its own. It needed the help of the Federal Reserve, which was established in late 1913 in order to create liquidity and prevent depressions and crises. According to Fisher, if wholesale and consumer prices remained relatively calm, everything would be fine. But if prices began to sag, threatening deflation, the Fed should intervene and expand credit.

In fact, wholesale and consumer prices in the United States were remarkably stable, and declined only slightly during the 1920s. Thus, the New Era monetarists thought everything was fine on the eve of the 1929 crash. In October 1929, a week before the stock market crash, Fisher made his infamous statement, "stocks appear to have reached a permanent plateau." Milton Friedman, a modern-day monetarist, refers to the 1920s as "The High Tide of the Federal Reserve," stating, "The Twenties were, in the main, a period of high prosperity and stable economic growth" (Friedman and Schwartz 1963, 296).

A fundamental flaw in Fisher's approach was his overemphasis on long-run macroeconomic equilibrium. In Fisher's world, the primary effect of monetary inflation was a general rise in prices, not structural imbalances, asset bubbles, and the business cycle. He focused almost exclusively on the price level, rather than the monetary aggregates or interest rates. But an "easy money" policy developed in the mid-1920s when the Fed artificially lowered interest rates to help strengthen the British pound, and this low-interest-rate policy created a manufacturing, real estate, and stock market boom that could not last.

Austrian Economists Warn of Impending Disaster

During the 1920s, there was a school of economics that did predict a monetary crisis: Specifically, the up and coming generation of Austrian economists, Ludwig von Mises (1881–1973) and Friedrich Hayek (1899–1992). Mises and Hayek argued, contrary to Fisher, that monetary inflation and easy-money policies are inherently unstable and create structural imbalances in the economy that cannot last. In Mises's view, money is "non-neutral," especially in the short run. The fateful decision by central banks to inflate and reduce interest rates in the 1920s inevitably created an artificial boom. Under an international gold standard, such an inflationary boom could only be short lived and must lead to a crash and depression.

When the dire predictions of Mises and Hayek came true in 1929–32, the economics profession paid attention. Economists from all over the world flocked to Vienna to attend the famous Mises seminar. Mises's works were translated into English and Hayek, his younger colleague, was invited to teach at the prestigious London School of Economics. Decades later, in 1974, Hayek won a Nobel Prize for his pathbreaking work in the 1930s.

Mises's revolutionary work was not the work of one individual; he drew upon the specie-flow mechanism of David Hume and David Ricardo; the "natural rate of interest" hypothesis of Swedish economist Knut Wicksell; and the capital model of his teacher, Eugen Böhm-

Bawerk. Like Fisher, Mises's first major book was on money. *The Theory of Money and Credit* (1971 [1912]) offered a monetary model that challenged Irving Fisher's Quantity Theory of Money.

The first and primary goal Mises tried to achieve was to integrate money into the economic system and the marginalist revolution. The classical and neoclassical economists treated money as a separate box, not subject to the same analysis as the rest of the system. Irving Fisher's equation of exchange, not marginal utility or price theory, formed the basis of monetary analysis. Economists such as Fisher spoke in aggregate terms—price level, money supply, velocity of circulation, and national output. Moreover, national currencies such as the dollar, the franc, the pound, and the mark, were viewed as units of account that were arbitrarily defined by government. As the German historical school declared, money is the creation of the state. Thus, microeconomics (the theory of supply and demand for individual consumers and firms) was split from macroeconomics (the theory of money and aggregate economic activity). Who would find the missing link and connect the two?

The Theory of Money and Credit linked micro and macro by first showing that money was originally a commodity (gold, silver, copper, beads, etc.), and therefore subject to marginal analysis like everything else. Mises showed that money is no different from any other commodity when it comes to marginal value. In microeconomics, the price of any good is determined by the quantity available and the marginal utility of that good. The same principle applies to money, only in the case of money, the "price" is determined by the general purchasing power of the monetary unit. The willingness to hold money ("cash balances") is determined by the marginal demand for cash balances. The interaction between the quantity of money available and the demand for it determines the price of the dollar. Thus, an increase in the supply of dollars will lead to a fall in its value or price.

Mises's application of marginal analysis on money is, of course, a confirmation of the first approximation of Fisher's Quantity Theory of Money. If you increase the money supply, the price of money will fall.

But then the question is, by how much?

Fisher, as you will recall, assumed that V (velocity) and T (transactions) were relatively constant, and therefore M (money supply) and

P (price level) would vary directly and proportionately. In *The Theory of Money and Credit,* Mises went further than Fisher. He contended that if even the nation's price index were stable, a business cycle could develop. Fisher's proposal of a stable price index "could not in any way ameliorate the social consequences of variations in the value of money," he wrote (Mises 1971 [1912], 402). Why not? Business activity could boom without a rise in commodity or consumer prices and, equally, the economy could collapse before general price deflation set in. According to Mises, *M* is the culprit. *M* is an independent variable that could create havoc in the economy, not by simply raising prices, as Fisher theoretized, but by introducing structural imbalances into the economy. In Mises's model, money is never neutral. It affects all the other variables in Fisher's equation of exchange—velocity *(V)*, prices *(P)*, and transactions *(T)*. The relationship between money and prices was scarcely proportional.

Wicksell and the Natural Rate of Interest

Moreover, if monetary policy pushed "market" interest rates below the "natural" rate, the central bank could create an unstable business cycle that could lead to financial disaster. With "natural" rate, Mises borrowed an idea from the brilliant Swedish economist Knut Wicksell (1851–1926), who defined the "natural" rate of interest to be the rate that equalizes the supply and demand for saving based on the social rate of time preference. For example, if the Swiss have a natural savings rate higher than the Swedish, the natural rate of interest will tend to be lower in Switzerland than in Sweden, assuming a neutral monetary policy by the government.

On the other hand, Wicksell defined the "market" rate of interest as the rate of interest banks charge for loans to individual customers and businesses. In a stable economy, Wicksell noted, the natural rate (time preference) is normally the same as the market rate (loan market). When the two are the same, you have macroeconomic stability. If the two part ways, however, trouble brews.

If the Federal Reserve artificially lowers the market rate of interest through an "easy money" policy below the natural rate, it creates a cumulative process of inflation and an unsustainable boom, especially in the capital markets. This could take a variety of forms, depending on how the money is spent—it could cause a bull market on Wall Street, a boom in construction and manufacturing, or a real estate bubble. However, according to Mises and Hayek, the inflationary boom cannot last. Eventually, inflationary pressures will raise interest rates and choke off the boom, resulting in a depression.

Hayek expanded on Mises's theory of the business cycle while serving under Mises as manager of the Austrian Institute of Economic Research. In *Prices and Production* (1935 [1931]), a compilation of a series of lectures given at the London School of Economics, Hayek created the "Hayekian triangles" to demonstrate the time-structure of production. The triangle represents spending at each stage of production—from natural resources to final consumption—with each stage adding value. According to Hayek, the structure of the triangle changes with interest rates, but if the market rate of interest falls below the natural rate, the size of the triangle increases and then shrinks.[3]

Mises also applied Böhm-Bawerk's theory of "roundaboutness" and the structure of capital. A government-induced inflationary boom would inevitably cause the roundabout production process to lengthen, especially in capital-goods industries, a process that could not be reversed easily during a slump. Once new funds are invested in machinery, tools, equipment, and buildings, capital would become heterogeneous, and it would not be easy to sell off assets, equipment, and inventories during a slowdown. In short, when a boom turns into a bust, it takes time, sometimes years, for the economy to recover.

Finally, Mises saw the international gold standard as a disciplinarian that would cut short any inflationary boom in short order. Borrowing from the Hume-Ricardo specie-flow mechanism, Mises outlined a series of events whereby an inflationary boom would quickly come to an end under gold:

1. Under inflation, domestic incomes and prices rise.

2. Citizens buy more imports than exports, causing a trade deficit.

3. The balance-of-payments deficit causes gold to flow out.

4. The domestic money supply declines, causing a deflationary collapse.

---

3. For a more complete explanation of Hayek's triangles, see chapter 12 of Skousen (2001, 294–95) and Garrison (2001).

The Austrian Model Ultimately Loses Popularity

Mises, Hayek, and Wicksell helped fill the gaps in neoclassical monetary economics, and helped complete the structure that Adam Smith had begun. But if their monetary theories of the business cycle had all the answers, why didn't they catch on? Primarily, their model was not appreciated until after the Great Depression took hold. And when the Great Depression didn't end quickly, as the Austrians predicted, economists started searching for a new model that could explain secular stagnation in a capitalist economy. Hayek and Mises advocated standard neoclassical solutions such as cutting wages and prices, lowering taxes, and reducing government interference in commerce and trade, but they adamantly counseled against reinflation and deficit spending. "It would only mean that the seed would already be sown for new disturbances and new crises," Hayek warned. The only solution to the Great Depression was "to leave it time to effect a permanent cure"—in other words, wait it out and let the market take its natural course (Hayek, 1935, 98–99). Such a prescription might have worked during a garden-variety recession, but it apparently was not enough to counter the full-scale deflationary collapse.

With the Austrians offering few explanations and no cure for the seemingly never-ending depression, economists eventually looked elsewhere for a solution. Who could come to the rescue and save capitalism? One economist did step forward to offer an exciting new theory of macroeconomics and a vigorous policy for curing the depression—a new model that excited the minds of a whole new generation of economists.

5

John Maynard Keynes

Capitalism Faces Its Greatest Challenge

A thousand years hence 1920–1970 will, I expect, be *the* time for
historians. It drives me wild to think of it. I believe it will make my
poor Principles, with a lot of poor comrades, into waste paper.[1]
—*Alfred Marshall (1915)*

Keynes was no socialist—he came to save capitalism, not to
bury it. . . . There has been nothing like Keynes's
achievement in the annals of social sciences.
—*Paul Krugman (2006)*

---

1. This prophetic statement was made in a letter from Alfred Marshall to a Cambridge
University colleague, Professor C. R. Fay, dated February 23, 1915. He made no reference
to Keynes as the instigator of this revolution, but Marshall did have a favorable opinion
of his student. See Pigou (1925, 489–90).

The capitalist system of natural liberty—founded by Adam Smith, revised by the marginalist revolution, and refined by Marshall, Fisher, and the Austrians—was under siege. The classical virtues of thrift, balanced budgets, low taxes, the gold standard, and Say's law were under attack as never before. The house that Adam Smith built was threatening to collapse.

The Great Depression of the 1930s was the most traumatic economic event of the twentieth century. It was especially shocking given the great advances achieved in Western living standards during the New Era twenties. Those living standards would be strained during 1929–33, the brunt of the depression. In the United States, industrial output fell by over 30 percent. Over one-third of the commercial banks failed or consolidated. The unemployment rate soared to over 25 percent. Stock prices lost 88 percent of their value. Europe and the rest of the world faced similar turmoil.

The Austrians Mises and Hayek, along with the sound-money economists in the United States, had anticipated trouble, but felt helpless in the face of a slump that just wouldn't go away. A nascent recovery under Roosevelt's New Deal began in the mid-1930s, but didn't last. U.S. unemployment remained at double-digit levels for a full decade and did not disappear until World War II. Europe didn't fare much better; only Hitler's militant Germany was fully employed as war approached. In the free world, fear of losing one's job, fear of hunger, and fear of war loomed ominously.

The length and severity of the Great Depression caused most of the Anglo-American economics profession to question classical laissez-faire economics and the ability of a free-market capitalist system to correct itself. The assault was on two levels—the competitive nature of capitalism (micro) and the stability of the general economy (macro).

Was the Classical Model of Competition Imperfect?

On the micro level, two economists simultaneously wrote books that independently challenged the classical model of competition. In 1933, Harvard University Press released *The Theory of Monopolistic Competition* by Edward H. Chamberlin (1899–1967), and Cambridge University Press published *Economics of Imperfect Competition* by

Joan Robinson (1903–83). Both economists introduced the idea that there are various levels of competition in the marketplace, from "pure competition" to "pure monopoly," and that most market conditions were "imperfect" and involved degrees of monopoly power. The Chamberlin-Robinson theory of imperfect competition captured the imagination of the profession and has been an integral feature of microeconomics ever since. It has strong policy implications: Laissez-faire is defective and cannot ensure competitive conditions in capitalism; the government must intervene through controls and antitrust actions to curtail the natural monopolistic tendencies of business.

The Radical Threat to Capitalism

But this threat was minor compared to the radical noncapitalist alternatives being proposed in macroeconomics. Marxism was all the rage on campuses and among intellectuals during the 1930s. Paul Sweezy, a Harvard-trained economist, had gone to the London School of Economics (LSE) in the early 1930s, only to return a full-fledged Marxist, ready to teach radical ideas at his alma mater. Sidney and Beatrice Webb returned from the Soviet Union brimming with optimism, firm in their belief that Stalin had inaugurated a "new civilization" of full employment and economic superiority. Was full-scale socialism the only alternative to an unstable capitalist system?

Who Would Save Capitalism?

More sober intellectuals sought an alternative to wholesale socialism, nationalization, and central planning. Fortunately, there was a powerful voice urging a middle ground, a way to preserve economic liberty without the government taking over the whole economy and destroying the foundations of Western civilization.

It was the voice of John Maynard Keynes, leader of the new Cambridge school. In his revolutionary 1936 book, *The General Theory of Employment, Interest and Money,* Keynes preached that capitalism is inherently unstable and has no natural tendency toward full employment. Yet, at the same time, he rejected the need to nationalize the economy, impose price-wage controls, and interfere with the microfoundations of supply and demand. All that was needed was for government to take control of a wayward capitalist steering wheel and get the car back on the road to prosperity. How? Not by slashing prices and wages—the classical approach—but by deliberately running federal deficits and spending money on public works that would expand "aggregate demand" and restore confidence. Once the economy got back on track and reached full employment, the government would no longer need to run deficits, and the classical model would function properly. As Keynes himself wrote, "But beyond this no obvious case is made out for a system of State Socialism which would embrace most of the economic life of the community" (Keynes 1973a [1936], 378). His message was really quite simple, yet revolutionary: "Mass unemployment had a single cause, inadequate demand, and an easy solution, expansionary fiscal policy" (Krugman 2006).

Keynes's model of aggregate demand management changed the dismal science to the optimists' club: man could be the master of his economic destiny after all. His claim that government could expand or contract aggregate demand as conditions required seemed to eliminate the cycle inherent in capitalism without eliminating capitalism itself. Meanwhile, a laissez-faire policy of economic freedom could be pursued on a microeconomic level. In short, Keynes's middle-of-the-road policies were viewed not as a threat to free enterprise, but as its savior. In fact, Keynesianism brought its chief rival theory, Marxism, to a total halt in advanced countries (Galbraith 1975 [1965], 132).

"Like a Flash of Light on a Dark Night"

The Keynesian revolution took place almost overnight, especially among the youngest and the brightest, who switched allegiance from the Austrians to Keynes. John Kenneth Galbraith wrote of the times, "Here was a remedy for the despair. . . . It did not overthrow the system but saved it. To the non-revolutionary, it seemed too good to be true. To the occasional revolutionary, it was. The old economics was still taught by day. But in the evening, and almost every evening from 1936 on, almost everyone discussed Keynes" (Galbraith 1975

[1965], 136). Milton Friedman, who later became a vociferous opponent of Keynesian theory, said, "By contrast with this dismal picture [the Austrian laissez-faire prescription], the news seeping out of Cambridge (England) about Keynes's interpretation of the depression and of the right policy to cure it must have come like a flash of light on a dark night. It offered a far less hopeless diagnosis of the disease. More importantly, it offered a more immediate, less painful, and more effective cure in the form of budget deficits. It is easy to see how a young, vigorous, and generous mind would have been attracted to it" (1974, 163).

The Keynesian model of aggregate demand management swept the profession even faster than the marginalist revolution, especially after World War II seemed to vindicate the benefits of deficit spending and massive government spending. It wasn't long before college professors, under the tutorage of Alvin Hansen, Paul Samuelson, Lawrence Klein, and other Keynesian disciples, began teaching students about the consumption function, the multiplier, the marginal propensity to consume, the paradox of thrift, aggregate demand, and $C + I + G$. It was a strange, new, exciting doctrine. And it was the beginning of a whole new area of study called "macroeconomics."[2]

The Dark Side of Keynes

Keynes may have offered a plausible cure for the depression, but his theoretical heresies also created a postwar environment favorable toward ubiquitous state interventionism, the welfare state, and boundless faith in big government. His theories encouraged excess consumption, debt financing, and progressive taxation over saving, balanced budgets, and low taxes. Critics saw Keynesian economics

---

2. With Keynes came the division of "macroeconomics," the study of economic aggregates such as the price level, the money supply, and Gross Domestic Product, and "microeconomics," the theory of individual and firm behavior. Paul Samuelson, who did not use the term in the first edition of his textbook, *Economics* (1948), says the distinction between "micro" and "macro" goes back to econometricians Ragnar Frisch and Jan Tinbergen, the first Nobel Prize winners in economics. But Roger Garrison notes that the Austrian economist Eugen Böhm-Bawerk wrote this sentence in January, 1891: "One cannot eschew studying the microcosm if one wants to understand properly the macrocosm of a developed country" (Böhm-Bawerk 1962: 117).

as a direct assault on traditional economic values and the most serious threat to the principles of economic freedom since Marxism. To them, Keynes's *General Theory* "constitutes the most subtle and mischievous assault on orthodox capitalism and free enterprise that has appeared in the English language" (Hazlitt 1977 [1960], 345). As Paul Krugman notes, "If your doctrine says that free markets, left to their own devices, produce the best of all possible worlds, and that government intervention in the economy always makes things worse, Keynes is your enemy" (Krugman 2006).

Despite occasional pronouncements that Keynes is dead, Keynesian thinking is still so pervasive in academia, the halls of parliament, and Wall Street, that *Time* magazine aptly voted Keynes the most influential economist of the twentieth century. Biographer Charles Hession writes, "More books and articles have been written about him than any other economist, with the possible exception of Karl Marx" (1984, xiv). Appropriately, *The New Palgrave* gives Keynes its longest biography—twenty pages, as compared to fifteen for Marx. And Keynes's latest biographer, Robert Skidelsky, places Keynes on a pedestal: "Keynes was a magical figure, and it is fitting that he should have left a magical work. There has never been an economist like him" (1992, 537).

Keynes Born Amid Britain's Ruling Elite

What kind of man was Keynes, who could engender such devotion and such hostility?

John Maynard Keynes (1883–1946) was an intellectual elitist from his earliest childhood. When asked once how to pronounce his name, he replied, "Keynes, as in brains." Born in 1883 (the year Marx died) in the center of Britain's most cerebral environment, he was the son of John Neville Keynes, an economics professor at Cambridge University and a friend of Alfred Marshall. Neville would actually outlive his son, Maynard, by three years, dying in 1949 at age ninety-seven. His mother, Florence Ada Keynes, also distinguished herself as Cambridge's first woman mayor. Keynes was always close to his mother, while his father was distant. His father wrote in his diary in 1891, when Maynard was only eight years old, "The only person he would like to be is his mother; at any rate, he would desire to resemble her in everything" (in Hession 1984, 11).

Keynes went to Britain's best private school, Eton, and then attended, as expected, Cambridge University, where he obtained a degree in mathematics in 1905. He would later write a controversial book on probability theory.

His friends considered him precocious, clever, and sometimes rude. His most distinguishing features were his "riotous eyes" and "leaping mind" (Skidelsky 1992, xxxi). Keynes viewed himself as "physically repulsive." Nevertheless, he was selected as one of only a dozen members of the Apostles, an exclusive secret society at Cambridge (not unlike the Skull and Bones at Yale). Membership is for life. Other noteworthy members have included the poet Alfred Lord Tennyson, biographer Lytton Strachey, and philosophers Bertrand Russell, G.E. Moore, and Alfred North Whitehead. The Apostles were a close-knit group, meeting every Saturday night to discuss papers.

The Truth About Keynes's Homosexuality

At the turn of the twentieth century, the Apostles, under the influence of G.E. Moore, developed a deep contempt for Victorian morality and bourgeois values. They even propounded the subversive idea that homosexuality was morally superior. Keynes was a practicing homosexual during his early adult life, although he apparently abandoned it upon marrying Lydia Lopokova in 1925. This fact was covered up by his official biographer, Roy Harrod, for fear it would destroy Keynes's reputation. In his introduction, Harrod explained, "In regard to his faults, I am not conscious of any suppression [of facts]. Criticisms have been made by the malicious or ill-informed which have no foundation in fact" (Harrod 1951, viii). Yet there was suppression. More recent histories by Robert Skidelsky (2003), D.E. Moggridge (1992), and Charles Hession (1984) spare few details of Keynes's sexual adventures. Moggridge even goes so far as to print Keynes's sexual engagement diary in an appendix (1992, 838–39).

Keynes's sexual proclivities may have been influenced by his family life (overprotective mother, weak father); the Eton school, an all-male institution where Greek philosophy taught that platonic love between men is spiritually higher than the carnal love between man and woman; and the collegiate ideas of G.E. Moore, who preached a disregard for morals and universal rules of conduct. Keynes firmly believed in living the "good life," without concern for right or wrong. "[It] is too late to change. I remain, and will always remain, an immoralist," he wrote (Hession 1984, 46).

Was Keynes a misogynist? Keynes's predilection for men may have affected his attitudes toward women in his early years. Like Marshall, he disliked the presence of female students in his classes. In 1909, while teaching at Cambridge, he wrote, "I think I shall have to give up teaching females after this year. The nervous irritation caused by two hours' contact with them is intense. I seem to hate every movement of their minds. The minds of the men, even when they are stupid and ugly, never appear to me so repellent" (Moggridge 1992, 183–34).

But Keynes shocked his homosexual friends in Bloomsbury when he announced his engagement and subsequent marriage to Lydia Lopokova, a Russian ballerina, in 1925. Based on private letters between Maynard and Lydia, their marriage was far from platonic. "Sexual relations certainly developed," biographer Robert Skidelsky writes (1992, 110–11; 2003, 300, 356–60). Keynes also developed friendships with women in the 1930s, including Joan Robinson.

But we are getting ahead of our story. After graduation, Keynes entered the British Civil Service, spending two years in the India office (although never visiting India). In 1909 he became a teaching fellow at Cambridge, and from 1911 to 1944 he served as the general editor of Cambridge's *Economic Journal*. He was not trained in economics, having taken only a single course from Alfred Marshall, but quickly acquired the skills to teach it.

Keynes Writes a Best-Seller

In 1919, following World War I, Keynes served as a senior Treasury official in the British delegation to the Versailles Peace Conference. Distressed by the proceedings, he resigned and wrote *The Economic Consequences of the Peace* (1920). It became a best-seller and propelled Keynes into fame and fortune.

Many critics consider it Keynes's best book. Writing in trenchant prose, he revealed peculiar personal characteristics of the Allied leaders.[3] Keynes condemned the Allies for imposing impractical and unrealistic reparations on the Germans. The defeated nations were required to pay the complete Allied costs of the war, including pay, pensions, and death benefits of troops—up to $5 billion "whether in gold, commodities, ships, securities or otherwise," before May 1, 1921. "The existence of the great war debts is a menace to financial stability everywhere," warned Keynes (1920, 279). A pessimistic Keynes predicted negative consequences in Europe. He implied that Germany would have no recourse but to inflate her way out. In a famous passage, Keynes noted, "Lenin was certainly right. There is no subtler, no surer means of overturning the existing basis of society than to debauch the currency. The process engages all the hidden forces of economic law on the side of destruction, and does it in a manner which not one man in a million is able to diagnose" (1920, 236).[4]

---

3. One of Keynes's eccentricities was his obsession with people's hands. He made a lifelong study of the size and shape of hands, which he regarded as a primary clue to character. He was so enamored of chirognomy—the reading of personality by the appearance of the hands—that he had casts made of his and his wife's hands, and even talked of making a collection of those of his friends (Harrod 1951:20). Whenever Keynes met a colleague, politician, or stranger, he focused immediately on the hands, often making a snap judgment about the person's character. Upon meeting President Woodrow Wilson at the Treaty of Versailles, he noted that his hands, "though capable and fairly strong, were wanting in sensitiveness and finesse" (Keynes 1920:40). At the same conference, Keynes expressed disappointment that French President Georges Clemenceau wore gloves (20–21). (No wonder Keynes did not take well to Adam Smith's doctrine of the invisible hand!) Upon meeting President Franklin D. Roosevelt the first time in 1934, Keynes was so preoccupied with examining FDR's hands that he faltered, "hardly knowing what I was saying about silver and balanced budgets and public works." Roosevelt reportedly was unimpressed with Keynes, and Keynes was disappointed as well. FDR's hand analysis: "Firm and fairly strong, but not clever or with finesse, shortish round nails like those at the end of a business-man's fingers" (Harrod 1951:20).

4. In a misguided review called *The Carthaginian Peace or the Economic Consequences of Mr. Keynes,* French economist Etienne de Mantoux later blamed Keynes for starting World War II. According to Mantoux, Keynes vastly underestimated Germany's capacity to pay the war reparations and convinced the world that the Versailles Peace Accords had crushed Germany and that therefore somehow the Nazi danger was minor. It's hard to imagine a more wrong-headed interpretation of Keynes's book. See Mantoux (1952).

Keynes Makes Another Brilliant Prediction in 1925

Keynes followed this success with another insightful analysis in 1925 when Britain, under Chancellor of the Exchequer Winston Churchill, returned to the gold standard at the overvalued prewar fixed exchange rate of $4.86. Keynes campaigned against this deflationary measure. In his booklet *The Economic Consequences of Mr. Churchill,* the Cambridge professor warned that deflation would force Britain to reduce real wages and retard economic growth (Keynes 1951 [1931], 244–70). Once again, Keynes proved prescient; Britain suffered from an economic malaise that only worsened as the Great Depression approached.

Unfortunately, Keynes's gift of prophecy disappeared in the late 1920s. In his *Tract on Monetary Reform* (which Milton Friedman rates as Keynes's greatest work), he joined the monetarist Irving Fisher in rejecting the gold standard, and later hailed the stabilizing influence of the U.S. dollar between 1923 and 1928 as a "triumph" of the Federal Reserve.

"We Will Not Have Any More Crashes in Our Time"

Like Fisher, Keynes was a New Era advocate who was bullish on stocks and commodities throughout the 1920s. In 1926, he met with Swiss banker Felix Somary, anxious to buy stocks. When Somary expressed pessimism about the future of the stock market, Keynes declared firmly, "We will not have any more crashes in our time" (Somary 1986 [1960], 146–47). Somary had been trained in Austrian economics at the University of Vienna and knew that the New Era boom was unsustainable. But Keynes, like Irving Fisher, ignored the Austrians and pinned his hopes on the Federal Reserve and price stabilization.

In late 1928, Keynes wrote two papers disputing that a "dangerous inflation" was developing on Wall Street, concluding that there was "nothing which can be called inflation yet in sight." Referring to both real estate and stock values in the United States, Keynes added, "I conclude that it would be premature today to assert the existence of over-investment. ... I should be inclined, therefore, to predict that stocks would not slump severely (i.e., below the recent low level) unless the market was discounting a business depression." Such would not be probable, he wrote, since the Federal Reserve Board would "do all in its power to avoid a business depression" (Keynes 1973b, 52–59; Hession 1984, 238–39).

Making Money from His Bedroom

Keynes should not have been so confident. By the late 1920s, he had developed a reputation for financial wizardry trading currencies, commodities, and stocks. He was chairman of the National Mutual Life Insurance Company and bursar of King's College in Cambridge. His personal account included a heavy commitment to commodities and stocks. He held long positions in futures contracts in rubber, corn, cotton, and tin, as well as several British automobile stocks.

Indeed, he was known for making trading decisions while still in bed. Reports Hession, "Some of this financial decision-making was carried out while he was still in bed in the morning; reports would come to him by phone from his brokers, and he would read the newspapers and make his decisions" (Hession 1984, 175).

Keynes Is Wiped Out by the Crash

Tragically, Keynes misread the times and failed to anticipate the crash. His portfolio was almost wiped out: he lost three-quarters of his net worth, primarily due to commodity losses (Moggridge 1983, 15–17; Skidelsky 1992, 338–43). In his *Treatise on Money*, published in 1930, he admitted that he had been misled by stable price indices in the 1920s, and that a "profit inflation" had developed (1930, 190–98).

However, Keynes, a stubborn investor, held onto his stocks and added substantially to his portfolio starting in 1932. Although he was incapable of getting out at the top, he had an uncanny ability to acquire stocks at the bottom of the market (Skousen 1992, 161–69). He bought securities that were clearly out of favor, such as utilities and gold stocks, and was so sure of his strategy that he bought heavily on margin. In 1944, he wrote a fellow money manager, "My central principle of investment is to go contrary to general opinion, on the ground that, if everyone is agreed about its merits, the investment is inevitably too dear and therefore unattractive" (Moggridge 1983, 111).

Keynes Still Manages to Die Spectacularly Rich

Keynes was so spectacularly successful in choosing stocks that his net worth reached £411,000 by the time he died in 1946. Given that his portfolio was worth only £16,315 in 1920, that's a 13 percent compounded annual return, far superior to what most professional money managers achieve and an amazing feat during an era when there was little or no inflation and, in fact, much deflation. And this extraordinary return was achieved despite fantastic setbacks in 1929–32 and 1937–38. Only David Ricardo had a superior record as a financial economist.

A Revolutionary Book Appears

Keynes's failure to predict the crash and the Great Depression deeply influenced his thinking. He was bitterly resentful of the speculators who drove prices down to ridiculously low levels and nearly put him in the poorhouse. He had long before rejected laissez-faire as a general organizing principle in society, but the 1929–33 crisis only strengthened his rejection of conventional classical economics. In BBC radio addresses, he lashed out at hoarders, speculators, and gold bugs, while urging deficit spending, inflation, and abandonment of the gold standard as solutions to the slump. He criticized Friedrich Hayek and the London School of Economics for believing that the economy was self-adjusting and for urging wage reductions and balanced budgets as solutions to the depression.

All the while, at his home in Cambridge, Keynes was working on a book creating a new model of economics, with the help of Richard Kahn, Joan Robinson, and the Cambridge Circus that developed around him. On New Year's Day 1935, Keynes wrote playwright George Bernard Shaw, "I believe myself to be writing a book on economic theory, which will largely revolutionise—not, I suppose, at once but in the course of the next ten years—the way the world thinks about economic problems" (Skidelsky 2003, 518). It was an arrogant prognostication, but one that proved to be right.

As already mentioned, *The General Theory of Employment, Interest and Money* first appeared in 1936.[5] Like other economists,

---

5. Some Keynesians, such as Charles Hession and John Kenneth Galbraith, emphatically insist that the correct title is *The General Theory of Employment Interest and Money*, without the comma. True, no commas were used on the cover of the original, but in the preface, Keynes added a comma after "employment."

Keynes identified with the great scientists of the past. Adam Smith and Roger Babson compared their analytical systems to those of Sir Isaac Newton, and Keynes emulated Albert Einstein. Keynes's book title refers to Einstein's general theory of relativity. His book, he said, created a "general" theory of economic behavior while he relegated the classical model to a "special" case and treated classical economists as "Euclidean geometers in a non-Euclidean world" (Skidelsky 1992, 487).

Like Marx, Keynes had high hopes that his magnum opus would be read by students and the general public and convinced Macmillan to price the 400-page treatise at only five shillings. But this was wishful thinking. *The General Theory* turned out to be Keynes's only unreadable book, full of technical jargon and incomprehensible language. Ricardo and Marx had their book of headaches and so did Keynes. The following simple Q and A will demonstrate a few of the difficulties found in *The General Theory*. (Thanks to Roger Garrison, economics professor at Auburn University, for providing this bit of satire.)

Keynes's Book of Headaches

Q: Please, Professor Keynes, what do you mean by "involuntary unemployment"?

A: "My definition is . . . as follows: Men are involuntarily unemployed if, in the event of a small rise in the price of wage-goods relative to the money-wage, both the aggregate supply of labour willing to work for the current money-wage and the aggregate demand for it at that wage would be greater than the existing volume of employment" (1973a [1936], 15).

Q: Humm . . . sounds very enlightening, Professor Keynes. Now tell us, please, what governs private investment in a market economy?

A: "Our conclusions can be stated in the most general form . . . as follows: No further increase in the rate of investment is possible when the greatest amongst the own-rates of own-interest of all available assets is equal to the greatest amongst the marginal efficiencies of all assets, measured in terms of the asset whose own-rate of own-interest is greatest" (236).

Q: Yes, I see. . . . One last question, Professor Keynes. Doesn't monetary expansion trigger an artificial boom?

A: "[A]t this point we are in deep water. The wild duck has dived down to the bottom—as deep as she can get—and bitten fast hold of the weed and tangle and all the rubbish that is down there, and it would need an extraordinarily clever dog to dive down and fish her up again" (183).

Even Paul Samuelson, a devote Keynesian, declared, "It is a badly written book, poorly organized; any layman who, beguiled by the author's previous reputation, bought the book was cheated of his five shillings. It is not well suited for classroom use. It is arrogant, bad-tempered, polemical, and not overly generous in its acknowledgements. It abounds in mares' nests or confusions. . . . Flashes of insight and intuition intersperse tedious algebra. An awkward definition suddenly gives way to an unforgettable cadenza. When finally mastered, its analysis is found to be obvious and at the same time new. In short, it is a work of genius" (Samuelson 1947 [1946], 148–89).[6]

And Paul Krugman writes that "although *The General Theory* is still worth reading and rereading," he admits that he "labored through" parts of it, and finds it helpful to describe the book as "a meal that begins with a delectable appetizer and ends with a delightful dessert, but whose main course consists of rather tough meat" (Krugman 2006).

The General Theory is still in print, but only because of the elucidating work of Keynes's disciples, especially Alvin Hansen and Paul Samuelson, who deciphered Keynes's convoluted jargon, translated it into plain English, and transformed the profession.

Keynes at War

Keynes was fifty-two when he completed *The General Theory,* his final major work. He was at the height of his powers. Keynes was

---

6. Biographer Charles Hession erected a novel theory that Keynes's revolutionary ideas and creative genius were the result of his androgynous background, which combined "the masculine truth of reason and the feminine truth of imagination" (Hession 1984: 107, 17–18). Skidelsky agrees, "Even his sexual ambivalence played its part in sharpening his vision" (1992: 537). But why should intuition and creativity be solely feminine and reason and logic solely masculine?

never a bookish scholar and recluse like his Cambridge colleagues Arthur Pigou or Dennis Robertson. He was a man of worldly affairs who loved the limelight and the social life, enjoyed the company of writers and artists, and was a devotee of cards, roulette, and speculations on Lombard Street and Wall Street. His magnetic personality attracted the highest leaders of government, who sought his counsel. He was a master of the written word and an entertaining speaker who regularly appeared on BBC radio.

After suffering a heart attack in 1937, Keynes had to slow down. He and his wife became active in promoting the arts and establishing the Arts Theatre in Cambridge. In 1940, when the war with Germany broke out, Keynes returned to the Treasury as an advisor and wrote an influential booklet, *How to Pay for the War*. He recommended restrictions on consumption and investment, and a forced savings program as a way to reduce demand and inflation.

In May 1942, Keynes's name was submitted to the king, nominating him to become Baron Keynes of Tilton, and in July he took his seat in the House of Lords. On his sixtieth birthday, Keynes was made High Steward of Cambridge, an honorary post. He thrived on the adulation and elitist status.

Near the end of the war, Keynes and his wife traveled to the United States to help negotiate a new international financial agreement. Keynes was one of the architects of the Bretton Woods agreement, which established a fixed exchange rate system based on gold and the dollar and created the International Monetary Fund (IMF) and the World Bank. Two years later, he died of a heart attack at the age of sixty-two.

Keynes's Disdain for Karl Marx and Marxism

Let us now turn to Keynes's approach to economics. It should be noted at the outset that Keynes had serious reservations about the economics of both Adam Smith and Karl Marx. The most influential economist of the twentieth century, Keynes was an interventionist and a supporter of Britain's Labour Party. Like Marx, he was no friend of laissez-faire. He argued that capitalism was inherently unstable and required government intervention. But that was as far as it went. Keynes couldn't stand Karl Marx or the communist experiment, which he regarded as "an insult to our intelligence" (Moggridge 1992, 470; Skidelsky 1992, 519; 2003, 514–18). Following a trip to Russia in 1925, Keynes wrote three articles for the *Nation,* debunking the Soviet "religion" as "unscrupulous," "ruthless," and "contrary to human nature." There was none of that naïve "I've seen the future" optimism for Keynes. Individual freedom and a liberal open society meant too much to him. "For me, brought up in a free air undarkened by the horrors of religion, with nothing to be afraid of, Red Russia holds too much which is detestable." He added, "How can I adopt a creed which, preferring the mud to the fish, exalts the boorish proletariat above the bourgeois and the intelligentsia who, with whatever faults, are the quality in life and surely carry the seeds of all human achievement? . . . We have everything to lose by the methods of violent change. In Western industrial conditions the tactics of Red Revolution would throw the whole population into a pit of poverty and death" (1951 [1931], 306). He lambasted Marx's magnum opus, *Capital,* as "an obsolete economic textbook" that was "scientifically erroneous" and "without interest or application for the modern world" (298–300).

In the middle of the Great Depression, the best and the brightest intellectuals embraced Marxism, but not Keynes. At a dinner among friends in 1934, Keynes said that, of all the "isms," Marxism was "the worst of all & founded on a silly mistake of old Mr Ricardo's [labor theory of value]" (Skidelsky 2003, 515). In a letter to playwright George Bernard Shaw, Keynes labeled *Das Kapital* "dreary, out-of-date, academic controversialising." He compared it to the Koran. "How could either of these books carry fire and sword round half the world? It beats me." In a second letter to Shaw dated January 1, 1935, Keynes complained of Marx's "vile manner of writing" (Skidelsky 1992, 520; 2003, 517).[7]

---

7. Marxists, in turn, have disdained the bourgeois Keynes and Keynesian economics. "Such a theory is a serious danger to the working class," wrote Marxist John Eaton in his little book, *Marx Against Keynes* (1951:12). According to Eaton, Keynesianism defends "wage slavery" and "policies of imperialism" (75). Eaton accused Keynes of not having "ever read and understood Marx's profoundly scientific analysis" in *Capital* (33). In short, Keynesian economics is the "vulgar economy of monopoly capitalism in crisis and decay" (85), according to Eaton, and thus is doomed to fail.

Keynes's Critique of Adam Smith and His Invisible Hand Doctrine

Keynes has been lauded as the savior of capitalism, but his model and policy recommendations were in many ways a direct repudiation and assault on Adam Smith's laissez-faire system. In the New Era twenties he wrote, "It is not true that individuals possess a prescriptive 'natural liberty' in their economic activities. . . . Nor is it true that self-interest generally is enlightened. . . . Experience does not show that individuals, when they make up a social unit, are always less clear-sighted than when they act separately" (Keynes 1951 [1931], 312). This speech, appropriately titled, "The End of Laissez-Faire," was given in 1926, a full decade before *The General Theory* was written. It was a clear attack on Adam Smith's system of natural liberty.

In the early 1930s, Keynes became increasingly disillusioned with capitalism, both morally and aesthetically. The ideas of Sigmund Freud were fashionable at the time, and Keynes adopted the Freudian thesis that moneymaking was a neurosis, "a somewhat disgusting morbidity, one of the semi-criminal, semi-pathological propensities which one hands over with a shudder to specialists in mental disease" (1951 [1931], 369). Later, in 1933, he indicted the capitalist system: "The decadent international but individualistic capitalism, in the hands of which we found ourselves after the war, is not a success. It is not intelligent, it is not beautiful, it is not just, it is not virtuous—and it doesn't deliver the goods. In short, we dislike it and are beginning to despise it. But when we wonder what to put in its place, we are perplexed" (Hession 1984, 258). This is a far cry from Adam Smith!

Keynes, the Heretic, Turns Classical Economics Upside Down

The General Theory did not aim to rebuild the classical model; it aimed to replace it with elaborate unconventional concepts and a new Weltanschauung. Until the 1930s, the economics profession had largely sanctioned the basic premises of the classical model of Adam Smith—the virtues of thrift, balanced budgets, free trade, low taxes, the gold standard, and Say's law. But Keynes turned the classical model upside down.

Instead of Smith's classical system being considered the general or universal model, Keynes relegated it to a "special case," applicable only in times of full employment. His own general theory of "aggregate effective demand" would apply during times of underemployed labor and resources, which, under Keynesianism, could exist indefinitely. Under such circumstances, Keynes offered the following principles:

1. An increase in savings can contract income and reduce economic growth. Consumption is more important than production in encouraging investment, thus reversing Say's law: "Demand creates its own supply" (1973a [1936], 18–21, 111).

2. The federal government's budget should be kept deliberately in a state of imbalance during a recession. Fiscal and monetary policy should be highly expansionary until prosperity is restored, and interest rates should be kept permanently low (128–31, 322).

3. Government should abandon its laissez-faire policy and intervene in the marketplace whenever necessary. According to Keynes, in desperate times it may be necessary to return to mercantilist policies, including protectionist measures (333–71).

4. The gold standard is defective because its inelasticity renders it incapable of responding to the expanding needs of business. A managed fiat money is preferable (235–56; 1971, 140). Keynes held a deep-seated disdain for the gold standard and was largely successful in dethroning gold as a worldwide monetary numeraire.

What Did Keynes Really Mean by "In the Long Run We Are All Dead"?

Keynes's cavalier statement, "In the long run we are all dead," is in many ways a symbol of his turning his back on classical economics.

Many economists consider his remark an affront to Frédéric Bastiat's classical view ("What Is Seen and What Is Not Seen") that economists must take into account the long-run and not just the short-run effects of government policies. For example, deficit spending may stimulate certain sectors of the economy in the short run, but what will be the impact in the long run? Tariffs may save some manufacturing jobs, but what impact will this have on consumers? As Henry Hazlitt declares, "The art of economics consists in looking not merely at the immediate but at the longer effects of any act or policy; it consists in tracing the consequences of that policy not merely for one group but for all groups" (1979 [1946], 17). And Ludwig von Mises, another critic of Keynes, concludes, "we have outlived the short-run and are suffering from the long-run consequences of [Keynesian] policies" (1980 [1952], 7). Keynes may have indeed used his dictum to support short-term policies like deficit spending, but he also used it in other contexts.

Keynes Attacks Monetarism

The first time Keynes made the famous remark quoted above, he used it to deride Irving Fisher's extreme monetarism, which claimed that monetary inflation has no ill effects in the long run but only raises prices (see chapter 4). Keynes retorted, "Now 'in the long run' this is probably true . . . but this long run is a misleading guide to current affairs. In the long run we are all dead. Economists set themselves too easy, too useless a task if in tempestuous seasons they can only tell us that when the storm is long past the ocean is flat again" (1971, 65). No doubt Hazlitt and Mises would find much to agree with in this statement.

Britain First!

Keynes also used his famous phrase in the context of British foreign policy in wartime. In 1937, when Churchill advocated rearmament and warned against appeasing Hitler, Keynes seemed to support short-term peace initiatives: "It is our duty to prolong peace, hour by hour, day by day, for as long as we can. . . . I have said in another context that it is a disadvantage of 'the long run' that in the long run we are all dead. But I could have said equally well that it is a great advantage of 'the short run' that in the short run we are still alive. Life and history are made up of short runs. If we are at peace in the short run, that is something. The best we can do is put off disaster" (Moggridge 1992, 611). Was Keynes advocating peace at any price?

After Pearl Harbor was attacked in December 1941, Keynes reacted with dismay to the British Foreign Office argument that free trade with America would be beneficial to Britain "in the long run." Keynes blustered, "The theory that 'to get our way in the long run' we must always yield in the short reminds me of the bombshell I threw into economic theory by the reminder that 'in the long run we are all dead.' If there was no one left to appease, the F.O. [Foreign Office] would feel out of a job altogether" (Moggridge 1992, 666). This was Keynes the mercantilist.

Keynes's Long Term

Keynes was truly a social millennialist who ultimately envisioned a world evolving to the point of infinite accumulation of capital. His utopian vision is best expressed in his essay, "Economic Possibilities for Our Grandchildren" (1951 [1931], 358–73). Keynes believed that by progressively expanding credit to promote full employment, the universal economic problem of scarcity would finally be overcome. Interest rates would fall to zero and mankind would reenter the Garden of Eden. In Keynes's mind, the gold standard severely limited credit expansion and preserved the status quo of scarcity. Thus, gold's inelasticity—which the classical economists considered its primary virtue—stood in the way of Keynes's paradise and needed to be abandoned in favor of fiat-money inflation (1951 [1931], 360–73). The Bretton Woods agreement was the first step toward removing gold from the world's monetary system. Keynes would undoubtedly be pleased to see gold playing such a moribund role in international monetary affairs in the twenty-first century.

In short, Keynes's goal was not to save Adam Smith's house, as his adherents contended, but to build another house entirely—the house that Keynes built. It was his belief that economists would live and work most of the time in Keynes's house, while using Smith's house occasionally, perhaps as a vacation home.

Is Capitalism Inherently Unstable?

Keynes rejected the classical notion that the capitalist system is self-adjusting over the long run. *The General Theory* was written specifically to create a model based on the view that the market system is inherently and inescapably flawed. According to Keynes, capitalism was unstable and therefore could become stuck indefinitely at varying degrees of "unemployed equilibrium," depending on the level of uncertainty in a fragile financial system. Keynes wanted to show that the economy could remain "in a chronic condition of sub-normal activity for a considerable period without any marked tendency either toward recovery or toward complete collapse" (1973a [1936], 249, 30). Paul Samuelson correctly understood the meaning of Keynes: "With respect to the level of total purchasing power and employment, Keynes denies that there is an invisible hand channeling the self-centered action of each individual to the social optimum" (Samuelson 1947, 151).

Keynes explained what he meant by "unemployment equilibrium," but used no diagram to illustrate it. In a masterful article, "Mr. Keynes and the Classics," British economist John Hicks developed a graphic framework (known as the IS-LM diagram) to demonstrate Keynes's version of full-employment equilibrium (the special classical theory) versus unemployment equilibrium (the general theory) (Hicks 1937). Today's textbooks use a similar diagram to demonstrate aggregate supply (*AS*) and aggregate demand (*AD*).

In Figure 5.1 we see how the economy is depressed at less than full employment. According to Keynes's model, the classical model only applies when the economy reaches full employment (Q_f), while the Keynesian general theory applies at any point along the *AS* curve where it intersects with the *AD* curve.

Who's to Blame? Irrational Investors!

Keynes blamed the instability of capitalism on the bad behavior of investors. *The General Theory* creates a macroeconomic model based essentially on a financial instability hypothesis. As Keynesian economist Hyman P. Minsky declares, "The essential aspect of Keynes's *General Theory* is a deep analysis of how financial

Figure 5.1 **Aggregate Supply (AS) and Aggregate Demand (AD) Model from a Keynesian Perspective**

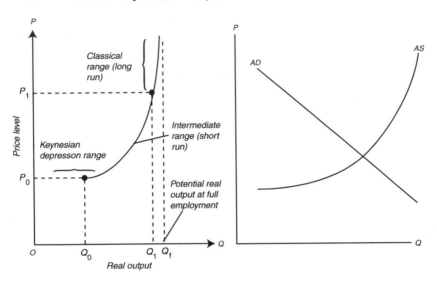

Source: Byrns and Stone (1987: 311). Reprinted by permission of Scott, Foresman and Co.

forces—which we can characterize as Wall Street—interact with production and consumption to determine output, employment, and prices" (1986, 100). Allan H. Meltzer at Carnegie Mellon University offers a similar interpretation, that Keynes's theory of employment and output was not so much related to rigid wages and prices as to expectations and uncertainty in the investment and capital markets (Meltzer 1988 [1968]).[8]

Numerous passages in *The General Theory* support this view. Keynes complained of the irrational short-term "animal spirits" of speculators who dump stocks in favor of liquidity during such crises. Such "waves of irrational psychology" could do much damage to long-term expectations, he said. "Of the maxims of orthodox finance none, surely, is more anti-social than the fetish of liquidity, the doctrine that it is a positive virtue on the part of investment institutions to

---

8. See also my version of this thesis in "Keynes as a Speculator: A Critique of Keynesian Investment Theory," in Skousen 1992: 161–69.

concentrate resources upon the holding of 'liquid' securities" (1973a [1936], 155). According to Keynes, the stock market is not simply an efficient way to raise capital and advance living standards, but can be likened to a casino or a game of chance. "For it is, so to speak, a game of Snap, of Old Maid, of Musical Chairs—a pastime in which he is victor who says Snap neither too soon nor too late, who passes the Old Maid to his neighbor before the game is over, who secures a chair for himself when the music stops" (1973a [1936], 155–56).

Keynes was speaking from experience. He reasoned that the 1929–33 crisis destroyed his portfolio without any rational economic cause—the panic was due to Wall Street's irrational demand for cash, what he termed "liquidity preference" and a "fetish of liquidity" (1973a [1936], 155).

The Culprit: Uninvested Savings

If Keynes were Sherlock Homes, the economist-investigator would point an accusing finger at Miss Thrifty in his murder mystery, "The Case of the Missing Savings." In Keynes's model, the key factor causing an indefinite slump is the de-linking of savings and investment. If savings failed to be invested, total spending in the economy would fall to a point below full employment. If savings were hoarded or left in excessive reserves in the banks, as was the case in the 1930s, the fetish for liquidity would make national invest-ment and output fall. Thus, thrift no longer served as a dependable social function.

In *The General Theory,* Keynes argued that as income and wealth accumulate under capitalism, the threat grows that savings will not be invested. He introduced a "psychological law" that the "marginal propensity to save" increases with income (1973a [1936], 31, 97). That is, as individuals earn more income and become wealthier, they tend to save a greater percentage of their income. Thus, there is a strong tendency for savings to rise disproportionately as national income increases. But wouldn't a growing capitalist economy al-ways be under pressure to invest those increased savings? Keynes responded, "Maybe, maybe not." If savings are not invested, the boom will turn into a bust.

Actually, this criticism of uninvested saving is an old saw with

Keynes. He acknowledged the necessity of thrift and self-denial during the nineteenth century in a delightful passage of *The Economic Consequences of the Peace* (1920, 18–22), stating that thrift "made possible those vast accumulations of fixed wealth and of capital improvement which distinguished that age from all others" (19). But in *A Treatise on Money* (1930), the Cambridge economist raised the likely possibility that saving and investment could grow apart, creating a business cycle. In a modern society, saving and investing are done by two separate groups. Saving is a "negative act of refraining from spending," while investment is a "positive act of starting or maintaining some process of production" (1930, 155). The interest rate is not an "automatic mechanism" that brings the two together—they can "get out of gear" (1951 [1931], 393) and savings can be "abortive." If investment exceeds savings, a boom occurs; if savings exceeds investment, a slump happens.[9]

During the depression of the 1930s, Keynes lashed out at frugal savers and hoarders who kept down "effective demand." The conventional wisdom in bad times has always been to cut costs, get out of debt, build a strong cash position, and wait for a recovery. Keynes was opposed to this "old-fashioned" approach, and he was joined by other economists, including British Treasury official Ralph Hawtrey and Harvard's Frank Taussig, in encouraging consumers to spend. In a radio broadcast in January 1931, Keynes asserted that thriftiness could cause a "vicious circle" of poverty, that if "you save five shillings, you

---

9. Historians Elizabeth and Harry Johnson even went so far as to suggest that Keynes's negative attitude toward saving was related to his misogynistic tendencies. The Johnsons noted that Keynes and his followers often referred to savings as female and investment as male. Female saving was usually seen in a negative light and male investment in a positive way. "The maleness of investment is attested to by among other things the frequent references by Joan Robinson and other Cambridge writers to 'the animal spirits' of entrepreneurs; the femaleness of savings is evident in the passive role assigned to savings in the analysis of the determination of employment equilibrium" (Johnson 1978:121). Keynes himself wrote in his *Treatise on Money*, "Thus, thrift may be the handmaid and nurse of enterprise. But equally she may not" (1930, 2:132). However, Keynes was sometimes ambiguous about the sexual identity of saving. In the same *Treatise*, Keynes commented on the lack of economic progress in Europe in the 1920s. "Ten years have elapsed since the end of the war. Savings have been on an unexampled scale. But a proportion of them has been wasted, spilt on the ground" (1930, 2:185). This is an allusion to the biblical story of Onan, who spilled his seed on the ground (Genesis 38: 8–9).

put a man out of work for a day." He encouraged British housewives to go on a buying spree and government to go on a building binge. He urged, "Why not pull down the whole of South London from Westminster to Greenwich, and make a good job of it. . . . Would that employ men? Why, of course it would!" (1951 [1931], 151–54).

Keynes's bias against thrift reached its zenith in *The General Theory,* where he referred to traditional views on savings as "absurd." He boldly wrote, "The more virtuous we are, the more determined by thrift, the more obstinately orthodox in our national and personal finance, the more our incomes will fall" (1973a [1936], 111, 211). Keynes praised the heterodox notions of underworld figures and monetary cranks, such as Bernard de Mandeville, J.A. Hobson, and Silvio Gessell, who held underconsumptionist views (333–71). He was undoubtedly influenced by the popularity of Major Douglas of the social credit movement and underconsumptionists Foster and Catchings during the 1920s.

An Antisaving Tradition

Keynes was not the first to question the virtue of thrift. Over the years, a small group of radical thinkers, known generally as underconsumptionists, have dissented from the traditional endorsement of thrift. They include Simonde de Sismondi, Karl Rodbertus, J.A. Hobson, and Karl Marx. Keynes expressed sympathy toward the "heretical" views of Major C.H. Douglas, an engineer who began the social credit movement in Canada in the 1920s and wrote several books championing "economic democracy" (1973a [1936], 370–71). Believing that saving created a permanent deficiency in a nation's purchasing power, Major Douglas advocated strict below-market price controls so that consumers could afford to buy the products they produced.

William T. Foster, past president of Reed College, and Waddill Catchings, an iron manufacturer and partner in the investment firm of Goldman Sachs, proposed a different scheme. Foster and Catchings wrote a series of books on a similar antisaving theme. "[E]very dollar which is saved and invested, instead of spent, causes one dollar of deficiency in consumer buying unless that deficiency is made up in some way" (Foster and Catchings 1927, 48). What way? Foster and Catchings advocated that the government issue new money credits to consumers to make up for consumer buying deficiency.

To generate interest in their theory and proposal, in 1927 they offered a prize of $5,000 to anyone who could refute them. They published the best essays a few months later, but the best critique was written by the Austrian economist Friedrich A. Hayek in 1929. His essay, "The 'Paradox' of Saving," was translated and published in *Economica* in May 1931.

According to Hayek, the Foster-and-Catchings dilemma depended on a single erroneous assumption. They assumed a "single-stage" model, so that investment depends entirely and immediately on consumer demand. Under such a restrictive assumption, "there would be no inducement [for consumers] . . . to save money . . . [or] . . . to invest their savings," noted Hayek (1939 [1929], 224, 247). With a capital-using, time-oriented period of production, Hayek demonstrated that increased savings lengthens the capitalistic process, increases productivity, and thereby enlarges profits, wages, and income sufficiently for consumers to buy the final product.[10]

Keynes Focuses on Spending as the Key Ingredient

In Keynes's mind, saving is an unreliable form of spending. It is only "effective" if savings are invested by business. Thus, savings that are hoarded under a mattress or piled up in a bank vault are a drain on the economy and aggregate demand.

Only "effective demand"—a powerful new term introduced in chapter 3 of *The General Theory*—counts. What consumers and businesses spend determines national output. Keynes defined effective demand as aggregate output *(Y)*, which is the sum of consumption *(C)* and investment *(I)*. Hence,

$$Y = C + I$$

Today we refer to *Y*, or "aggregate effective demand," as gross domestic product (GDP). GDP is defined as the value of final output of goods and services during the year. Simon Kuznets, a Keynesian statistician, developed national income accounting in the early 1940s as a way to measure Keynes's aggregate effective demand. Keynes effectively demonstrated

---

10. Foster and Catchings rejected all arguments and never paid the prize money.

that if savings are not invested by business, GDP does not reach its potential; recession or depression indicates a lack of effective demand.

Demand Creates Its Own Supply

What was Keynes's solution to recession? Increase effective demand! If demand is stimulated through additional spending, more goods have to be produced and the economy should recover. In this sense, Keynes turned Say's law upside down. Demand creates supply, not the other way around.

To increase Y (national output), the choices are limited in a recession. During a downturn, the business community might be afraid to risk its capital on I (investment). Equally, consumers might be unwilling to increase consumption (C) due to the uncertainty of their incomes. Both investors and consumers are more likely to pull in their horns when left to their own devices.

Adding G to the Equation

There is only one way out, wrote Keynes. Get government to start spending. Keynes added G (government) to the national income equation, so that

$$Y = C + I + G$$

Keynes saw government (G) as an independent agent capable of stimulating the economy through the printing presses and public works. An expansionary government policy could raise "effective demand" if resources were underutilized, and it could do so without hurting consumption or investment. In fact, during a recession, a rise in G would encourage both C and I and thereby boost Y.

Digging Holes in the Ground: Keynes Endorses an Activist Fiscal Policy

Keynes overturned the classical solution to a slump, which had been to "tighten one's belt" by cutting prices, wages, and wasteful spending while waiting out the slump. Instead, during a recession, he recommended deliberate deficit spending by the federal government to jump-start the economy. He endorsed an even more radical approach during a deep depression like that of the 1930s: government spending could be totally wasteful and it would still help. "Pyramid-building, earthquakes, even wars may serve to increase wealth," he proclaimed (1973a [1936], 129). Of course, "It would, indeed, be more sensible to build houses and the like," but productive building was not essential. According to Keynes, spending is spending, no matter what the objective, and it has the same beneficial effect—increasing aggregate demand.

Keynes Favors Public Works over Monetary Inflation

Keynes felt that tinkering with fiscal policy (changes in spending and taxes) was more effective than monetary policy (changes in the money supply and interest rates). He had lost faith in monetary policy and the Federal Reserve in the 1930s, when interest rates were so low that reducing them wouldn't have made much difference (see Figure 5.2). Inducing the Federal Reserve to expand the money supply would not be very effective either, because banks refused to lend excess reserves anyway. Keynes called this a "liquidity trap." The new money would just pile up unspent and uninvested because of "liquidity preference," the desire to hold cash during a severe depression (1973a [1936], 207).

How the Multiplier Generates Full Employment

Public works would serve several benefits. First, public works are positive spending, putting people to work and money into business's pockets. Moreover, they have a multiplier effect, based on the nation's marginal propensity to consume.

The multiplier, a concept introduced by Richard Kahn, was a powerful new tool in the Keynesian tool box, demonstrating that a "small increment of investment will lead to full employment" (Keynes 1973a [1936], 118). Suppose in a recession that the government hires construction workers and suppliers to construct a new federal building costing $100 million. These previously unemployed workers are now getting paid. In the first round of spending, $100 million is added to the economy.

Now suppose that the public's marginal propensity to consume is 90

Figure 5.2 **The General Theory Was Written When Interest Rates Were at Their All-Time Lows**

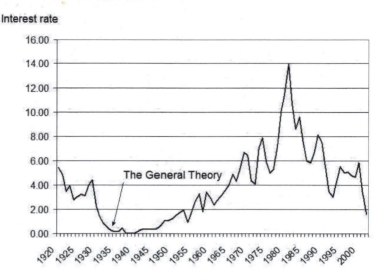

percent, that is, these workers spend 90 cents of every new dollar earned. (Another way of saying it: their marginal propensity to save is 10 percent.) In the second round of spending, $90 million is added to the economy.

Then there is a third round. After the workers spend their new money, that $90 million becomes the revenues of other businesses— shopping malls, gas stations, supermarkets, car dealerships, and movie theaters. These business may in turn hire new workers to handle the new demand, paying them more wages, too, and these workers also spend 90 percent of that income. They receive an additional $81 million (90 percent of $90 million) of spending power. Ultimately, the public investment has a multiplier effect that generates round after round of gradually declining spending. By the time the new spending has run its course, the aggregate spending has increased tenfold. Keynes's formula for the multiplier *(k)* is,

$$k = \frac{1}{1 - MPC}$$

where *MPC* = marginal propensity to consume.

Since $MPC = .90$ in the example above, $k = 10$. As Keynes stated, "the multiplier k is 10; and the total employment caused by . . . increased public works will be ten times the primary employment provided by the public works themselves, assuming no reduction of investment in other directions" (1973a [1936], 116–17).

Keynes Makes a Mischievous Assumption

Note that in the Keynesian model, only consumption spending generates additional income and employment in the economy. Keynes assumes that saving is sterile, that it aborts into cash hoarding or excess bank reserves. Thus, the Keynesian model as originally proposed is considered a "depression" model. As we shall see in the next chapter, this was a crucial mistake that led to much mischief and misunderstanding in economics in the postwar era.

Keynes Offers a Drastic Measure to Stabilize Capitalism

The Cambridge leader was not satisfied with temporary measures such as public works and deficit spending to reestablish full employment. Once maximum output was reached, he reasoned, there is no reason to believe it will stay there. Investment is unpredictable and ephemeral, Keynes said. Long-term expectations, a stable business climate, and savings equal to investment could never be guaranteed as long as irrational "animal spirits" operated in a laissez-faire financial marketplace. What was Keynes's solution? He favored a gradual but comprehensive "socialisation of investment" as the "only means of securing an approximation to full employment" (1973a, 378). This was by no means "state socialism," but it could mean government ownership of the entire capital market. Keynes also sanctioned a small "transfer tax" on all securities sales as a way to dampen speculative fever.[11]

---

11. Nobel laureate James Tobin has entertained a similar measure, known as the Tobin tax on stock and foreign exchange transactions, a legal step that would surely reduce liquidity and enlarge the bid-ask spreads on stocks and foreign exchange.

6

A Turning Point in Twentieth-Century Economics

> Keynsesian economics is . . . the most serious blow that the
> authority of orthodox economics has yet suffered.
> —*W.H. Hutt* (1979, 12)

Two factors created the right atmosphere for the Keynesian revolution to sweep the economics profession after World War II. First, the depth and length of the Great Depression seemed to justify the Keynesian-Marxian view that market capitalism was inherently unstable and that the market could be stuck at unemployed equilibrium indefinitely.

Economic historians noted that the only governments that appeared to make headway in eliminating unemployment in the 1930s were totalitarian regimes in Germany, Italy, and the Soviet Union. Curiously, Keynes himself acknowledged in the introduction to the German edition of *The General Theory,* that his theory "is much more easily adapted to the conditions of a totalitarian state, than is the theory of the production and distribution of a given output produced under conditions of free competition and a large measure of laissez-faire" (1973a [1936], xxvi).

Second, World War II came along right after the publication of *The General Theory,* giving strong empirical evidence of Keynes's policy prescription. Government spending and deficit financing increased dramatically during World War II, unemployment disappeared, and economic output soared. War was "good" for the economy, just as Keynes suggested (1973a [1936], 129). As historian Robert M. Collins wrote, "World War II set the stage for the triumph of Keynesianism by providing striking evidence of the effectiveness of government expenditures on a huge scale" (1981, 12). The following quote from a popular textbook repeated what other textbooks were saying in the postwar period: "Once the massive, war-geared expenditure of the 1940s began, income responded sharply and unemployment evaporated. Government expenditures on goods and services, which had been running at under 15 percent of GNP during the 1930s, jumped to 46 percent by 1944, while unemployment reached the incredible low of 1.2 percent of the civilian labor force" (Lipsey, Steiner, and Purvis 1987, 573).

Paul Samuelson Raises the Keynesian Cross

As noted earlier, Keynes died in 1946, right after the war. It would be left to his disciples to lead the charge and create a "new economics." Fortunately for Keynes, a young wunderkind was ready to fill his shoes. His name was Paul Samuelson, and he would write a textbook that would dominate the profession for more than an entire generation.

The year was 1948, one of those watershed years that occasionally crops up in economics. Remember 1776, 1848, and 1871? In early 1948, the Austrian émigré Ludwig von Mises, secluded in his New York apartment, was typing a short article, "Stones into Bread, the Keynesian Miracle," for a conservative publication, *Plain Talk*. "What is going on today in the United States," he declared solemnly, "is the final failure of Keynesianism. There is no doubt that the American public is moving away from the Keynesian notions and slogans. Their prestige is dwindling" (Mises 1980 [1952], 62).

Perhaps it was wishful thinking, but Mises could not have misread the times more egregiously in 1948. It was in that very year that the new economics of John Maynard Keynes was being hailed by Keynes's rapidly growing number of disciples as the wave of the future and the savior of capitalism. Literally hundreds of articles and dozens of books had been published about Keynes and the new Keynesian model since Keynes wrote *The General Theory of Employment, Interest and Money*.

The Other Cambridge

The year 1948 was also when Seymour E. Harris, chairman of the economics department at Harvard, produced an edited volume entitled *Saving American Capitalism*. This was a sequel to his 1947 edited work, *The New Economics*. Both best-sellers were filled with laudatory articles by prominent economists preaching the new economics of Keynes.

Darwin had one bulldog to propagate his revolutionary theory, but Keynes had three in the United States—Seymour Harris, Alvin Hansen, and Paul A. Samuelson. They all came from the "other Cambridge"—Cambridge, Massachusetts. Both Harris and Hansen were conservative Harvard teachers who had converted to Keynesianism and devoted their energies to convincing students and colleagues of the efficacy of this strange new doctrine.

The American advancement of Keynesian economics represented a subtle but clear shift from Europe to the New World. Before the war, London and Cambridge in the United Kingdom shaped the economic world. After the war, the magnets for the best and the brightest graduate students were Boston, Chicago, and Berkeley. Students came from all over the world to do their work in the United States, and not just in economics.

The Year of the Textbook

Finally, 1948 was the year in which an exciting new breakthrough textbook came forth from Harvard's neighboring university, the Massachusetts Institute of Technology (MIT). Written by the "brash whippersnapper go-getter" Paul Samuelson (his own words!), *Economics* was destined to become the most successful textbook ever published in any field. Sixteen editions have sold more than 4 million copies and have been translated into over forty languages. No other textbook, including those of Jean-Baptiste Say, John Stuart Mill, and Alfred Marshall, can compare. Samuelson's *Economics* survived a half-century of dramatic changes in the world economy and the economics profession: peace and war, boom and bust, inflation and deflation, Republicans and Democrats, and an array of new economic theories.

Samuelson's textbook was popular not so much because it was well written, but because it elucidated and simplified the basics of Keynesian macroeconomics through the deft use of simple algebra and clear graphs. It took the profession by storm, selling hundreds of thousands of copies every year. Samuelson updated the textbook every three years or so, a practice that every textbook publisher now imitates. *Economics* sold over 440,000 copies at the height of its popularity in 1964. Even a conservative institution such as Brigham Young University, my alma mater, used the Samuelson textbook.

The Acme of Professional Success

Samuelson is known for more than just popularizing Keynesian economics. He is considered the father of modern macroeconomic theorizing. He has made innumerable contributions to pure mathematical economics, for which he has been both honored and blamed—honored for making economics a pure logical science, and blamed for carrying the Ricardian vice and Walrasian equilibrium analysis to an extreme, devoid of any empirical work. (See chapters 2 and 4.)

For his popular and scientific works, the academic community has awarded Samuelson virtually every honor it confers. He was the first American to win the Nobel Prize in economics, in 1970. He was awarded the first John Bates Clark Medal for the brightest economist under forty, and beyond economics, he received the Albert Einstein Medal in 1971. There's even an annual award named after him, the Paul A. Samuelson Award, given for published works in finance. His articles have appeared in all the major (and many minor) journals. He was elected president of the American Economic Association (AEA), has received innumerable honorary degrees from various universities, and has been the subject of many Festschrifts, gatherings at which scholars honor a fellow colleague with essays about his work.

"The Young, Brash Wunderkind"

Paul A. Samuelson was born in Gary, Indiana, in 1915 to Jewish parents, and moved to Chicago, where he received his B.A. in 1935—at the tender age of twenty—from the University of Chicago. Chicago in the 1930s, as it is today, was the citadel of laissez-faire economic thought. In those days, it was run by Frank Knight, Jacob Viner, and Henry Simons, among others. Paul's first class in economics was taught by Aaron Director, who was perhaps the most libertarian among the faculty and who later became Milton Friedman's brother-in-law. Both Friedman and George Stigler were graduate students at the time. Director's laissez-faire philosophy failed to take in the youthful reformist Samuelson, who enjoyed being an intellectual heretic in a conservative institution and who was influenced by a father known as a "moderate socialist." Moreover, during the depression, most of the leaders of the Chicago school advocated deficit spending and other government activist policies as temporary measures. Samuelson did inherit one concept from Chicago that he carried with him until he encountered Keynes—monetarism. He called himself a "jackass" for having been taken in (Samuelson 1968, 1).

Alvin Hansen Switches Sides to Become the "American Keynes"

After Chicago, Samuelson immediately went to Harvard, where he witnessed an amazing transition. His teacher, Alvin Hansen (1887–1975), a long-standing classical economist, converted to Keynesianism. Most older economists at first rejected Keynes's heretical ideas, including Hansen, who was at the University of Minnesota. Only Marriner Eccles, the exceptional Utah banker who became head of the Federal Reserve, and Lauchlin Currie, an economic aide to Roosevelt, were prominent Keynesian advocates.

Then, in the fall of 1937, Hansen transferred to Harvard and suddenly—at the age of fifty—recognized the revolutionary nature of Keynes. He would become an outspoken exponent—the "American Keynes." His fiscal policy seminar attracted many enthusiastic students, including Samuelson, and convinced many colleagues, including Seymour Harris. Keynes had to be translated into plain English and easy-to-understand graphs and math, and Hansen was the principal interpreter, from *Fiscal Policy and Business Cycles* (1941) to *A Guide to Keynes* (1953). Hansen also campaigned for the Employment Act of 1946. According to Mark Blaug, "Alvin Hansen did more than any other economist to bring the Keynesian Revolution to America" (Blaug 1985, 79).

"Stagnation Thesis" Discredits Hansen and Almost Destroys Samuelson's Reputation

However, Hansen fell into a trap. He logically extended Keynes's unemployment equilibrium theory into a "secular stagnation thesis." (Keynes himself believed that conditions of the 1930s could persist indefinitely.) In his presidential address before the AEA in 1937, Hansen boldly announced that the United States was stuck in a "mature economy" rut from which it could not escape, due to its lack of technological innovations, the American frontier, and the population growth rate. His stagnation thesis was vigorously attacked by George Terborgh in his book *The Bogey of Economic Maturity* (1945) and then soundly disproved by a vibrant recovery after World War II. The stigma of this unfulfilled prediction haunted Hansen throughout his life.

Paul Samuelson, under the Hansen stagnation spell, almost suffered the same fate. In 1943, he wrote an article warning that unless the government acted vigorously after the end of the war, "there would be ushered in the greatest period of unemployment and industrial dislocation which any economy has ever faced." In a two-part article in published in *The New Republic* in the autumn of 1944, Samuelson predicted a replay of the 1930s depression (Sobel 1980, 101–02).

Although he, along with most Keynesians, was proved inaccurate about the postwar period, Samuelson gradually began expressing strong optimism about the U.S. economy in successive editions of his textbook. "Our mixed economy—wars aside—has a great future before it" (1964, 809).

Samuelson found it an exciting time to be an economist: "To have been born as an economist before 1936 was a boon—yes. But not to have been born too long before!" (in Harris 1947, 145). He applied the following familiar lines from William Wordsworth's *The Prelude* (Book 11, lines 108-9, previously quoted in chapter 2):

> Bliss was it in that dawn to be alive,
> But to be young was very Heaven!

Samuelson completed his dissertation in 1941, and it won the David A. Wells Award that year. (It was published in 1947 as *Foundations of Economic Analysis*.) In this work, Samuelson broke with Alfred Marshall by contending that mathematics, not literary expression, should be the primary exposition of economics.

But after graduation Samuelson discovered that heaven was not so sweet. He declared his preference to teach at Harvard, but his youthful exuberance, arrogant personality, and Jewish background all worked against him. His cocky attitude had long irritated his chairman, Harold

Hitchings Burbank, and the department offered him only an instructor-ship. Determined to stay in Cambridge, he accepted a position at the relatively unheralded department of economics at the Massachusetts Institute of Technology.

Harvard soon came to regret its mistake. By 1947, Samuelson had been awarded the first John Bates Clark Medal for being the brightest young economist, his school had granted him a full professorship, and MIT had been ranked as one of the best economics departments in the country. And Samuelson was only thirty-two! A year later he would drop the bomb that would be the envy of every economics department: the first edition of *Economics,* Samuelson's new testa-ment of macroeconomics. Harvard professor Otto Eckstein remarked, "Harvard lost the most outstanding economist of the generation" (Sobel 1980, 101).

How Samuelson Came to Write His Famous Textbook: "A Singular Opportunity"

In the early postwar period, Harvard students studied economics from outdated textbooks that said nothing about the war and little about the new economics of Keynes. "Students at Harvard and MIT often had that glassy-eyed look," commented Samuelson. His department head asked him to write a new text. Three years later, after toiling through nights and summers ("my tennis suffered"), *Economics* was born.

Attacked from Both Sides

The first edition, published by McGraw-Hill, sold over 120,000 cop-ies through 1950 and just kept selling. But it soon came under attack from the business community, on the one hand, which complained of its socialistic tendencies, and the Marxists, on the other hand, who complained of its capitalistic tendencies. William F. Buckley, Jr., protested in *God and Man at Yale* (1951) that Samuelson's text-book was antibusiness and progovernment. An organization called the Veritas Foundation published *Keynes at Harvard* and identified Keynesianism with Fabian socialism, Marxism, and fascism. On the other side, Marxists took umbrage at Samuelson's assertion that

Marx's predictions about the capitalist system were "dead wrong." A massive two-volume critique, *Anti-Samuelson* (1977), was published to counter Samuelson and introduce Marxism to students. Samuelson was pleased to hear that in Stalin's day, *Economics* was kept on a special reserve shelf in the library, along with books on sex, forbidden to all but specially licensed readers. "Actually," responded Samuelson, "when your cheek is smacked from the Right, the pain may be assuaged in part by a slap from the Left" (1998, xxvi). Meanwhile, Samuelson offered a seemingly balanced brand of economics that found mainstream support. While he favored heavy involvement in "stabilizing" the economy as a whole, he appeared relatively laissez-faire in the micro sphere, supporting free trade, competition, and free markets in agriculture.

The High Tide of Keynesian Economics

The success of Keynesian economics and Samuelson's textbook reached its zenith in the early 1960s. The MIT professor became president of the AEA in 1961, the year John F. Kennedy was inaugurated president. Samuelson, along with Walter Heller and other top Keynesians, was a close advisor to Kennedy and helped steer through Congress the Kennedy tax cut of 1964, a Keynesian program designed to stimulate economic growth through deliberate deficit financing. It appeared to work, as the economy flourished through the mid-1960s. By that time, Samuelson's textbook reigned atop the profession, selling more than a quarter of a million copies a year. And a year after the Nobel Prize in economics was established in 1969 by the Bank of Sweden, the prize went to Paul A. Samuelson.

Samuelson's textbook has been on the decline since the turbulent and inflationary 1970s, and today—a half-century after the first edition—it no longer tops the list in popularity. However, the new front-runners (especially Campbell McConnell's textbook, which has been among the top sellers for years) are mostly considered clones of Samuelson. Since 1985, new editions of *Economics* have been coauthored by Yale professor William D. Nordhaus, and Samuelson's hair has turned from blond to brown to gray in his sunset years. Yet "his memory dazzles even when it fails," writes an admirer (Elzinga 1992, 878).

Figure 6.1   The Keynesian Cross of National Income Determination: How Saving and Investment Determine Income

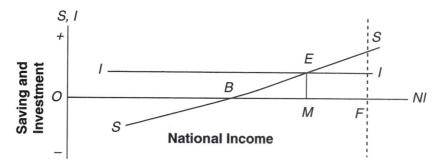

HOW SAVING AND INVESTMENT DETERMINE INCOME

Source: Samuelson (1948: 259). Reprinted by permission of McGraw-Hill.

Samuelson's Goal: To Raise the Keynesian Cross Atop a New House of Economics

What was Paul Samuelson trying to achieve? There is no real Samuelson school of economics; he considers himself "the last generalist in economics." (But what about Kenneth Boulding?) The MIT professor's intention was, first and foremost, to introduce Keynesianism to the classroom: the multiplier, the propensity to consume, the paradox of thrift, countercyclical fiscal policy, national income accounting, and $C + I + G$ were all new topics introduced in the first edition of *Economics* in 1948. Only John Maynard Keynes was honored with a biographical sketch in early editions, and only Keynes, not Adam Smith or Karl Marx, was labeled "a many-sided genius" (Samuelson 1948, 253).

The "Keynesian cross" income-expenditure diagram, invented by Samuelson and reproduced in Figure 6.1, was printed on the cover of the first three editions. The Keynesian cross incorporates all the elements of the new "general" theory. In the diagram in Figure 6.1, note that saving *(S)* increases with national income *(NI)*. As people earn more, they save more. However, investment *(I)* is autonomous and independent of saving. It is set at a fixed amount because, according to Keynes's theory, investment is fickle and varies with the "animal spirits" and expectations of investors and businessmen. So the investment schedule is set at any level, unrelated to income. Equilibrium *(M)* is set at the point where $S = I$, which you will note falls short of full-employment income *(F)*. Thus, the Keynesian cross reflects underemployment equilibrium.

This static equilibrium model represents Samuelson's (and Keynes's) view that capitalism is inherently unstable and can be stuck indefinitely at less than full employment *(M)*. No "automatic mechanism" guarantees full employment in the capitalist economy (Samuelson and Nordhaus 1985, 139). Samuelson compared capitalism to a car without a steering wheel; it frequently runs off the road and crashes: "The private economy is not unlike a machine without an effective steering wheel or governor," he wrote. "Compensatory fiscal policy tries to introduce such a governor or thermostatic control device" (Samuelson 1948, 412). Krugman compares the market economy to a system that needs a "new alternator" (Krugman 2006).

How the Multiplier Works Magic

How does compensatory fiscal policy work? There are two ways for the economy to grow and reach full employment under Keynesian theory: Shift investment schedule I upward, or shift saving schedule S to the right.

First, let's look at investment. Schedule I can be shifted upward by restoring business confidence, primarily through increased government spending or tax cuts. Both techniques have a multiplier effect—either a $100 billion spending program or a tax cut can create $400 billion in new income.

But Samuelson noted that under the Keynesian system, government spending has a higher multiplier than a tax cut. Why? Because 100 percent of a federal program is spent, while only a portion of a tax cut is spent—some of it is saved. Samuelson called his discovery the "balanced budget multiplier." Thus, a new federal spending program is preferred over a tax cut by Keynesians because the expenditure side is considered a more potent weapon against recession than a tax cut.

Figure 6.2   **Samuelson's "Paradox of Thrift"**

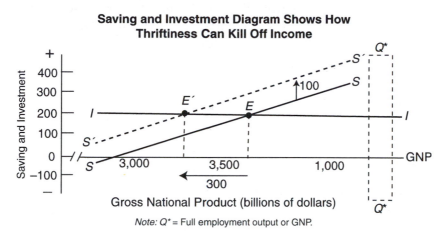

**Saving and Investment Diagram Shows How
Thriftiness Can Kill Off Income**

Note: Q^* = Full employment output or GNP.

Source: Samuelson and Nordhaus (1989: 184). Reprinted by permission of McGraw-Hill.

The Paradox of Thrift Denies Adam Smith

The second way out of a recession is to increase the public's propensity to consume, which would shift saving schedule S to the right.

Note that in the Keynesian model, if the public decides to save more during an economic downturn, it only makes matters worse. Consumers buy less, producers lay off workers, and households end up saving less. An increased supply of savings cannot lower interest rates and encourage investment under the crude Keynesian model because interest rates are assumed to be constant. In the Figure 6.1 diagram, more savings means that the saving schedule S shifts backward to the left, and has no effect on raising the I schedule.

Samuelson called this phenomenon the "paradox of thrift" (see Figure 6.2)—an increase in desired thrift results in less total savings! "Under conditions of unemployment, the attempt to save may result in less, not more, saving," he declared (1948, 271). Keynes, of course, said practically the same thing, only more eloquently: "The more virtuous we are, the more determinedly thrifty, the more obstinately orthodox in our national and personal finance, the more our incomes will have to fall" (Keynes 1973a [1936], 111).

Samuelson delighted in this attack on the orthodoxy of Adam Smith and Benjamin Franklin. Smith found thrift a universal virtue, writing that "What is prudence in the conduct of every private family, can scarce be folly in that of a great kingdom" (1965 [1776], 424). Franklin counseled every child, "A penny saved is a penny earned." But Samuelson labeled this thinking a "fallacy of composition." "What is good for each person separately need not be good for all," he countered. Moreover, Franklin's "old virtues [of thrift] may be modern sins" (1948, 270). As one modern-day textbook put it, "While savings may pave the road to riches for an individual, if the nation as a whole decides to save more, the result could be a recession and poverty for all" (Baumol and Blinder 1988, 192).

The Keynesians readily endorsed savings as a virtue during periods of full employment, but Samuelson was convinced it seldom happened. "[F]ull employment and inflationary conditions have occurred only occasionally in our recent history," he wrote. "Much of the time there is some wastage of resources, some unemployment, some insufficiency of demand, investment, and purchasing power" (1948, 271). This paragraph remained virtually the same throughout the first eleven editions of his textbook.[1]

Savings as Leakage

Echoing Keynes, Samuelson declared war on uninvested savings, which could "leak" out of the system and "become a social vice" (1948, 253). He produced a diagram (see Figure 6.3) separating savings from investment. The diagram shows savings leaking out of the system, unconnected to the investment hydraulic handle above. (This diagram led observers to call the model "hydraulic Keynesianism," with the emphasis on priming the pump through government spending.)

---

1. Amazingly, Samuelson recently protested being labeled an "antisaving Keynesian" (Samuelson 1997). After noting that Martin Feldstein publicly complained that economists at Harvard also attacked savings in his college days, Samuelson said he regularly appeared before Congress to urge more saving and investment and less consumption. My response: Then why didn't he say so in his textbook?

Figure 6.3 **Saving Leaks Out of the System While the Hydraulic Investment Press Pumps Up the Economy**

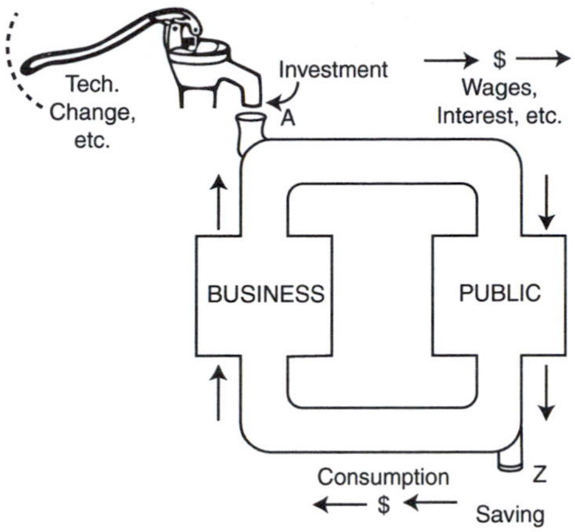

Source: Samuelson (1948: 264). Reprinted by permission of McGraw-Hill.

Is Consumption More Important Than Saving?

The Keynesian model leads to the odd conclusion that consumption is more productive than saving. As noted above in the Keynesian cross model, an increase in the "propensity to consume" (a lower saving rate) leads to full employment. Keynes applauded "all sorts of policies for increasing the propensity to consume," including confiscatory inheritance taxes and the redistribution of wealth in favor of lower-income groups, who consume a higher percentage of their income than the wealthy (1973a [1936], 325). Canadian economist Lorie Tarshis, the first to write a Keynesian textbook, warned that a high rate of saving is "one of the main sources of our difficulty," and one of the goals of the federal government should be "reducing incentives to thrift" (Tarshis 1947, 521–12).

Keynesian economist Hyman Minsky confirmed this unorthodox approach when he said, "The policy emphasis should shift from the encouragement of growth through investment to the achievement of full employment through consumption production" (Minsky 1982, 113). Of course, all of this Keynesian theory goes counter to traditional classical growth theory that a high level of saving is a key ingredient to economic growth.

Is Keynesianism Politically Neutral?

Samuelson contended that the Keynesian "theory of income determination" is politically "neutral." For example, "it can be used as well to defend private enterprise as to limit it, as well to attack as to defend government fiscal interventions" (1948, 253). But the evidence disputes this claim.

For instance, the balanced-budget multiplier (which Samuelson considers one of his proudest "scientific discoveries") favors government spending programs over tax cuts as a countercyclical policy. According to Samuelson, progressive taxation (imposing higher tax rates on the wealthy) has a "favorable" redistributionist effect on the economy: "To the extent that dollars are taken from frugal wealthy people rather than from poor ready spenders, progressive taxes tend to keep purchasing power and jobs at a high level" (1948, 174).

Samuelson also endorsed Social Security taxes, farm aid, unemployment compensation, and the rest of the welfare state as "built-in stabilizers" in the economy. The index of Samuelson's textbook consistently lists "market failures" (including imperfect competition, externalities, inequalities of wealth, monopoly power, and public goods) but not "government failures." His bias is overwhelmingly evident.

Apologist for the National Debt

In early editions, Samuelson denied that the national debt was a burden. The first edition favors the "we owe it to ourselves" argument: "The interest on an internal debt is paid by Americans to Americans; there is no direct loss of goods and services" (1948, 427). In the seventh edition (1967a), after raising the specter of "crowding out" of private investment, Samuelson went on to say: "On the other hand, incurring debt when there is no other feasible way to move the C + I + G equilibrium intersection up toward full employment actually represents a negative burden on the intermediate future to the degree that it induces more current capital formation than would otherwise take place!" (1967a, 346). At the end of an appendix on the national debt, Samuelson compared federal debt financing to private debt financing, such as AT&T's "never-ending" growth in debt (1967a,

358). By implication, he suggested that government debt could also grow continually, rather than necessarily being balanced over the business cycle.[2]

In sum, Keynesian economics as presented by Samuelson became an apology for big-government capitalism in the postwar period. "A laissez-faire economy cannot guarantee that there will be exactly the required amount of investment to insure full employment" (1967a, 197–78). Only a powerful state can.

Critics Begin a Long Battle Against Keynesian Economics

Samuelson claimed in his first edition that the Keynesian system was "increasingly accepted by economists of all schools of thought" (1948, 253). Judging from the popularity of Samuelson's textbook, he was right. In the 1950s and 1960s, scholars in the major economics departments spent their entire careers doing empirical studies on the consumption function, the multiplier, national income statistics, and other Keynesian aggregates. Keynesian macroeconomics also became popular among journalists, because it was easy to understand (increasing consumer spending is "good for the economy"), and among politicians, because deficit spending bought votes. Robert Solow, Samuelson's colleague at MIT and a Nobel laureate, summarized the new orthodoxy when he proclaimed with considerable pride that "short-term macroeconomic theory is pretty well in hand. . . . All that is left is the trivial job of filling in the empty boxes" (1965, 146).

The Pigou Effect: The First Assault

But over time critics have chipped away at the Keynesian structure. The first objection was the "liquidity trap" doctrine, Keynes's fear that the economy could be trapped indefinitely in a deep depression where interest rates are so low and "liquidity preference" so high that reducing interest rates further would have no effect (Keynes 1973a

---

2. A popular work coinciding with Samuelson's support of deficit spending was *A Primer on Government Spending,* by Robert L. Heilbroner and Peter L. Bernstein. It stated, "Recent experience indicates that the economy grows faster when the government runs a deficit and slower when revenues exceed outlays" (1963, 119).

[1936], 207). The man who first countered the liquidity-trap doctrine was Arthur C. Pigou, ironically the straw man Keynes vilified in *The General Theory*. In a series of articles in the 1940s, Pigou said that Keynes overlooked a beneficial side effect of a deflation in prices and wages: deflation increases the real value of cash, Treasury securities, cash-value insurance policies, and other liquid assets of individuals and business firms. The increased value of these liquid assets raises aggregate demand and provides the funds to generate new buying power and hire new workers when the economy bottoms out (Pigou 1943, 1947). This positive real wealth effect, or what Israeli economist Don Patinkin later named the "real balance effect" in his influential *Money, Interest and Prices* (1956), did much to undermine the Keynesian doctrine of a liquidity trap and unemployed equilibrium.

The Pigou "wealth" or "real balance" effect can also be extended to the issue of wage cuts during a downturn. Keynes rejected the classical argument that wage cuts are necessary to adjust the economy to new equilibrium conditions, from which a solid recovery could occur. Arguing against the conventional view that persistent unemployment is caused by excessive wage rates, Keynes claimed that wage cuts would simply depress demand further and do nothing to reduce unemployment. But Keynes and his followers confused wage rates with total payroll. Facing a recession and widespread unemployment, business leaders recognize that a reduction in wage rates can actually boost net employment and total payroll. Cutting wages allows firms to hire more workers at the bottom of a slump. When the economy bottoms out, well-managed companies begin hiring more workers at low wages, so that even though the wage rate remains low, the total payroll increases, and thus puts the economy back on the road to recovery (Hazlitt 1959, 267–69; Rothbard 1983 [1963], 46–48).

Growth Data Contradict Antithrift Doctrine

Economic historians had serious doubts almost immediately about the Keynesian antipathy toward saving, which has always been considered a key ingredient to long-term economic growth. They point especially to European and Asian countries, such as Germany, Switzerland, Japan, and Southeast Asia, whose growth rates have benefited tremendously from high rates of saving during the postwar period. Nobel laureate

Figure 6.4 **Connection Between Growth and Savings Rates**

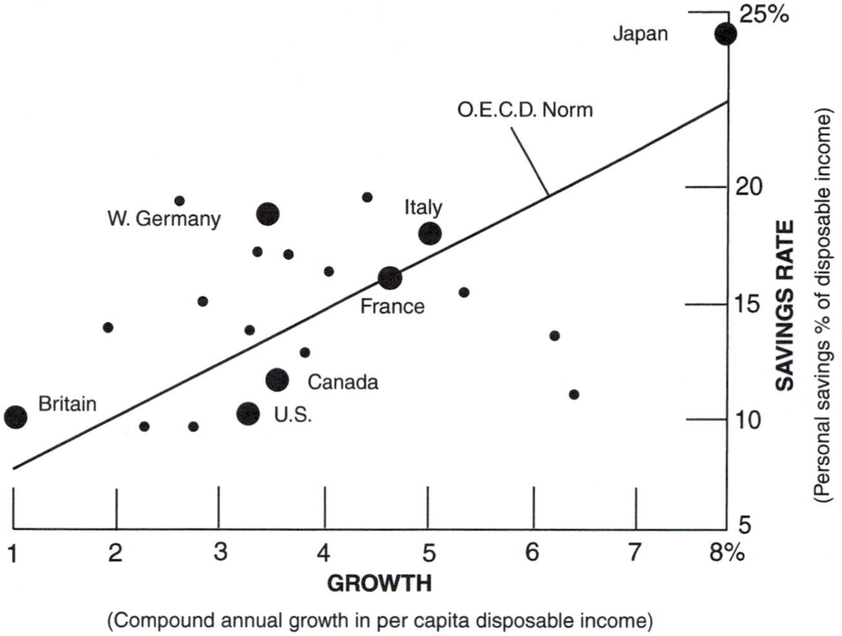

(Compound annual growth in per capita disposable income)

Source: Franco Modigliani (1986: 303).
Reprinted by permission of The Nobel Foundation.

Franco Modigliani, as well as top textbook writer Campbell McConnell, both Keynesians, have recognized the direct relationship between saving rates and economic growth. For example, the graph in Figure 6.4 was included in Franco Modigliani's Nobel Prize paper in 1986.

Historically, the evidence is overwhelming: higher saving rates lead to higher growth rates–just the opposite of the standard Keynesian prediction. As one recent Keynesian textbook declared after teaching students about the paradox of thrift: "The fact that governments do not discourage saving suggests that the paradox of thrift generally is not a real-world problem" (Boyes and Melvin 1999, 265).

But then why teach the paradox of thrift at all? Not only is it historically unproved, but it is fundamentally flawed. The problem is that Keynesians treat savings as if it disappears from the economy, that it is simply hoarded or left languishing in bank vaults, uninvested. In reality, saving is simply another form of spending, not on current consumption, but on future consumption. The Keynesians stress only the negative side of saving, the sacrifice of current consumption, while ignoring the positive side, the investment in productive enterprise. As noted in chapter 4, the Austrian economist Eugen Böhm-Bawerk stressed the positive side of saving: "For an economically advanced nation does not engage in hoarding, but invests its savings. It buys securities, it deposits its money at interest in savings banks or commercial banks, puts it out on loan, etc." (1959 [1884], 113).

Saving Has a Multiplier, Too!

Saving is in fact a better form of spending because it offers a potentially infinite payoff in future productivity (thus Franklin's refrain, "A penny saved is a penny earned"). If the public saves more generally, the pool of savings enlarges, interest rates decline, old equipment is replaced, and more research and development, new technology, and new production processes evolve. The future benefits are incalculable. Meanwhile, funds spent on pure consumer goods are used up within a certain period, or depreciated over time.

The Keynesian multiplier (k) is higher as the public consumes more. But proponents assume that the savings remain uninvested—a false assumption under normal conditions. In truth, both components of income—consumption and savings—are spent. Thus, the multiplier (k) is infinite! The saving component also has a multiplier effect in the economy as it is invested in the intermediate production stages. Moreover, the savings k is theoretically more productive than the consumption k because it is not used up as fast.

Going back to Samuelson's hydraulic model (Figure 6.2), saving does not leak out of the system, but goes back into the system to improve the factors of production (land, labor, and capital) through new technology, education, and training. Figure 6.5 demonstrates how saving, consumption, and the economy really operate.

The Ekins diagram in Figure 6.5 is what Samuelson should have published over the years in his textbook instead of the hydraulic model. In this chart, the ultimate purpose of economic activity is to provide increasing utility. Note how in the diagram, consumption is used up. It is consumption—not saving—that "leaks" out and is consumed as utility. Saving, on the other hand, is invested back into the economic

Figure 6.5   **The Growth Model Driven by Saving/Investment (Paul Ekins)**

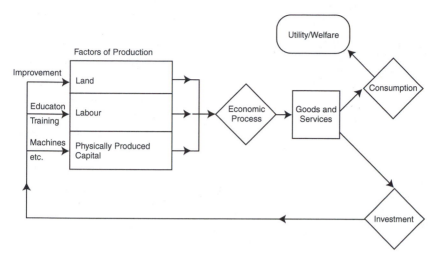

Source: Ekins and Max-Neef (1992: 148). Reprinted by permission of Routledge.

process over and over again, facilitating new investment and improving our standard of living (utility/welfare). An amazing contrast.

A Critical Flaw in the Keynesian Model

The central problem with the Keynesian model is that it fails to comprehend the true nature of the production-consumption process. The Keynesian system assumes that the only thing that matters is current demand for final consumer goods—the higher the consumer demand, the better. Despite talk that Keynes is dead, this Keynesian preoccupation with consumer demand is almost universally accepted in the establishment media today. For example, Wall Street monitors retail sales figures to determine the direction of the economy and the markets. They seem to be disappointed if consumers don't spend enough—as if they want the Christmas season to last all year!

Yet is consumer spending the cause or the effect of prosperity? If everyone went on a buying spree at the local department store or grocery store, would investment in new products and technology expand? Certainly investment in consumer goods would expand, but increased expenditures for consumer goods would do little or nothing to construct a bridge, build a hospital, pay for a research program to cure cancer, or provide funds for a new invention or a new production process.

According to business-cycle analysts, retail sales and other measures of current consumer spending are lagging indicators of economic activity. Almost all of the components of the U.S. Commerce Department's Index of Leading Economic Indicators are production and investment oriented, for example, contracts and orders for plant equipment, changes in manufacturing and trade inventories, changes in raw material prices, and the stock market, which represents long-term capital investment (Skousen 1990, 307–12). Typically in a business cycle, consumption starts declining after the recession has already started; similarly, consumer spending picks up after the economy begins its recovery stage.

This myth of a consumer-driven economy persists in part because of a misunderstanding of national income accounting. The media frequently report that consumer spending accounts for two-thirds of GDP. Recall that GDP = $C + I + G$, and typically in the United States:

C =   70 percent
I =   12 percent
G =   18 percent

Therefore, the media conclude that, since consumption accounts for approximately two-thirds of GDP, the economy must be consumer-driven.

Not so. GDP is defined as the value of all *final* goods and services produced in a year. It ignores all intermediate production in the economy at the wholesale, manufacturing, and natural-resource stages. If one measures spending at all levels of production, the results are surprisingly different.

I have created a national income statistic called gross domestic expenditures (GDE), which measures gross sales at all stages of production.[3] Using this new, broader definition of total spending in the economy, it becomes apparent that consumption represents only about

---

3. See Skousen (1990, 185–92) for details of this new statistic. Recently, the U.S. Department of Commerce has developed a new statistic called "gross output" that approaches my GDE (although it leaves out gross wholesale and retail figures). See Table 8 in U.S. Department of Commerce, "Gross Output by Industry, 1987–98," *Survey of Current Business* (2000), p. 48.

one-third of economic activity, and that business spending (investment plus goods-in-process spending) accounts for more than half of the economy. Thus, business investment is far more important than consumer spending in the United States (and in most other nations).

The Keynesian macroeconomic model suffers from the defect of oversimplification—it assumes only two stages, consumption and investment, and it assumes that investment is a direct function of current consumption only. If current consumption increases, so will investment, and vice versa.

How the Economy Really Works

William Foster and Waddill Catchings committed this same error. As Hayek pointed out in his critique of the Foster-Catchings debate, investment is actually multistaged and changes form and structure when interest rates rise or fall. Investment is not simply a function of current demand, but of future demand; both long-term and short-term interest rates influence investment and capital formation (Hayek 1939 [1929]). For example, suppose the public decides to save more of their income for a better future. Spending for cars, clothing, entertainment, and other forms of current consumption might level off or even fall. But this temporary slowdown in consumption does not cause a broad-based recession. Instead, the increased savings leads to lower interest rates, which encourage businesses, especially in capital-goods industries and research and development, to expand operations. Lower interest rates mean lower costs. Businesses can now afford to upgrade computers and office equipment, construct new plants and buildings, and expand inventories. Lower interest rates can even reverse the slowdown in car sales by offering cheaper financing to prospective car buyers. Contrary to the dire predictions of the Keynesians, an increase in the propensity to save pays for itself. It does not lead to a "recession and poverty for all" (Baumol and Blinder 1988, 192). Only the structure of production and consumption changes, not the total amount of economic activity.

An Example: Building a Bridge

A hypothetical example could be useful in reinforcing the benefits of increased savings. Suppose St. Paul and Minneapolis are separated by a river and that the only transportation between the two cities is by barge. Travel between the twin cities is expensive and time-consuming. Finally, the city fathers call a meeting and decide to build a bridge. Everyone agrees to cut back on current spending and put their savings to work to build the bridge. In the short run, retail sales, employment, and profits in local department stores decline. Yet new workers and new investment funds are assigned to the building of the bridge. In the aggregate, there is no reduction in output and employment. Moreover, once the bridge is completed, the twin cities benefit immensely from lower travel costs and increased competition between St. Paul and Minneapolis. In the end, the twin cities' sacrifice has been transformed into a higher standard of living.

Say's Law Redux: Production Is More Important Than Consumption

In essence, the Keynesian demand-driven view of the economy fails to recognize another force that is even stronger than current demand—the demand for future consumption. Spending money on current consumer goods and services will do nothing to change the quality and variety of goods and services of the future. Such change requires new savings and investment.

Thus, we return to the truism of Say's law: Supply (production) is more important than demand (consumption). Consumption is the effect, not the cause, of prosperity. Production, saving, and capital formation are the true cause.

Keynes created another straw man in *The General Theory*. The straw man was J.-B. Say and his famous law of markets. Steven Kates calls *The General Theory* "a book-length attempt to refute Say's Law." But to do this, Keynes gravely distorted Say's law and classical economics in general. As Kates disclosed in his remarkable *Say's Law and the Keynesian Revolution*, "Keynes was wrong in his interpretation of Say's Law and, more importantly, he was wrong about its economic implications" (Kates 1998, 212). In the introduction to the French edition of *The General Theory*, published in 1939, Keynes focused on Say's law as the central issue of macroeconomics. "I believe that economics everywhere up to recent times has been dominated . . . by the doctrines associated with the name of J.-B. Say. It is true that his 'law of markets' has long been abandoned by most economists; but they have not extricated themselves from his basic assumptions and particularly from his fallacy that demand is created by supply. . . . Yet a theory so based is clearly incompetent to tackle the problems of unemployment and of the trade cycle" (1973a [1936], xxxv).

Unfortunately, Keynes failed to understand Say's law. He incorrectly paraphrased it as "supply creates its own demand" (1973a [1936], 25), a distortion of the original meaning. In effect, Keynes altered Say's law to mean that everything produced is automatically bought. Hence, according to Keynes, Say's law cannot explain the business cycle. Keynes falsely concluded, "Say's Law . . . is equivalent to the proposition that there is no obstacle to full employment" (26). Interestingly, Keynes never quoted Say directly, and some historians have thus surmised that Keynes never read Say's actual *Treatise*, relying instead on Ricardo's and Marshall's comments on Say's law of markets. (For a detailed discussion of Say's law, see chapter 2 of this book.) Keynes went on to say that the classical model under Say's law "assumes full employment" (15, 191). Other Keynesians have continued to make this point, but nothing could be further from the truth. Conditions of unemployment do not prohibit production and sales from taking place that form the basis of new income and new demand.

Say actually used his own law to explain recessions. As such, Say's law specifically formed the basis of a classical theory of the business cycle and unemployment. As Kates states, "The classical position was that involuntary unemployment was not only possible, but occurred often, and with serious consequences for the unemployed" (Kates 1998, 18).

Say's law concludes that recessions are not caused by failure of the level of demand (Keynes's thesis), but by failure in the structure of supply and demand. According to Say's law, an economic slump occurs when producers miscalculate what consumers wish to buy, thus causing unsold goods to pile up, production to be cut back, workers to be laid off, income to fall, and finally, consumer spending to drop. As Kates elucidates, "Classical theory explained recessions by showing how errors in production might arise during cyclical upturns which would cause some goods to remain unsold at cost-covering prices" (1998, 19). The classical model was a "highly-sophisticated theory of recession and unemployment" that was "obliterated" with one fell swoop by the illustrious Keynes (Kates 1998, 20, 18).[4]

Keynes's Nemesis

On one point Keynes was right: Say's law is Keynes's nemesis. It specifically refutes Keynes's basic thesis that a deficit in aggregate demand causes a recession and that artificially stimulating consumer spending through government deficits is a cure for depression. To quote Kates, "Say clearly understood that economies can and do enter prolonged periods of economic depression. But what he was at pains to argue was that increased levels of unproductive consumption are not a remedy for a depressed level of economic activity, and contribute nothing to the wealth creation process. Consumption, whether productive or unproductive, uses up resources, while only productive consumption is capable of leaving something of an equivalent or even higher value in its place" (1998, 34).

Let us return to Samuelson's model of income determination—the Keynesian cross he invented to represent unemployment equilibrium (see Figure 6.1). We see now that saving and investment do not involve two separate schedules at all. Except in extreme circumstances, savings are invested. As income increases, savings and investment both increase together. Thus, there is no intersection of S and I at a single point and therefore no determination of macro equilibrium. The Keynesian cross crumbles under its own weight.

The Inflationary Seventies: Keynesian Economics on the Defensive

Experience is often a far greater teacher than high theory. While the theoretical battle over Keynesian economics ensued during the postwar era, no event raised more doubts about the Keynes-Samuelson model than the inflationary crises of the 1970s, when oil and commodity

---

4. In his broad-based book, Kates highlights other classical economists, including David Ricardo, James Mill, Robert Torrens, Henry Clay, Frederick Lavington, and Wilhelm Röpke, who extended this classical model of Say's law. Many classical economists focused on how monetary inflation exacerbated the business cycle.

Figure 6.6   **The Phillips Curve Trade-Off Between Inflation and Full
Employment**

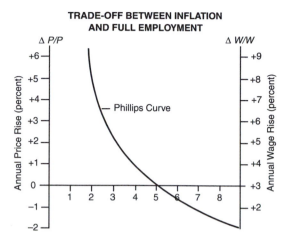

Source: Samuelson (1970: 810). Reprinted by permission of McGraw-Hill.

prices skyrocketed while industrial nations roiled in recession. Under
standard Keynesian analysis of aggregate demand, inflationary recession was not supposed to happen.

Keynesians relied heavily on the Phillips curve, a concept popularized in the 1960s and based upon empirical studies on wage rates and
unemployment conducted in Great Britain by economist A.W. Phillips
(1958). Many economists were convinced that there was a trade-off
between inflation and unemployment. Reproducing an idealized Phillips
trade-off curve (see Figure 6.6), Samuelson described the "dilemma for
macro policy": if society desires lower unemployment, it must be willing to accept higher inflation; if society wishes to reduce the high cost
of living, it must be willing to accept higher unemployment. Between
these two tough choices, Keynesians considered unemployment a more
serious evil than inflation (Samuelson 1970, 810–12).

But in the 1970s and 1980s, the idealized Phillips trade-off fell
apart—Western nations found that higher inflation did not reduce
unemployment, but made it worse. The emergence of an inflationary
recession and the collapse of the Phillips curve caused economists
to question for the first time their textbook models. In their search
for alternative explanations, a sudden renaissance of new economic
theories arose—from Marxism to Austrian economics.

Figure 6.7   **Aggregate Supply (AS) and Aggregate Demand (AD) Model Explains an Inflationary Recession**

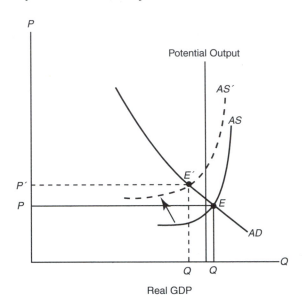

Source: Samuelson (1998: 385). Reprinted by permission of McGraw-Hill.

Keynesian Economics Makes a Comeback: The Creation of Aggregate Supply and Demand

Yet Keynesian economics was able to make a surprising recovery with the discovery of a new tool that could explain the crises of the 1970s: aggregate supply and demand, or *AS-AD*. When Bill Nordhaus signed up as coauthor of the twelfth edition (1985), Samuelson's *Economics* added the new *AS-AD* diagrams. Samuelson and other Keynesians used *AS-AD* to explain the inflationary recession of the 1970s (see Figure 6.7).

As Samuelson stated, "Supply shocks produce higher prices, followed by a decline in output and an increase in unemployment. Supply shocks thus lead to a deterioration of all the major goals of macroeconomic policy" (Samuelson and Nordhaus 1998, 385).

Alan Blinder, a leading Keynesian, also used *AS-AD* to explain the contortions in the traditional Phillips curve. According to Blinder, prior to the 1970s, fluctuations in aggregate demand had dominated the data. In the 1970s, however, aggregate supply dominated, and the result was stagflation. "That inflation and unemployment rose together following the OPEC shocks in 1973–74 and in 1979–80 in no ways contradicts a Phillips-curve trade-off" (Blinder 1987, 42).

Thus, Keynesian economics recovered from the 1970s crises and *AS-AD* diagrams filled the pages of modern textbooks. In the words of G.K. Shaw, modern Keynesian theory "not only resisted the challenge but also underwent a fundamental metamorphosis, emerging ever more convincing and ever more resilient" (Shaw 1988, 5). The remaining Keynesian precepts achieved a certain kind of "permanent revolution."

Post-Keynesian Economics Today

What's left of modern Keynesian theory? Was Keynesianism a "permanent" revolution, as G.K. Shaw says, or an unfortunate interlude, as Leland Yeager calls it, a temporary "diversion" from the neoclassical model? Keynes and his disciples still hold fast to a central belief that the system of Adam Smith is inherently precarious, especially under a laissez-faire global financial system, and requires government intervention (expansionary fiscal and monetary policy) to maintain a high level of "aggregate effective demand" and full employment. Paul Krugman (2006) identifies four Keynesian ideas that permeate today's economics:

1. Economies often suffer from a lack of aggregate demand, which leads to involuntary unemployment.

2. The market response to shortfalls in demand operates slowly and painfully.

3. Government policies can make up for this shortfall in demand, reducing unemployment.

4. Monetary policy may not always be sufficient to stimulate private sector spending; government spending must at times step into the breach.

Keynesianism still permeates our economic way of thinking, such as when the media warns that falling consumer confidence poses a threat to the economy, or when politicians promise that their tax cuts will create jobs by putting spending money in people's pockets, or when they warn consumers that saving their tax cut won't stimulate the economy.

In our final chapter, we see how promarket economists have raised serious objections to Keynesianism, both on a theoretical and empirical level. As a result, the economics profession has witnessed a gradual return to a "neoclassical" position. But clearly, after Keynes, the house of Adam Smith will never be the same.

7

Conclusion

Has Adam Smith Triumphed Over
Marx and Keynes?

> In the aftermath of the Keynesian revolution, too many
> economists forgot that classical economics provides the right
> answers to many fundamental questions.
> —*N. Gregory Mankiw (1994)*

> To judge from the climate of opinion, we have
> won the war of ideas. Everyone—left or right—talks
> about the virtues of markets, private property,
> competition, and limited government.
> —*Milton Friedman (1998)*

At the end of the twentieth century, the editors of *Time* magazine gathered around to choose the Economist of the Century. They chose John Maynard Keynes, who more than any other economist provided the theoretical underpinning of an active role for an enlarged welfare state during the post–Great Depression era. And yet Keynes left economics in a state of disequilibrium when he died after World War II. His disciples had clearly taken the profession too far away from the classical tradition. During the heyday of Keynesianism, which lasted into the late 1960s, too many economists were fearful that thrifty consumers might damage the economy, that progressive taxation and federal deficits could do no harm, that monetary policy didn't matter, and that centrally planned economies such as the Soviet Union could grow faster than the free West. The spirit of Keynes, and even Marx, dominated the political and intellectual atmosphere.

Milton Friedman Leads a Monetary Counterrevolution

However, by the early 1960s, a counterrevolution had begun that went a long way toward restoring the virtues of free markets and classical economics. The primary force behind this revolt against Keynesianism was the Chicago school of economics, led by Milton Friedman (1912–2006). His fierce, combative style and ideological roots were ideally suited for the task of taking on the Keynesians. Moreover, he had impeccable credentials in technical economics to command respect from the profession. Friedman earned his Ph.D. in economics from Columbia University; he won the highly prestigious John Bates Clark Medal two years after Paul Samuelson won it; and he taught economics at one of the premier institutions in the country, the University of Chicago. In 1967, he was elected president of the American Economic Association. His focus on monetary policy and the quantity theory of money was particularly attractive in an age of inflation. In 1976, on the 200th anniversary of both the Declaration of Independence and the publication of *The Wealth of Nations,* it was fitting that Friedman won the Nobel Prize. Adam Smith was his mentor. "The invisible hand has been more potent for progress than the visible hand for retrogression," he wrote in his best-seller, *Capitalism and Freedom* (1982 [1962], 200). It is worth noting that *Time* magazine came very close to naming Friedman the Economist of the Century because of his unique ability to "articulate the importance of free markets and the dangers of undue government intervention" (Pearlstine 1998, 73).

Except for Friedman, the free-market response to Keynesian theory was almost completely ineffectual. Ludwig von Mises, the dean of the Austrian school, wrote little about Keynes; his magnum opus, *Human Action* (1966), makes only a handful of references. Friedrich Hayek, the leading anti-Keynesian in the 1930s, made the strategic error of ignoring *The General Theory* when it came out in 1936, a decision he later regretted. During World War II, Hayek lost interest in economics and went on to write about political philosophy in works such as *The Road to Serfdom* (1944) and *The Constitution of Liberty* (1960). Other free-market economists, such as Henry Hazlitt and Murray Rothbard, wrote largely from outside the profession and had marginal influence.

How did Friedman almost single-handedly change the intellectual climate back from the Keynesian model to the neoclassical model of

Adam Smith? After acquiring academic credentials, he focused on scholarly technical work, particularly empirical evidence to test the Keynesian model. He learned the importance of sophisticated quantitative analysis from Simon Kuznets, Wesley Mitchell, and other stars at the National Bureau of Economic Research.

Friedman started teaching at Chicago in 1946, where he stayed until his official retirement in 1977. Following Frank Knight's retirement in 1955, Friedman continued the Chicago tradition and even strengthened it with an upgraded version of Irving Fisher's quantity theory of money, which he applied to monetary policy. He wrote on numerous topics related to monetary economics, culminating in the research and writing of his most famous empirical study, *A Monetary History of the United States, 1867–1960,* which was published by the prestigious National Bureau of Economic Research and Princeton University, and coauthored by Anna J. Schwartz (1963).

Essentially, his monumental study thoroughly contradicted the Keynesian view that monetary policy was ineffective. According to Friedman, it was quite the opposite. His magnum opus demonstrated the unrelenting power of money and monetary policy in the ups and downs of the U.S. economy, including the Great Depression and the postwar era. Even Yale's James Tobin, a friendly critic, recognized its greatness: "This is one of those rare books that leaves their mark on all future research on the subject" (1965, 485).

Friedman had a twofold mission in researching and writing *Monetary History*. First, he wanted to dispel the prevailing Keynesian notion that "money doesn't matter," that somehow an aggressive expansion of the money supply during a recession or depression cannot be effective, like "pushing on a string." Friedman and Schwartz showed time and time again that monetary policy was indeed effective in both expansions and contractions. Friedman's work on monetary economics became increasingly important and applicable as inflation headed upward in the 1960s and 1970s. His most famous line is "Inflation is always and everywhere a monetary phenomenon" (Friedman 1968, 105).

Friedman Discovers the Real Cause of the Great Depression

That money mattered was an important proof, but the research by Friedman and Schwartz revealed a deeper purpose. One startling sentence in the entire 860-page book changed forever how economists and historians would view the cause of the most cataclysmic economic event of the 20th century: "From the cyclical peak in August 1929 to the cyclical trough in March 1933, the stock of money fell by over a third" (Friedman and Schwartz 1963, 299).

For thirty years, an entire generation of economists did not really know the extent of the damage the Federal Reserve had inflicted on the U.S. economy from 1929 to 1933. They had been under the impression that the Fed had done everything humanly possible to keep the depression from worsening, but like "pushing on a string," were impotent in the face of overwhelming deflationary forces. According to the official apologia of the Federal Reserve System, it had done its best, but was powerless to stop the collapse. Friedman radically altered this conventional view. "The Great Contraction," as Friedman and Schwartz called it, "is in fact a tragic testimonial to the importance of monetary forces" (Friedman and Schwartz 1963, 300). The government had acted "ineptly," turning a garden-variety recession into the worst depression of the century by raising interest rates and failing to counter deflationary forces and bank collapses. On another occasion, Friedman explained, "Far from being testimony to the irrelevance of monetary factors in preventing depression, the early 1930s are a tragic testimony to their importance in producing a depression" (1968, 78–79).

One of the reasons for this ignorance about monetary policy is that the government did not publish aggregate money supply figures until Friedman and Schwartz developed the statistical concepts of M1 and M2 in their book (1963). Friedman commented, "If the Federal Reserve System in 1929 to 1933 had been publishing statistics on the quantity of money, I don't believe that the Great Depression could have taken the course that it did" (Friedman and Heller 1969, 80). See Figure 7.1 for the money supply figures during the 1929–32 crash.

Did the Gold Standard Cause the Great Depression?

Keynesians have blamed the international gold standard for precipitating the Great Depression. "Far from being synonymous with stability, the gold standard itself was the principal threat to financial stability and

Figure 7.1 **The Dramatic Decline in the Money Stock, 1929–33**

THE GREAT CONTRACTION
The Stock of Money and Its Proximate Determinants, Monthly,
1929–March 1933

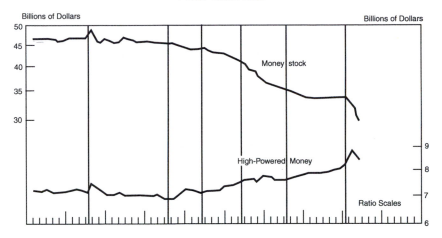

Source: Friedman and Schwartz 1963: 333. Reprinted by permission of Princeton University Press.

economic prosperity between the wars," contends Barry Eichengreen (1992, 4). Critics of the gold standard have pointed out that in a crucial time, 1931–32, the Federal Reserve raised the discount rate for fear of a run on its gold deposits. If only the United States had not been shackled by a gold standard, they argued, the Federal Reserve could have avoided the reckless credit squeeze that pushed the country into depression and a banking crisis.

But Friedman and Schwartz dispute this widely held belief. They point out that the U.S. gold stocks rose during the first two years of the contraction, but the Fed once again acted ineptly. "We did not permit the inflow of gold to expand the U.S. money stock. We not only sterilized it, we went much further. Our money stock moved perversely, going down as the gold stock went up" (Friedman and Schwartz 1963, 360–61). The U.S. gold stock reached an all-time high in the late 1930s. In short, even under the defective gold exchange standard, there may have been room to avoid a devastating worldwide depression and monetary crisis.

Is Free-Market Capitalism Unstable?

On a more philosophical scale, Friedman's monetary research countered a core assumption behind Keynesian economics—that free-enterprise capitalism was inherently unstable and could be stuck at less than full employment indefinitely unless the government intervened to increase "effective demand" and restore its vitality. As James Tobin put it, the "invisible" hand of Adam Smith required the "visible" hand of Keynes (Breit and Spencer 1986, 118). Friedman concluded differently: "The fact is that the Great Depression, like most other periods of severe unemployment, was produced by government mismanagement rather than any inherent instability of the private economy" (1982 [1962], 38). Furthermore, he wrote: "Far from the depression being a failure of the free-enterprise system, it was a tragic failure of government" (1998, 233). From this time forward, thanks to the profound work of Friedman and Schwartz, most textbooks gradually replaced "market failure" with "government failure" in their sections on the Great Depression.

Friedman came to the conclusion that once the monetary system is stabilized, and prices and wages remain flexible, Adam Smith's system of natural liberty could flourish. In contrast to Keynes, Friedman faithfully maintained that the neoclassical model represents the "general" theory and only a monetary disturbance by the government's central bank can derail a free-market economy. In short, according to Friedman, the business cycle is government-, not market-, induced, and monetary stability is an essential prerequisite for economic stability.

The Quantity Theory of Money: Friedman vs. Keynes

Friedman also took issue with Keynes and his disciples over the quantity theory of money. Recall Fisher's equation of exchange,

$$MV = PT,$$

where M = the quantity of money, V = velocity of circulation, P = price level, and T = transactions, or real output of goods and services.

Keynes argued in *The General Theory* that monetary policy was largely impotent because if you increased M, V would decline, since the new funds would simply go into bank reserves and not be loaned out. Hence, monetary policy would be incapable of stimulating the economy. However, Friedman discovered in his empirical work that V always moved in the same direction as M. When M increased, so did V, and vice versa. An increase in M could generate a recovery. Friedman concluded that even though "Keynes's theory is the right kind of theory in its simplicity. . . . I have been led to reject it because I believe it has been contradicted by experience" (Friedman 1986, 48).

Friedman Raises Doubts About the Multiplier

The Chicago economist began his attack on Keynesianism in his 1962 book *Capitalism and Freedom*, where he questioned the effectiveness and stability of Keynesian countercyclical finance. He debunked the concept of the multiplier, calling it "spurious." "The simple Keynesian analysis implicitly assumes that borrowing the money does not have any effect on other spending" (Friedman 1982 [1962], 82). Inflation and crowding out of private investment are two possible outcomes of Keynesian deficit spending. Subsequent studies have demonstrated that the spending multiplier has historically never reached the heights of 5–7 as the Keynesians originally estimated, while the money multiplier has proven to be consistently higher.

Regarding the role of fiscal policy, Friedman noted that the federal budget is the "most unstable component of national income in the postwar period." The Keynesian balance wheel is usually "unbalanced," and it has "continuously fostered an expansion in the range of government activities at the federal level and prevented a reduction in the burden of federal taxes" (1982 [1962], 76–77).

Friedman Takes On the Phillips Curve

In his American Economics Association (AEA) presidential address, published in 1968, Friedman introduced the "natural rate of unemployment" concept to counter the Phillips curve. As noted in chapter 6, Keynesians quickly incorporated the Philips curve to justify a liberal fiscal policy; to them, inflation could be tolerated if it meant lower unemployment. A "little inflation" could do no harm and considerable good.

Friedman objected, arguing that "there is always a temporary trade-off between inflation and unemployment; there is no permanent trade-off." Accordingly, any effort to push unemployment below the "natural rate of unemployment" must lead to an accelerating inflation. Moreover, "the only way in which you ever get a reduction in unemployment is through *unanticipated inflation*," which is unlikely. Friedman concluded that any acceleration of inflation would eventually bring about higher, not lower, unemployment. Thus, efforts to reduce unemployment by expansionary government policies could only backfire in the long run as the public anticipated its effect (Friedman 1969, 95–110). In the late 1960s, Friedman even predicted that unemployment and inflation could rise together, a phenomenon known as stagflation.

By the late 1970s, Friedman was proven right. The Phillips curve became unrecognizable as inflation and unemployment started rising together, opposite to what had happened in Britain in the 1950s. In a famous statement, British prime minister James Callaghan confessed in 1977, "We used to think you could spend your way out of a recession. . . . I tell you, in all candor, that that option no longer exists; and that insofar as it ever did exist, it only worked by injecting bigger doses of inflation into the economy followed by higher levels of unemployment at the next step. This is the history of the past twenty years" (Skousen 1992, 12). In his Nobel lecture, Friedman warned that the Phillips curve had become positively inclined, with unemployment and inflation rising simultaneously.

Out of this Phillips curve controversy rose a whole new "rational expectations" school, led by Robert Lucas, Jr., who won the Nobel Prize in 1995. Rational expectations undermine the theory that policymakers can fool the public into false expectations about inflation. Accordingly, government policies are frequently ineffective in achieving their goals.

Rules Versus Authority

One principle Friedman learned from Henry Simons, a monetarist mentor at Chicago, was that strict monetary rules are preferable to discretionary decision making by government authorities. "Any system which gives so much power and so much discretion to a few men that [their] mistakes—excusable or not—can have such far-reaching effects is a bad system," he wrote (Friedman 1982 [1962], 50). Among many choices, including the gold standard, Friedman has favored a "monetary rule" whereby the money supply (usually M2) is increased at a steady rate equal to the long-term growth rate of the economy.

One of the problems with Friedman's monetary rule is how to define the money supply. Is it M1, M2, M3, or what? It is hard to measure in an age of money market funds, short-term CDs, overnight loans, and Eurodollars. Notwithstanding theoretical support for a monetary rule, central bankers have largely focused on "inflation targeting," that is, price stabilization and interest rate manipulation, as a preferable method.

The Shadow of Marx and the Creative Destruction of Socialism

The Herculean efforts of Milton Friedman, Friedrich Hayek, and other libertarian economists were not the only reason neoclassical economics has made a stupendous comeback. The other reason is the collapse of Marxist-inspired Soviet communism and the socialist central planning model in the early 1990s. Since then, globalization has opened the floodgates to freer economic policies, especially within developing countries. Nations that for decades engaged in systematic policies of nationalization, protectionism, import substitution, foreign exchange controls, and corporate cronyism have opened their borders to foreign investment, denationalization and privatization, deregulation, and other market policies. Even the World Bank, once a severe critic of the capitalist model, has shifted dramatically in favor of market solutions to underdevelopment problems (with some important exceptions). The radical model of Marx and the socialists was clearly losing ground.

But it wasn't always that way. In fact, during most of the twentieth century, heavy-handed central planning was considered more efficient and more productive than laissez-faire capitalism. At the depths of the Great Depression, radical thinking dominated the atmosphere in intellectual and political circles. Suspicious of free-market capitalism, many were attracted to central planning and the Soviet model.

Ludwig von Mises and Friedrich Hayek were in the minority in questioning the collectivist zeitgeist and offering a critique of socialism on purely economic grounds. Hayek published Mises's 1920 article, "Economic Calculation in the Socialist Commonwealth," and other essays in a volume entitled *Collectivist Economic Planning* (Hayek 1935). In these articles, Mises and Hayek, among others, contended that competitive prices provided critical information necessary for a well-run, coordinated economy between producers and consumers. Vital information is inherently local in nature, Hayek noted, and if channeled through a distant central planning board, actions determined by the state would distort the signals necessary to run an economy efficiently. For a central authority to "assume all the knowledge . . . is . . . to disregard everything that is important and significant in the real world" (Hayek 1984, 223). In sum, decision making must be decentralized, and profit incentives and property rights must be established.

But Mises's and Hayek's arguments were largely ignored as a result of counterarguments and historical trends. In the 1930s and 1940s, Nazi Germany and the Soviet Union were heralded as apparent economic success stories. Journalists returned from tours of Russia exclaiming "I have been to the future, and it works" (Malia 1999, 340). In 1936, Sidney and Beatrice Webb came back with glowing reports of a "new civilization" and the "re-making of man," a vibrant nation with full employment, good working conditions, free education, free medical services, child care and maternity benefits, and the widespread availability of museums, theaters, and concert halls. Oskar Lange, a Polish socialist, and Fred M. Taylor, president of the AEA, contended that central planning boards could imitate the market's success. Austrian economist and Harvard professor Joseph Schumpeter chided Mises and Hayek by concluding, "Can socialism work? Of course it can," adding even more damagingly, "The capitalist order tends to destroy itself and centralist socialism is . . . a likely heir apparent" (Schumpeter 1950 [1942], 167).

Foreign Aid and Development Economics

After World War II, European and Latin American countries began experimenting with socialism on a gigantic scale, nationalizing industry after industry, raising taxes, imposing wage–price controls, inflating the money supply, creating national welfare programs, and engaging in all kinds of collectivist mischief.

The postwar Marshall Plan demonstrated the efficacy of government aid, and the new Keynesian approach to development of Third World countries became state-driven growth. International development organizations, such as the World Bank and the Alliance for Progress, were established to assist developing nations suffering from disease, famine, low literacy rates, high unemployment, rapid population growth, and agriculture-based economies. MIT's W.W. Rostow wrote his "noncommunist manifesto," *The Stages of Economic Growth* (1960), which, along with the Harrod-Domar model, promoted the centralized nation-state and high levels of government-driven capital formation via foreign aid and government investment as the key to sustained growth.

Economists were convinced by data from the Central Intelligence Agency (CIA) that Soviet-style socialist planning had produced high levels of economic growth, even exceeding that experienced by market economies in the West. Paul Samuelson was one who became convinced of Soviet economic superiority. By the fifth edition of his *Economics* textbook, Samuelson began including a graph indicating that the gap between the United States and the USSR was narrowing and possibly even disappearing (1961, 830). In the twelfth edition, the graph was replaced with a table declaring that, between 1928 and 1983, the Soviet Union had grown at a remarkable 4.9 percent annual growth rate, higher than that of the United States, the United Kingdom, or even Germany and Japan (Samuelson and Nordhaus 1985, 776). Ironically, right before the Berlin Wall was torn down, Samuelson and Nordhaus confidently declared, "The Soviet economy is proof that, contrary to what many skeptics had earlier believed [a reference to Mises and Hayek], a socialist command economy can function and even thrive" (1989, 837).

Even conservative Yale economist Henry C. Wallich, a former member of the Federal Reserve Board, was so convinced by CIA statistics that he wrote a whole book arguing that freedom leads to lower economic growth, greater inequality, and less competition. In *The Cost of Freedom,* he concluded, "The ultimate value of a free economy is not production, but freedom, and freedom comes not as a profit, but at a cost" (Wallich 1960, 146).

One ardent critic of the Keynesian development model was P.T.

Bauer of the London School of Economics. In the postwar period, Bauer waged a lonely battle against foreign aid, comprehensive central planning, and nationalization. According to Bauer, state planning was neither benevolent nor sustainable, but would lead to a concentration of power in the hands of a political elite that would inevitably create a corrupt and abusive system. In one of his classic essays, he wrote about how the tiny colony of Hong Kong prospered despite no central planning, its lack of natural resources, including water, and despite being the most densely populated place in the world (Bauer 1981, 185–90). But Bauer's views were largely ignored until the 1980s.

"Mises was right!"

The collapse of the Soviet Union and Eastern-bloc communism virtually ended the century-old debate over comparative economic systems and changed the minds of many economists about the virtues of socialism. A prominent example is Robert Heilbroner, a socialist who toyed with Marxism in his early years. He would later write *The Worldly Philosophers* (1999 [1953]), a popular history of economics. Under the influence of Schumpeter and Adolph Lowe, among others, Heilbroner joined the rest of the profession and concluded that Mises was wrong and socialism could work. He maintained that position for decades.

In the late 1980s, shortly before the collapse of the Berlin Wall, Heilbroner began to reconsider his views. In a stunning article in the *New Yorker* entitled "The Triumph of Capitalism," Heilbroner wrote that the longstanding debate between capitalism and socialism was over and capitalism had won. He went on to say, "The Soviet Union, China, and Eastern Europe have given us the clearest possible proof that capitalism organizes the material affairs of humankind more satisfactorily than socialism: that however inequitably or irresponsibly the marketplace may distribute goods, it does so better than the queues of the planned economy; however mindless the culture of commercialism, it is more attractive than state moralism; and however deceptive the ideology of a business civilization, it is more believable than that of a socialist one" (Heilbroner 1989, 98).

In a follow-up article after the demise of the Eastern bloc, Heilbroner was even more explicit: "Socialism has been a great tragedy this century. . . . There is no doubt that the collapse marks its end as a model of economic clarity." Furthermore, the debate between the socialists and Mises had to be reexamined in light of contemporary events. "It turns out, of course, that Mises was right," declared Heilbroner (1990, 91–92).

New Empirical Work Confirms Mises's Thesis

The fall of the Soviet Union brought about a major revision of economic history under communism. Based on research coming out of the previously secret KGB files in Moscow, historians confirmed negative views about social central planning that Mises, Hayek, and Bauer elucidated. In her work about Soviet Russia in the 1930s entitled *Everyday Stalinism,* Sheila Fitzpatrick countered the old conventional view held by Sidney and Beatrice Webb and George Bernard Shaw that the Soviet system during the 1930s was a glorious "new civilization." On the contrary, Fitzpatrick wrote, "With the abolition of the market, shortages of food, clothing, and all kinds of consumer goods became endemic. As peasants fled the collective villages, major cities were soon in the grip of an acute housing crisis, with families jammed for decades in tiny single rooms in communal apartments. . . . It was a world of privation, overcrowding, endless queues, and broken families, in which the regime's promises of future socialist abundance rang hollow. . . . Government bureaucracy often turned everyday life into a nightmare" (Fitzpatrick 1999, dustjacket).

Nations Grow Faster Under Economic Freedom

In addition, recent studies comparing the economic growth of nations and their degree of freedom have confirmed Mises's thesis. According to the work of James Gwartney and Robert Lawson, countries with the greatest level of economic liberty enjoy the highest standard of living (see Figure 1.2 in chapter 1).

And so ends a critical chapter in the history of economics. Mises, long dead, was finally vindicated. The words of the physicist Max Planck apply here: "Science progresses funeral by funeral."

As we begin the twenty-first century, the winds of change are everywhere. As Francis Fukuyama declared in *Time* magazine, "If socialism signifies a political and economic system in which the government controls a large part of the economy and redistributes wealth to produce social equality, then I think it is safe to say the likelihood of its making a comeback anytime in the next generation is close to zero" (2000, 111).

The Winds of Change in Development Economics

With the downfall of Eastern-bloc communism, the paramount question became how to dismantle the socialist state and reestablish capitalism and the culture that goes with it. The watchwords became denationalization, privatization, deregulation, and flat tax rates. Developing countries, which in the past had depended on foreign aid and government programs to stimulate the economy, now opened up their economies to trade and foreign investment.

Since the collapse of the Soviet central planning model, Rostow's thesis has been largely discredited and Bauer's less orthodox views have triumphed. Even Rostow admitted, "There are, evidently, serious and correct insights in the Bauer position" (Rostow 1990, 386). Recently, the World Bank has moved toward Bauer's side. In a 1993 study of the Four Tigers and the East Asian economic miracle, it concludes, "The rapid growth in each country was primarily due to the application of a set of common, market-friendly economic policies, leading to both higher accumulation and better allocation of resources" (World Bank 1993, vi).

Perhaps the best example of change in development economics is reflected in the work of Muhammad Yunus, president of the Grameen Bank in Bangladesh and founder of the micro-credit revolution. In his book, *Banker to the Poor,* Yunus tells how he grew up under the influence of Marxist economics. But after earning a Ph.D. in economics at Vanderbilt University, he saw firsthand "how the market [in the United States] liberates the individual. . . . I do believe in the power of the global free-market economy and in using capitalist tools. . . . . I also believe that providing unemployment benefits is not the best way to address poverty." He strongly opposes foreign aid from the World Bank and the International Monetary Fund. Believing that "all human beings are potential entrepreneurs," Yunus is convinced that poverty can be eradicated by loaning poor people the capital they need to engage in profitable businesses, not by giving them a government handout or engaging in population control (Yunus 1999, 203–07).

In 2006, Yunus won the Nobel Peace Prize. But his former Marxist colleagues call it a capitalist conspiracy. "What you are really doing," a communist professor told Yunus, "is giving little bits of opium to the poor people. . . . Their revolutionary zeal cools down. Therefore, Grameen is the enemy of the [communist] revolution" (Yunus 1999, 204).

Neoclassical Economics Today

Where does economic thinking stand today? We have seen throughout this history of the Big Three that each economist has at times stood taller than the other two. During times of strong economic performance, Adam Smith has been on top; during crises and depression, Keynes and Marx have stood out. Since the end of World War II, we have seen a gradual advance in esteem for the founder of modern economics, Adam Smith, and this despite occasional monetary crises, recessions, natural disasters, terrorist attacks, and complaints about inequality, trade deficits, and wasteful government programs.

A growing number of economists recognize that the neoclassical model is the keystone of economic analysis. In microeconomics, this means incorporating the principles of supply and demand, and profit and loss, which, under broad-based competition, leads to an efficient allocation of resources, economic growth, and a self-regulating economy. Under competition and a reasonable system of justice, man's natural tendency toward self-assertion leads to social well-being. As Adam Smith wrote over 200 years ago, "Little else is required to carry a state to the highest degree of opulence from the lowest barbarism, but peace, easy taxes, and a tolerable administration of justice" (Danhert 1974, 218).

In macroeconomics, it means teaching the classical model of thrift, a stable monetary policy, fiscal responsibility, free trade, widespread economic and political freedom, and a consistent rule of law for the justice system. As James Gwartney notes, "It turns out that the legal system—the rule of law, security of property rights, an independent judiciary, and an impartial court system—is the most important function of government, and the central element of both economic freedom and civil society, and is far more statistically significant than the other variables," including size of government, monetary system, trade, and regulation (Skousen 2005, 32). Gwartney and coauthor Lawson point to a number of countries that lack a decent legal system and as a result suffer from corruption, insecure property rights, poorly enforced contracts, and inconsistent regulatory environments, particularly in Latin America, Africa, and the Middle East. "The enormous benefits of the market network—gains from trade, specialization, expansion of the market, and mass production techniques—cannot be achieved without a sound legal system" (Gwartney and Lawson 2005, 35). All these basic principles were established over 200 years ago in Adam Smith's *Wealth of Nations.*

A Surprise Counterrevolution at Harvard

The shift back to market principles and the classical model of Adam Smith is best illustrated by the recent work of Harvard's Gregory Mankiw. In his textbook, *Macroeconomics,* written in the early 1990s, Mankiw surprised the profession by beginning with the classical model and ending with the short-term Keynesian model, the reverse of the standard Samuelson pedagogy.

Recall that Keynes in 1936 attempted to replace the Adam Smith model with his own "general theory" of the economy. The classical model, Keynes insisted, was actually a "special case" of the general theory, and only applied at times of full employment. Now we see that Mankiw, who considers himself a "neo-Keynesian," has once again made the classical model of Smith the real general theory and the Keynesian model of aggregate supply and demand the "special" case, relegated to the back of the book. It was a brilliant, revolutionary—or rather counterrevolutionary—move, a reflection of a changing fundamental philosophy.

Dubbing the classical model "the real economy in the long run," Mankiw pinpointed the effects of an increase in government spending—that rather than act as a multiplier, it "crowds out" private capital. "The increase in government purchases must be met by an equal decrease in [private] investment. . . . Government borrowing reduces national saving" (Mankiw 1994, 62).

In previous textbooks, Samuelson and his colleagues emphasized the cyclical nature of capitalism and how the economy could be stabilized through Keynesian policies. In contrast, in *Macroeconomics,*

Mankiw discussed economic growth up front, ahead of the chapters on the business cycle. Using the Solow growth model, Mankiw took a strong prosaving approach. Accordingly, "the saving rate is a key determinant of the steady state capital stock and high level of output. If the saving rate is low, the economy will have a small capital stock and a low level of output" (1994, 62). What is the effect of higher savings? "An increase in the rate of saving raises growth until the economy reaches a new steady state." Far from accepting the paradox of thrift, Mankiw wrote favorably about those nations with high rates of saving and investment, and even includes a case study on the miracles of Japanese and German postwar growth (examples virtually ignored in Samuelson's textbook). Mankiw therefore supports policies aimed at increasing the rates of saving and capital formation in the United States, including the possibility of altering Social Security from a pay-as-you-go system to a fully funded plan, though he did not discuss outright privatization (1994, 103–34).

Unemployment is another issue Mankiw approached in a non-Keynesian way. What causes unemployment? Relying on Friedman's "natural" rate of unemployment, insurance and similar labor legislation reduce incentives for the unemployed to find work. He provided evidence that unionized labor and the adoption of minimum-wage and living-wage laws actually increases the unemployment rate. Finally, he offered a case study on Henry Ford's famous $5 workday as an example of higher productivity and increasing wages.

He approvingly quoted Milton Friedman on monetary policy: "Inflation is always and everywhere a monetary phenomenon." Mankiw used numerous examples, including hyperinflation in interwar Germany, to confirm the social costs of inflation (1994, 161–69).

Mankiw has followed up with a new *Principles of Economics* textbook, published since 1997. Like his intermediate text, it is devoted almost entirely to classical economics, relegating the Keyensian model to the end chapters. Amazingly, Mankiw's textbook does not mention most of the standard Keynesian analysis: no consumption function, no Keynesian cross, no propensity to save, no paradox of thrift, and only a brief reference to the multiplier. Thus, we have a sea change in economics, and this coming from Cambridge, Massachusetts, the same place the Keynesian revolution originated in America.

Samuelson: Fiscal Policy Dethroned!

Even Paul Samuelson has been forced to change his focus in recent editions of his text, in part because of the force of history, in part due to the influence of his coauthor, Bill Nordhaus. Samuelson's fiftieth anniversary edition (1998) is telling. In addition to the replacement of the paradox of thrift with a prosavings section and the statement that "a large public debt is likely to reduce long-run economic growth" (Samuelson and Nordhaus 1998, 652), the biggest shock is Samuelson's abandonment of fiscal policy. This sixteenth edition highlights this statement in color: "Fiscal policy is no longer a major tool of stabilization in the United States. Over the foreseeable future, stabilization policy will be primarily handled by Federal Reserve monetary policy" (1998, 655).

In short, Milton Friedman, Friedrich Hayek, and the free-market proponents may have lost the debate early on, but they seem to have won the war. "The growing orientation toward the market," concluded Samuelson, "has accompanied widespread desire for smaller government, less regulation, and lower taxes" (1998, 735). Samuelson expressed dismay at this outcome, ending his fiftieth anniversary edition on a sour note by calling the new global economy "ruthless" and characterized by "growing" inequality and a "harsh" competitive environment. But the deed—the triumph of the market and classical economics—appears irreversible. Friedman and Hayek, representing the two schools of free-market economics (Chicago and Vienna) have combined forces for a one-two punch that has reversed the tide of ideas (Yergin and Stanislaw 1998, 98).

From Dismal Science to Imperial Science: May a Thousand Flowers Bloom

Spearheaded by economists from the University of Chicago, the reestablishment of classical free-market economics in the classroom and the halls of government has resulted in a surprising plethora of applications to social and economic problems. Kenneth E. Boulding (1919–93), longtime professor at the University of Colorado and former AEA president, always believed that economics should be eclectic and shared with other disciplines. Now his dream is being fulfilled. Like an invading army, the science of Adam Smith is over-running the whole of social science—law, criminal justice, finance, management, politics, history, sociology, environmentalism, religion, and even sports.

Economics used to be the "dismal science," a term of derision coined by the English critic Thomas Carlyle in the 1850s. But attitudes are quickly changing in the twenty-first century by applying its micro principles of competition, incentives, and opportunity cost to solve a host of public and private problems. In short, twenty-first-century economics is the "imperial science" (Skousen 2001, 7–10).

Here are just a few examples of the expanding role of economics in other areas: Gary Becker has been instrumental in applying the principles of supply and demand to the human behavioral sciences in areas such as racial discrimination, crime, and marriage. Ronald Coase, Richard Posner, and Richard Epstein have contributed to the development of law and economics.

Harry Markowitz, Merton Miller, William Sharpe, Burton Malkiel, and Fischer Black, among others, have created the field of financial economics, especially the application of efficiency markets to Wall Street. Robert Fogel and Douglass C. North have applied statistical analysis (known as "cliometrics") to a variety of historical events and trends. Robert Mundell, Art Laffer, and Paul Craig Roberts have advanced the "supply side" impact of economics on the issues of taxes, regulation, and trade, and have been a major force in the movement toward low flat taxes instead of progressive taxes.

Market-oriented economists have also applied their tools to public finance issues. During the 1950s and 1960s, the field was dominated by Keynesians, led by Richard Musgrave with his textbook, *Public Finance in Theory and Practice* (1958). Musgrave saw the need for a three-pronged government policy: (1) allocation—to provide public goods that the private sector could not; (2) distribution—to redistribute wealth and institute social justice; and (3) stabilization—to steady an inherently vacillating capitalist economy.

Musgrave debated James Buchanan, a professor at George Mason University and one of the founders of the public-choice school. In their 1998 published debate, Musgrave defended social insurance, progressive taxation, and the growth of the public sector as the "price we pay for civilization" (Buchanan and Musgrave 1999, 75). Addressing today's worries about an overbloated government, Musgrave wrote, "Is the state of our civilization really that bad? . . . There is much that should go on the credit side of the ledger. The taming of unbridled capitalism and the injection of social responsibility that began with the New Deal. . . . . Socializing the capitalist system . . . was needed for its own survival and for building a good society" (1999, 228). He also mentioned the "enormous gains" by blacks and women in the twentieth century.

Buchanan, on the other hand, blamed democratic politics for a "bloated" public sector, "with governments faced with open-ended entitlement claims," resulting in "moral depravity" (Buchanan 1999, 222). He argued in favor of constraining government through constitutional rules and limitations. He succinctly described the difference between the two: "Musgrave trusts politicians; we [Buchanan] distrust politicians" (Buchanan and Musgrave 1999, 88).

Who won the debate? Musgrave's views are still prevalent in Keynesian textbooks, but his books are seldom cited and long out of print. On the other hand, James Buchanan won a Nobel Prize in 1986 and public-choice theory has been added to most curricula. Even Samuelson cites the public-choice work of Buchanan and Gordon Tullock in his latest textbook.

According to public-choice theory, the incentives and discipline found in the marketplace are frequently missing from government. Voters have little incentive to control the excesses of legislators, who in turn are more responsive to powerful interest groups. As a result, government subsidizes the vested interests of commerce and other groups while imposing costly, wasteful regulations and taxes on the general public. Buchanan and other public-choice theorists have recommended a series of constitutional rules and restrictions to alter the misguided public sector into acting more responsibly (Buchanan and Tullock 1962).

Economic Historian Resolves the Mysteries of the Great Depression

Another example of the revisionist history is a new interpretation of the Great Depression by historian Robert Higgs of Seattle University. According to Higgs, there were essentially three transitional periods in this critical event: the Great Contraction (1929–32), the Great Duration (1933–39), and the Great Escape (1940–46). What caused the Great Depression? Why did it last so long? Did World War II really restore prosperity?

As we learned earlier in this chapter, Milton Friedman was instrumental in addressing the cause of the Great Contraction. It was not free enterprise, but the government-controlled Federal Reserve that pushed the economy over the edge in 1929–32.

What produced the decade-long stagnation of the world economy that in turn caused a paradigm shift from classical economics to Keynesianism? Higgs provides an answer that economists had only vaguely considered. In an in-depth study of the 1930s, Higgs focused on the lack of private investment during this period. Most economists recognize that investment is the key to recovery in a slump. Higgs showed how the New Deal initiatives greatly hampered private investment time and time again, destroying much-needed investor and business confidence. These programs included the National Recovery Act, prolabor legislation, government regulation, and stiff tax increases (Higgs 2006, 3–29).

In another brilliant analysis, Higgs attacked the orthodox view that World War II saved us from the depression and restored the economy to full employment. The war gave only the appearance of recovery because everyone was employed. In reality, however, private consumption and investment declined while Americans fought and died for their country. A return to genuine prosperity—the true Great Escape—did not happen until after the war was over, when most of the wartime controls were lifted and most of the resources used in the military were returned to civilian production. Only after the war did private investment, business confidence, and consumer spending return to the fore (Higgs 2006, 61–80).

Ignoring the government *(G)* in GDP figures leads to a better understanding of what occurred during World War II. Consumption *(C)* and investment *(I)* slowed and even declined slightly during 1940–45, then rose sharply after the war in 1946–48.

Not everyone has accepted these relatively new findings, but a growing consensus contends that "government failure" has to take much of the responsibility for the troublesome 1930–45 period of the U.S. economy.

Figure 7.2   The Growth of Government in Five Industrial Nations

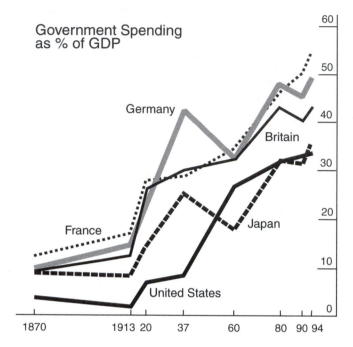

Source: Economist (April 6, 1996). Reprinted by permission.

Today's Debates: The New Challenge of Keynes and Marx

The application of market principles has expanded in every direction in the recent past, but the triumph of free-market economics is far from complete. Many victories have been won on paper, but not in policy. Despite U.S. president Bill Clinton's observation that "[t]he era of big government is over," the size of government in industrial nations has reached gigantic proportions (see Figure 7.2).

On the positive side, it appears that the government sizes have reached their upper bounds. In most countries, the private sector is now growing faster than the public sector. This is especially true in developing countries (government as a percentage of GDP has fallen from 80 percent to 20 percent in China, for example). But that trend could reverse itself quickly if economic conditions change and a nation or region suffers another slump or crisis. Witness the growth of government following the terrorist attacks in the United States and around the world in 2001.

Despite privatization, deregulation, and supply-side tax cuts, governments are still intrusive, revenue hungry, and bureaucratic. Free-market economists have much to offer legislators and business that can help them improve efficiency.

It would be inaccurate and highly misleading to suggest that Keynes, or even Marx, is dead. Quite the contrary. Keynesian and Marxist thinking still carry a strong voice today. If a country falls into a military conflict, a deep slump, or other crisis, the Keynesian model immediately comes to the forefront: maintain spending at all costs, even if it means significant deficit financing. The misleading Keynesian notion that consumer spending, rather than saving, capital formation, and technology, drives the economy, is still very much in vogue in the halls of government and in financial circles. Countries such as China and Japan are criticized for saving too much; Keynesians insist that they need to stimulate "domestic demand" if they hope to advance. Fear that a laissez-faire global financial world is subject to unexpected and debilitating crises is common among both Keynesians and Marxists. They also express deep concern that the entrepreneurs, speculators, and the wealthy class in general are benefiting more from the new global economy and the political process than the middle and lower classes. "Tax cuts help the rich more than the poor" is a common refrain. Critics of the market also constantly complain about growing inequality of income, wealth, and opportunity, despite claims to the contrary by free-market economists. They are sharply critical of free-trade agreements and the potential loss of jobs to producers in China, Mexico, and other developing countries.

The central role of government monetary policy is a global concern. Fiscal policy may have been dethroned as a stabilization tool, but central bank policy might fail to do its job in maintaining macroeconomic stability. Monetary authorities have been known to blunder, overshooting their interest-rate or inflation targets. Their response to every crisis, whether it be a currency crisis or economic downturn, seems to be to adopt an "easy money" policy by injecting liquidity into the system and cutting interest rates below the natural rate. The result has been an increasing structural imbalance and asset bubbles in stocks, real estate, and other sectors. How far they can go with such unstable policies without creating a major global financial crisis remains to be seen. The price of gold is a valuable monitor of global economic instability, and it has been rising lately.

Environmentalism is a major subject of debate. How can nations grow and increase their standards of living without destroying the air, polluting the water, devastating the forests, and causing global warming? The debate goes back to Thomas Malthus (chapter 2) and is related to historical and present-day concerns over unlimited growth and limited resources. In this ecological debate, economists, while not alarmists, have made numerous contributions to minimizing pollution and other environmental problems. To solve the "tragedy of the commons," for example, market economists have emphasized the need to establish defensive resource rights in water, fishing, and forestland, so that owners have the proper incentives to preserve these resources in a balanced way. In the case of air pollution, economists have recommended pollution fees and marketable permits to pollute. Pollution fees are taxed on polluters, penalizing them in proportion to the amount they discharge, a common practice in Europe. Marketable permits allow polluters to sell their permits to other firms, and have successfully reduced the rate of pollution in the United States (Anderson and Leal 2001).

Stiglitz's Challenge: Is Market Imperfection Pervasive?

Joseph Stiglitz, Columbia professor and winner of the Nobel Prize in 2001 for his work in the economics of information, is a Keynesian who has taken a hardened stance against Adam Smith and the competitive equilibrium model. The invisible hand, according to Stiglitz, is either "simply not there, or at least ... if there, it is palsied" (Stiglitz 2001, 473). He declares that market imperfections and market failures are so pervasive and so serious that the market is always inefficient and requires government correction. Imperfect information exists in labor, products, money, trade, and capital markets.[1] Serious unemployment

---

1. Neo-Keynesians have contributed extensively to the new field of "behavioral economics," which questions the efficiency/rational expectations model of the Chicago school, and proposes ways to counter the tendency of individuals to make financial mistakes, such as undersaving, over-consuming, and underperforming the stock market averages. See, for example, Richard Thaler (2004) and Robert Shiller (2005). However, not all behavioral economists are Keynesian. See Jeremy Siegel (2005).

could exist even without minimum wage laws or labor unions, he contends. During the Great Depression, "had there been more wage and price flexibility, matters might have been even worse," he states (2001, 477). According to Stiglitz, involuntary unemployment is still a problem! Gary Becker, Milton Friedman, and other Chicago economists may claim that the competitive marketplace discourages discrimination, unemployment, and poverty, but Stiglitz's hometown of Gary, Indiana, "even in its heyday . . . was marred by poverty, periodic unemployment, and massive racial discrimination" (2001, 473).

Stiglitz makes another paradigm shift back to a Keynesian model of imperfect information that "undermines" the foundations of competitive analysis, including the denial of the "law" of supply and demand, the law of the single price, and the efficient market hypothesis (2001, 485). Why? Because information in a decentralized market economy is "asymmetric"—"different people know different things," which in turn can lead to "thin or non-existent markets" (2001, 488–89). What Hayek views as positive, Stiglitz sees as negative.

Market economists counter Stiglitz by arguing that while imperfect information may indeed be pervasive, the outcome of the imperfect competitive market system acts "as if" it is perfectly competitive. For example, experimental economics seems to confirm this "as if" approach. Vernon L. Smith, Nobel laureate from George Mason University and founder of experimental economics, ran an experiment to test the Chamberlin-Robinson "imperfect competition" model. Recall from chapter 5 that this model suggested that a small number of sellers (or buyers) creates an imperfect form of competition, causing prices to rise, and output to fall. The imperfect monopolistic model was therefore inefficient, and gave support to government antitrust actions to break up big businesses and force more competition into the industry.

However, Smith made an interesting observation. When he reduced the number of buyers and sellers to only a few in his experiments, the results were the same—the final price approached the same competitive price that was achieved with a large number of buyers and sellers. By implication, competition within an industry is not necessarily reduced when it is limited to only a few large companies (Smith 1987, 241–46).

Smith's observation confirmed the earlier work of George Stigler,

Harry Johnson, and other members of the Chicago school that competition is strong even among only a few large firms. Monopolistic
firms tend to keep prices competitive because of the ever-present threat
of entry by other large firms. The world is "as if" fully competitive
(Bhagwati 1998, 411–12).

The Return of Adam Smith's Vision

We have come a long way since Adam Smith proposed that the path to
economic growth, prosperity, and social justice lies in nations' granting citizens the maximum freedom possible to pursue their public and
private interests under a tolerable system of justice. But Adam Smith's
system of natural liberty has been challenged in every generation since
his *Wealth of Nations* was published in 1776. Today is no exception.

Adam Smith's vision of unfettered markets flourished initially
across the English channel among J.-B. Say, Frédéric Bastiat, and
the French *philosophes,* but it was not long before the revolutionary
Smith came under attack from the least likely place—his own British
school. Thomas Robert Malthus and David Ricardo turned the optimistic world of Adam Smith upside down into the abyss of the iron
law of subsistence wages. John Stuart Mill joined the social reformers in seeking a utopian alternative to the so-called dismal science
and, when voluntary means were not forthcoming, along came the
irrepressible radical Karl Marx, who plunged economics into a new
age of alienation, class struggle, exploitation, and crisis.

Just as we were about to give up on our almost-dead protagonist,
three good Samaritans revived the life of Adam Smith—Stanley
Jevons, Carl Menger, and Leon Walras. The marginalist revolution
restored the Smithian soul, and with the help of Alfred Marshall in
Britain and John Bates Clark in the United States, among others, it
resurrected Smith and transformed him into a whole new classical
man. Despite efforts to renounce the new capitalist model by Thorstein
Veblen and other institutionalists, the critics were effectively countered, especially by Max Weber. The neoclassical paradigm stood tall,
ready to make contributions to the new scientific age.

The golden age of neoclassical economics continued to face hurdles
as Irving Fisher, Knut Wicksell, and Ludwig von Mises searched for
the ideal monetary standard to house Adam Smith, but no consensus

had been achieved by time the 1929 stock market crash plunged the world into the worst depression of modern times. Once again, Adam Smith faced imminent demise. Marxists were in the wings waiting to take over when a new doctor, John Maynard Keynes, presented the world with new medicine, with which he proposed to save Adam Smith and restore him as the father of capitalism. But Keynes turned out to be a temporary savior only, as the long-run effects of his medicine led to an overbloated patient. It would take the inventiveness of Milton Friedman and Friedrich Hayek, intellectual descendants of Adam Smith, to correctly diagnose the cause of the distress and restore the model underlining a competitive, robust economy.

No doubt the bold challenges made by Marx and Keynes and their disciples have had a positive effect. They have caused market economists to respond to their deft criticisms and improve the classical model that Adam Smith created. Today the neoclassical market framework is stronger than ever before, and its applications are ubiquitous.

In 1930, at the beginning of the Great Depression, John Maynard Keynes wrote an optimistic essay, "Economic Possibilities for Our Grandchildren." After lambasting his disciples who predicted never-ending depression and permanent stagnation, Keynes foresaw a bright future. Goods and services would become so abundant and cheap that leisure would be the greatest challenge. What productive things can be done in one's spare time? According to Keynes, capital would become so inexpensive that interest rates might fall to zero. Interest rates have not fallen to zero, but our standards of living have advanced remarkably, at least in most areas of the world. Keynes concluded, "It would not be foolish to contemplate the possibility of a greater progress still" (Keynes 1963 [1930], 365).

Market forces are on the march. The collapse of the Keynesian paradigm and Marxist communism has turned "creeping socialism" into "crumbling socialism." There is no telling how high the world's standard of living can reach through expanded trade, lower tariffs, a simplified tax system, school choice, Social Security privatization, a fair system of justice, and a stable monetary system. Yet bad policies, wasted resources, and class hatred die slowly. As Milton Friedman once wrote, "Freedom is a rare and delicate flower" (1998, 605). Unless market economists are vigilant, natural liberty and universal prosperity will be on the defensive again.

Bibliography

Anderson, Terry L., and Donald R. Leal. 2001. *Free Market Environmentalism.* 2d ed. New York: Palgrave.

Arrow, Kenneth J., and F.H. Hahn.1971. *General Competitive Analysis.* San Francisco: Holden-Day.

Barzun, Jacques. 1958 [1941]. *Darwin, Marx, Wagner.* 2d ed. New York: Doubleday.

Bastiat, Frédéric. 1998 [1850]. *The Law.* New York: Foundation for Economic Education.

Bauer, P.T. 1981. *Equality, the Third World and Economic Delusion.* Cambridge, MA: Harvard University Press.

Baumol, William J., and Alan S. Blinder. 1988. *Economics: Principles and Policy.* 4th ed. New York: Harcourt Brace Jovanovich.

_____. 2001. *Economics: Principles and Policies.* 8th ed. Ft. Worth, TX: Harcourt College Publishers.

Bean, Charles R. 1994. "European Unemployment: A Survey." *Journal of Economic Literature* 32, 2 (June): 573–619.

Berman, Marshall. 1999. *Adventures in Marxism.* New York: Verso.

Bhagwati, Jagdish. 1998. *A Stream of Windows.* Cambridge: MIT Press.

Black, R.D. Collison, A.W. Coats, and Craufurd D.W. Goodwin, eds. 1973. *The Marginal Revolution in Economics.* Durham, NC: Duke University Press.

Blaug, Mark. 1978. *Economic Theory in Retrospect.* 3d ed. Cambridge, UK: Cambridge University Press.

_____. 1985. *Great Economists Since Keynes.* Cambridge, UK: Cambridge University Press.

_____. 1986. *Great Economists Before Keynes.* Atlantic Heights, NJ: Humanities Press International.

_____. 1999. *Who's Who in Economics.* 3d ed. Cheltenham, UK: Edward Elgar.

Blinder, Alan S. 1987. *Hard Heads, Soft Hearts.* Reading, MA: Addison-Wesley.

Blumenberg, Werner. 1998 [1962]. *Karl Marx: An Illustrated Biography.* London: Verso.

Boaz, David. 1997. *Libertarianism: A Primer.* New York: The Free Press.

Böhm-Bawerk, Eugen.1959 [1884]. *Capital and Interest.* South Holland, IL: Libertarian Press.

———. 1962. "The Austrian Economists." In *Shorter Classics of Böhm-Bawerk.* South Holland, IL: Libertarian Press. Originally appeared in *Annals of the American Academy of Political and Social Sciences* (January 1891).

Boswell, James. 1933. *Life of Johnson.* 2 vols. New York: Oxford University Press.

Bottomore, Tom, ed. 1991. *A Dictionary of Marxist Thought.* 2d ed. Oxford: Blackwell.

Boyes, William, and Michael Melvin. 1999. *Macroeconomics.* 4th ed. Boston: Houghton Mifflin.

Breit, William, and Roger W. Spencer, eds. 1986. *Lives of the Laureates.* Cambridge, MA: MIT Press.

Brennan, Geoffrey, and Philip Pettit. 1993. "Hands Invisible and Intangible." *Synthese* 94: 191–225.

Bronfenbrenner, Martin. 1967. "Marxian Influences in 'Bourgeois' Economics." *American Economic Review* 57, 2 (May): 624–35.

Brown, William Montgomery. 1935. *Teachings of Marx for Girls and Boys.* Galion, Ohio: Bradford-Brown Educational Co.

Buchanan, James M., and Gordon Tullock. 1962. *The Calculus of Consent.* Ann Arbor: University of Michigan Press.

Buchanan, James M., and Richard A. Musgrave. 1999. *Public Choice and Public Finance: Two Contrasting Views of the State.* Cambridge, MA: MIT Press.

Buchholz, Todd G. 1999. *New Ideas from Dead Economists.* 2d ed. New York: Penguin.

Buckley, William F., Jr. 1951. *God and Man at Yale.* Chicago: Regnery.

Bush, George W. 2002. "President Honors Milton Friedman for Lifetime Achievements." www.whitehouse.gov/news/releases/2002/05/20020509-1.html.

Byrns, Ralph T., and Gerald W. Stone. 1989. *Economics.* 4th ed. Glenville, IL: Scott, Foresman.

Carlyle, Thomas. 1904. *Critical and Miscellaneous Essays.* London: Charles Scribner's Sons.

Chamberlin, Edward H. 1933. *The Theory of Monopolistic Competition.* Cambridge, MA: Harvard University Press.

Clark, John Bates. 1914. *Social Justice Without Socialism.* Boston: Houghton Mifflin.

_____. 1965 [1899]. *The Distribution of Wealth.* New York: Augustus M. Kelley.

Coase, Ronald H. 1976. "Adam Smith's View of Man." *Journal of Law and Economics* 19: 529–46.

Colb, Ralph, Jr. 1982. "The Myth of the Marx-Darwin Letter." *History of Political Economy* 14, 4: 461–82.

Collins, Robert M. 1981. *The Business Response to Keynes, 1929–1964.* New York: Columbia University Press.

Cox, Michael, and Richard Alm. 1999. *The Myths of Rich and Poor.* New York: Free Press.

Danhert, Clyde E., ed. 1974. *Adam Smith, Man of Letters and Economist.* New York: Exposition.

D'Aulaire, Ingrid, and Edgar D'Aulaire. 1962. *D'Aulaire's Book of Greek Myths.* New York: Doubleday.

Denby, David. 1996. *Great Books.* New York: Simon and Schuster.

Desai, Maghnad. 2004. *Marx's Revenge.* New York: Verso.

Dewey, Donald. 1987. "John Bates Clark." In *The New Palgrave: A Dictionary of Economics.* Vol. 1, 428–31. London: Macmillan.

Diggins, John Patrick. 1996. Max Weber: *Politics and the Spirit of Tragedy.* New York: Basic Books.

_____. 1999. *Thorstein Veblen, Theorist of the Leisure Class.* Princeton, NJ: Princeton University Press.

Dorfman, Joseph. 1934. *Thorstein Veblen and His America.* New York: Augustus M. Kelley.

Downs, Robert B. 1983. *Books That Changed the World.* 2d ed. New York: Penguin.

D'Souza, Dinesh. 2005. "How Capitalism Civilizes Greed." www.dineshdsouza. com/articles/civilizinggreed.html.

Dobbs, Zygmund. 1962. *Keynes at Harvard.* New York: Probe.

Eaton, John. 1951. *Marx Against Keynes.* London: Lawrence and Wishart.

Eichengreen, Barry. 1992. *Golden Fetters: The Gold Standard and the Great Depression.* New York: Oxford University Press.

Ekins, Paul, and Manfred Max-Neef. 1992. *Real-Life Economics: Understanding Wealth Creation.* London: Routledge.

Elzinga, Kenneth G. 1992. "The Eleven Principles of Economics." *Southern Economic Journal* 58, 4 (April): 861–79.

Engels, Friedrich. 2000 [1844]. *The Condition of the Working Class in England.* New York: Pathfinder.

Feuerbach, Ludwig. 1957 [1841]. *The Essence of Christianity.* New York: Harper Torchbooks.

Fisher, Irving. 1963 [1911]. *The Purchasing Power of Money.* 2d ed. New York: Augustus M. Kelley.

Fitzgibbons, Athol. 1995. *Adam Smith's System of Liberty, Wealth, and Virtue.* New York: Clarendon.

Fitzpatrick, Sheila. 1999. *Everyday Stalinism.* New York: Oxford University Press.

Foster, William T., and Waddill Catchings. 1927. *Business Without a Buyer.* Boston: Houghton Mifflin.

Friedman, Milton. 1968. *Dollars and Deficits.* New York: Prentice-Hall.

———. 1969. *The Optimum Quantity of Money and Other Essays.* London: Macmillan.

———. 1974. "Comment on the Critics." In *Milton Friedman's Monetary Framework,* ed. Robert J. Gordon, 132–37. Chicago: University of Chicago Press.

———. 1978. "Adam Smith's Relevance for 1976." In *Adam Smith and the Wealth of Nations: 1776–1976 Bicentennial Essays,* ed. Fred R. Glahe. Boulder: Colorado Associated University Press, 7–20.

———. 1981. *The Invisible Hand in Economics and Politics.* Singapore: Institute of Southeast Asian Studies.

———. 1982 [1962]. *Capitalism and Freedom.* Chicago: University of Chicago Press.

———. 1986. "Keynes's Political Legacy." In *Keynes's General Theory: Fifty Years On,* ed. John Burton. London: Institute of Economic Affairs.

Friedman, Milton, and Rose Friedman. 1980. *Free to Choose: A Personal Statement.* New York: Harcourt Brace Jovanovich.

———. 1998. *Two Lucky People.* Chicago: University of Chicago Press.

Friedman, Milton, and Walter W. Heller. 1969. *Monetary vs. Fiscal Policy.* New York: W.W. Norton.

Friedman, Milton, and David Meiselman. 1963. "The Relative Stability of Monetary Velocity and the Investment Multiplier in the United States, 1897–1958." In *Stabilization Policies.* Report from the Commission on Money and Credit. Englewood Cliff, NJ: Prentice-Hall, 165–268.

Friedman, Milton, and Anna J. Schwartz. 1963. *A Monetary History of the United States, 1867–1960*. Princeton, NJ: Princeton University Press.

Fromm, Eric. 1966. *Marx's Concept of Man*. New York: Continuum.

Fukuyama, Francis. 2000. "Will Socialism Make a Comeback?" *Time*, May 22, 110–12.

Galbraith, John Kenneth. 1975 [1965]. "How Keynes Came to America." In *Essays on John Maynard Keynes*, ed. Milo Keynes, 132–41. Cambridge, UK: Cambridge University Press.

Garrison, Roger B. 1985. "West's 'Cantillon and Adam Smith': A Comment." *Journal of Libertarian Studies* 7, 2 (Fall): 287–94.

———. 2001. *Time and Money*. London: Routledge.

Glahe, Fred R., ed. 1978. *Adam Smith and the Wealth of Nations: 1776–1976 Bicentennial Essays*. Boulder: Colorado Associated University Press.

———. 1993. *Adam Smith's An Inquiry into the Nature and Causes of the Wealth of Nations: A Concordance*. Landam, MD: Rowman and Littlefield.

Gordon, H. Scott. 1967. "Discussion on *Das Kapital*: A Centenary Appreciation." *American Economic Review* 52, 2 (May): 640–41.

Gutiérrez, Gustavo. 1973. *A Theology of Liberation: History, Politics, and Salvation*, trans. Caridad Inda and John Eagleson. Maryknoll, NY: Orbis Books.

Gwartney, James D., and Robert A. Lawson. 2004. *Economic Freedom of the World*. Vancouver: Fraser Institute.

Gwartney, James D., Robert A. Lawson, and Walter E. Block. 1996. *Economic Freedom of the World: 1975–1995*. Vancouver: Fraser Institute.

Hahn, Frank. 1982. "Reflections on the Invisible Hand." *Lloyds Bank Review*, April, 1–21.

Hansen, Alvin. 1941. *Fiscal Policy and Business Cycles*. New York: W.W. Norton.

———. 1953. *A Guide to Keynes*. New York: McGraw-Hill.

Harrington, Michael. 1976. *The Twilight of Capitalism*. New York: Macmillan.

Harris, Sharon. 1998. "The Invisible Hand Is a Gentle Hand." HarryBrowne.org/articles/InvisibleHand.htm (September 14).

Harris, Seymour E., ed. 1947. *The New Economics: Keynes' Influence on Theory and Public Policy*. New York: Alfred A. Knopf.

———. 1948. *Saving American Capitalism*. New York: Alfred A. Knopf.

Harrod, Roy. 1951. *The Life of John Maynard Keynes*. New York: Harcourt, Brace.

Hart, Michael H. 1978. *The 100: A Ranking of the Most Influential Persons in History*. New York: Hart.

———. 1992. *The 100: A Ranking of the Most Influential Persons in History*. 2d ed. New York: Citadel.

Hayek, Friedrich. 1935 [1931]. *Prices and Production*. 2d ed. London: George Routledge and Sons.

———, ed. 1935. *Collectivist Economic Planning*. London: George Routledge and Sons.

———. 1939 [1929]. "The 'Paradox' of Thrift." In *Profits, Interest and Investment*. London: Routledge, 199–263.

———. 1944. *The Road to Serfdom*. Chicago: University of Chicago Press.

———. 1960. *The Constitution of Liberty*. Chicago: University of Chicago Press.

_____. 1976. "Introduction: Carl Menger." In *Principles of Economics*, ed. Carl Menger. New York: New York University Press.

_____. 1984. *The Essence of Hayek,* ed. Chiaki Nishiyama and Kurt R. Leube. Stanford, CA: Stanford University Press.

Hazlitt, Henry. 1959. *The Failure of the "New Economics."* Princeton, NJ: D. Van Nostrand.

_____. 1977 [1960]. *The Critics of Keynesian Economics.* 2d ed. New York: Arlington House.

_____. 1979 [1946]. *Economics in One Lesson.* 3d ed. New York: Arlington House.

Heilbroner, Robert. 1961. *The Worldly Philosophers.* 2d ed. New York: Simon and Schuster.

_____. 1986. *The Essential Adam Smith.* New York: W.W. Norton.

_____. 1989. "The Triumph of Capitalism." *New Yorker,* January 23, 98–109.

_____. 1990. "Reflections After Communism." *New Yorker,* September 10, 91–100.

————. 1999 [1953]. *The Worldly Philosophers.* 7th ed. New York: Simon and Schuster.

Heilbroner, Robert, and Peter L. Bernstein. 1963. *A Primer on Government Spending.* New York: Random House.

Hession, Charles H. 1984. *John Maynard Keynes.* New York: Macmillan.

Hicks, John R. 1937. "Mr. Keynes and the 'Classics'; A Suggested Interpretation." *Econometrica* 5:2 (April), 147–59.

Higgs, Robert. 2006. *Depression, War, and the Cold War.* New York: Oxford University Press.

Hirschman, Albert O. 1997. *The Passions and the Interests.* 2d ed. Princeton, NJ: Princeton University Press.

Hobbes, Thomas. 1996 [1651]. *Leviathan.* New York: Oxford University Press.

Howard, M.C., and J.E. King. 1989. *A History of Marxian Economics, 1823–1929.* Princeton, NJ: Princeton University Press.

Hutt, W.H. 1979. *The Keynesian Episode: A Reassessment.* Indianapolis, IN: Liberty Press.

Iannaccone, Laurence. 1991. "The Consequences of Religious Market Structure." *Rationality and Society* 3, 2 (April): 156–77.

Ingrao, Bruna, and Giorgio Israel. 1990. *The Invisible Hand: Economic Equilibrium in the History of Science.* Cambridge, MA: MIT Press.

Jevons, W. Stanley. 1965 [1871]. *The Theory of Political Economy.* 5th ed. New York: Augustus M. Kelley.

Johnson, Elizabeth, and Harry G. Johnson. 1978. *The Shadow of Keynes.* Oxford: Basil Blackwell.

Jorgensen, Elizabeth, and Henry Jorgensen. 1999. *Thorstein Veblen: Victorian Firebrand.* Armonk, NY: M.E. Sharpe.

Jouvenel, Bertrand de. 1999. *Economics and the Good Life: Essays on Political Economy,* ed. Dennis Hale and Marc Landy. New Brunswick, NJ: Transaction.

Joyce, Helen. 2001. "Adam Smith and the Invisible Hand." http://plus.maths.org/issue14/features/smith/feat.pdf.

Kates, Steven. 1998. *Say's Law and the Keynesian Revolution.* Cheltenham, UK: Edward Elgar.

Keynes, John Maynard. 1920. *Economic Consequences of the Peace.* New York: Harcourt, Brace.

———. 1923. *A Tract on Monetary Reform.* London: Macmillan.

———. 1930. *A Treatise on Money.* 2 vols. London: Macmillan.

———. 1951 [1931]. *Essays in Persuasion.* New York: W.W. Norton.

———. 1963 [1930]. *Essays in Biography.* New York: W.W. Norton.

———. 1971. *Activities 1906–1914: India and Cambridge. The Collected Works of John Maynard Keynes.* Vol. 15. London: Macmillan.

———. 1973a [1936]. *The General Theory of Employment, Interest and Money.* London: Macmillan.

———. 1973b. *The General Theory and After, Part I, Preparation. The Collected Works of John Maynard Keynes.* Vol. 13, ed. by Donald Moggridge. London: Macmillan.

Klamer, Arjo, and David Colander. 1990. *The Making of an Economist.* Boulder, CO: Westview.

Knight, Frank H. 1959. "Review of Ricardian Economics." *Southern Journal of Economics* 25, 3 (January): 363–65.

———. 1982 [1947]. *Freedom and Reform.* Indianapolis, IN: Liberty Fund.

Krugman, Paul. 2006. "Introduction to *The General Theory of Employment, Interest and Money.*" www.pkarchive.org/economy/GeneralTheoryKeynesIntro.html.

Kuttner, Robert. 1985. "The Poverty of Economics." *Atlantic Monthly* (February): 74–84.

Lai, Cheng-chung. 2000. *Adam Smith Across Nations.* New York: Oxford University Press.

Leamer, Edward. 1983. "Let's Take the Con out of Economics." *American Economic Review* 73, 1 (March): 31–43.

Lebergott, Stanley. 1976. *The American Economy.* Princeton, NJ: Princeton University Press.

Lenin, V.I. 1970. *Selected Works.* 12 vols. Moscow: Progress.

Leontief, Wassily. 1938. "The Significance of Marxian Economics for Present-Day Economic Theory." *American Economic Review* 28, 2 (March supplement): 1–9.

Lichtheim, George. 1970. *A Short History of Socialism.* New York: Praeger.

Liebknecht, Wilhelm. 1968 [1901]. *Karl Marx Biographical Memoirs.* New York: Greenwood.

Linder, Marc. 1977. *Anti-Samuelson.* 2 vols. New York: Urizen.

Lindsey, Brink. 2002. *Against the Dead Hand: The Uncertain Struggle for Global Capitalism.* New York: John Wiley.

Lipsey, Richard G., Peter O. Steiner, and Douglas D. Purvis. 1987. *Economics.* 8th ed. New York: Harper & Row.

Lux, Kenneth. 1990. *Adam Smith's Mistake.* Boston: Shambhala.

McCloskey, Deirdre. 1998 [1985]. *The Rhetoric of Economics.* 2d ed. Madison, WI: University of Wisconsin Press.

Macfie, A.L. 1967. *The Individual in Society: Papers on Adam Smith.* London: George Allen & Unwin.

McGovern, Arthur F. 1980. *Marxism: An American Christian Perspective.* Maryknoll, NY: Orbis Books.

Macleod, H.D. 1896. *The History of Economics.* London: Bliss, Sands.

Malia, Martin. 1999. *Russia Under Western Eyes*. Cambridge, MA: Harvard University Press.

Malthus, Thomas Robert. 1985 [1798]. *An Essay on the Principle of Population*. New York: Penguin. (This edition contains the original 1798 first edition and *A Summary View of the Principle of Population*, published in 1830.)

Mandel, Ernest. 1976. "Introduction." *Capital*. Vol. 1. New York: Penguin.

Mandeville, Bernard. 1997 [1714]. *The Fable of the Bees, and Other Writings*. New York: Hackett.

Mankiw, N. Gregory. 1994. *Macroeconomics*. 2d ed. New York: Worth.

_____. 1997. *Principles of Economics*. New York: Dryden Press.

Mantoux, Etienne de. 1952. *The Cathagian Peace*. Pittsburgh, PA: University of Pittsburgh Press.

Marshall, Alfred. 1920 [1890]. *Principles of Economics*. 8th ed. London: Macmillan.

Marx, Karl. 1976 [1867]. *Capital*. Vol. 1. New York: Penguin.

———. 1980. *The Holy Family, or Critique of Critical Criticism*. New York: Firebird.

———. 1988. *The Economic and Philosophic Manuscripts of 1844*. New York: Prometheus.

———. 1995. *The Poverty of Philosophy*. New York: Prometheus.

_____. 2000. *Selected Writings*. 2d ed. Oxford: Oxford University Press.

Marx, Karl, and Friedrich Engels. 1964 [1848]. *The Communist Manifesto*. New York: Monthly Review Press.

———. No date. *Collected Works (Letters 1860–64)*. Vol. 41. New York: International Publishers.

Mayo, Elton. 1945. *The Social Problems of an Industrious Civilization*. Cambridge, MA: Harvard University Press.

Meltzer, Allan H. 1988 [1968]. *Keynes's Monetary Theory: A Different Interpretation*. Cambridge, UK: Cambridge University Press.

Menger, Carl. 1976 [1871]. *Principles of Economics*, trans. James Dingwall and Bert F. Hoselitz. New York: New York University Press.

Mill, John Stuart. 1884 [1848]. *Principles of Political Economy*, ed. J. Laurence Laughlin. New York: D. Appleton.

_____. 1989 [1859]. *On Liberty*. Cambridge, UK: Cambridge University Press.

Minsky, Hyman P. 1982. *Can "It" Happen Again? Essays on Instability and Finance*. Armonk, NY: M.E. Sharpe.

_____. 1986. *Stabilizing an Unstable Economy*. New Haven, CT: Yale University Press.

Mises, Ludwig von. 1966. *Human Action*. 3d ed. Chicago: Regnery.

_____. 1971 [1912]. *The Theory of Money and Credit*. 2d ed. New York: Foundation for Economic Education.

_____. 1972. *The Anti-Capitalist Mentality*. Spring Mills, PA: Libertarian Press.

———. 1980 [1952]. *Planning for Freedom*. 4th ed. Spring Mills, PA: Libertarian Press.

Modigliani, Franco. 1986. "Life Cycle, Individual Thrift, and the Wealth of Nations." *American Economic Review* 76, 3 (June): 297–313.

Moggridge, D.E. 1983. "Keynes as an Investor." In *The Collected Works of John Maynard Keynes*, 1–113. Vol. 12. London: Macmillan.

_____. 1992. *Maynard Keynes*. London: Routledge.

Montesquieu, Charles. 1989 [1748]. *The Spirit of the Laws*, ed. Anne Cohler, Basia Miller, and Harold Stone. Cambridge, UK: Cambridge University Press.

Muller, Jerry Z. 1993. *Adam Smith in His Time and Ours*. Princeton, NJ: Princeton University Press.

Musgrave, Richard A. 1958. *Public Finance in Theory and Practice*. New York: Macmillan.

North, Gary. 1993. "The Marx Nobody Knows." In *Requiem for Marx*, ed. Uri N. Maltsev. Auburn, AL: Ludwig von Mises Institute.

Novak, Michael. 1991. *Will It Liberate? Questions About Liberation Theology*. New York: Madison Books.

Padover, Saul K. 1978. *Karl Marx: An Intimate Biography*. New York: McGraw-Hill.

Patinkin, Don. 1956. *Money, Interest and Price*. New York: Harper & Row.

Payne, Robert. 1968. *Marx*. New York: Simon & Schuster.

_____. 1971. *The Unknown Marx*. New York: New York University Press.

Pearlstine, Norman. 1998. "Big Wheels Turning." *Time*, December 7, 70–73.

Phillips, A.W. 1958. "The Relationship Between Unemployment and the Rate of Change in Money Wage Rates in the United Kingdom, 1861–1957." *Economica* 25 (November): 283–99.

Pigou, Arthur C., ed. 1925. *Memorials of Alfred Marshall*. London: Macmillian.

Pigou, Arthur C. 1943. "The Classical Stationary State." *Economic Journal* 53 (December): 343–51.

_____. 1947. "Economic Progress in a Stable Environment." *Economica* 14 (August): 180–88.

Plaut, Eric A., and Kevin Anderson. 1999. *Marx on Suicide*. Evanston, IL: Northwestern University Press.

Popper, Karl. 1972. *Conjectures and Refutations*. 4th ed. London: Routledge and Kegan Paul.

Powell, Jim. 2000. *The Triumph of Liberty*. New York: The Free Press.

Raddatz, Fritz J. 1978. *Karl Marx: A Political Biography*. Boston: Little, Brown.

Rae, John. 1895. *Life of Adam Smith*. London: Macmillan.

Rand, Ayn. 1964. *The Virtue of Selfishness*. New York: Signet.

Rashid, Salim. 1998. *The Myth of Adam Smith*. Cheltenham, UK: Edward Elgar.

Read, Leonard E. 1999. "I, Pencil." Irvington, NY: Foundation for Economic Education. (Originally published in *Freeman*, December 1958.)

Ricardo, David. 1951. *On the Principles of Political Economy and Taxation*, ed. Piero Sraffa. Cambridge, UK: Cambridge University Press.

Robinson, Joan. 1933. *Economics of Imperfect Competition*. London: Macmillan.

Roemer, John E. 1988. *Free to Lose*. Cambridge, MA: Harvard University Press.

Rogge, Benjamin A., ed. 1976. *The Wisdom of Adam Smith*. Indianapolis, IN: Liberty Press.

Ross, Ian Simpson. 1995. *The Life of Adam Smith*. Oxford: Clarendon.

Rostow, W.W. 1960. *The Stages of Economic Growth*. Cambridge: Cambridge University Press.

_____. 1990. *Theorists of Economic Growth from David Hume to the Present*. New York: Oxford University Press.

Rothbard, Murray N. 1980. "The Essential Von Mises." In *Planning for Freedom*, by Ludwig von Mises, 234–70. 4th ed. Spring Mills, PA: Libertarian Press.

_____. 1983 [1963]. *America's Great Depression*. 4th ed. New York: Richardson and Snyder.

_____. 1995a. *Economic Thought Before Adam Smith*. Hants, UK: Edward Elgar.

_____. 1995b. *Classical Economics*. Hants, UK: Edward Elgar.

Rothschild, Emma. 2001. *Economic Sentiments: Adam Smith, Condorcet, and the Enlightenment*. Cambridge, MA: Harvard University Press.

St. Clair, Oswald. 1965. *A Key to Ricardo*. New York: Augustus M. Kelley.

Samuelson, Paul. 1947. *Foundations of Economic Analysis*. Cambridge, MA: Harvard University Press.

_____. 1948. *Economics*. New York: McGraw-Hill.

_____. 1957. "Wages and Interest: A Modern Dissection of Marxian Economic Models." *American Economic Review* 47, 6 (May): 884–910.

———. 1960. "American Economics." In *Postwar Economic Trends in the U.S.*, ed. Ralph E. Freeman. New York: Harper.

_____. 1961. *Economics*. 5th ed. New York: McGraw-Hill.

_____. 1962. "Economists and the History of Ideas." *American Economic Review* 52, 1 (March): 1–18.

———. 1964. *Economics*. 6th ed. New York: McGraw-Hill.

———. 1966. *Collected Scientific Papers of Paul A. Samuelson*. Vol. 2. Cambridge, MA: MIT Press.

———. 1967a. *Economics*. 7th ed. New York: McGraw-Hill.

———. 1967b. "Marxian Economics as Economics." *American Economic Review* 57, 2 (May): 616–23.

———. 1968. "What Classical and Neoclassical Monetary Theory Really Was." *Canadian Journal of Economics* 1 (February): 1–15

———. 1970. *Economics*. 8th ed. New York: McGraw-Hill.

———. 1976. *Economics*. 10th ed. New York: McGraw-Hill.

———. 1977. *The Collected Scientific Papers of Paul A. Samuelson*. Vol. 4. Cambridge, MA: MIT Press.

———. 1990. "Foreword." In *The Principles of Economics Course*, ed. Phillips Saunders and William B. Walstad. New York: McGraw-Hill.

———. 1997. "Credo of a Lucky Textbook Author." *Journal of Economic Perspectives* 11, 2 (spring): 153–60.

Samuelson, Paul A., and William D. Nordhaus. 1985. *Economics*. 12th ed. New York: McGraw-Hill.

———. 1989. *Economics*. 13th ed. New York: McGraw-Hill.

_____. 1998. *Economics*. 16th ed. New York: Irwin-McGraw-Hill.

Say, Jean-Baptiste. 1971 [1880]. *A Treatise on Political Economy*, trans C.R. Prinsep. 4th ed. New York: Augustus M. Kelley.

Schor, Juliet B. 1991. *The Overworked American*. New York: Basic Books.

Schumacher, E.F. 1973. *Small Is Beautiful*. London: Penguin.

Schumpeter, Joseph. 1950 [1942]. *Capitalism, Socialism and Democracy*. New York: Harper.

_____. 1954. *History of Economic Analysis*. New York: Oxford University Press.

Schwartzchild, Leopold. 1947. *Karl Marx, the Red Prussian*. New York: Grosset and Dunlap.

Schweickart, David. 2002. *After Capitalism*. London: Rowman and Littlefield.

Seymour-Smith, Martin. 1998. *The 100 Most Influential Books Ever Written*. Toronto: Citadel.

Shaw, G.K. 1988. *Keynesian Economics: The Permanent Revolution*. Hants, UK: Edward Elgar.

Shiller, Robert J. 2005. *Irrational Exuberance*. 2nd ed. Princeton: Princeton University Press.

Shleifer, Andrei, and Robert W. Vishny. 1998. *The Grabbing Hand: Government Pathologies and Their Cures*. Cambridge, MA: Harvard University Press.

Siegel, Jeremy J. 2005. *The Future for Investors*. New York: Crown/Business.

Simon, Julian L., ed. 1995. *The State of Humanity*. Cambridge, UK: Blackwell.

———. 1996. *The Ultimate Resource 2*. Princeton, NJ: Princeton University Press.

Skidelsky, Robert. 1992. *John Maynard Keynes: The Economist as Saviour, 1920–1937*. London: Macmillan.

———. 2003. *John Maynard Keynes: Economist, Philosopher, Statesman*. New York: Penguin Books.

Skousen, Mark. 1990. *The Structure of Production*. New York: New York University Press.

———, ed. 1992. *Dissent on Keynes: A Critical Appraisal of Keynesian Economics*. New York: Praeger.

———. 2001. *The Making of Modern Economics*. Armonk, NY: M.E. Sharpe.

———. 2005. *Vienna and Chicago, Friends or Foes?* Washington, DC: Capital Press.

Smith, Adam. 1947. "Letter from Adam Smith to William Strahan." In *Supplement to David Hume, Dialogues Concerning Natural Religion*, ed. Norman Kemp Smith. Indianapolis, IN: Bobbs-Merrill, 248.

———. 1965 [1776]. *An Inquiry into the Nature and Causes of the Wealth of Nations*. New York: Modern Library.

———. 1982 [1759]. *The Theory of Moral Sentiments*, ed. D.D. Raphael and A.L. Macfie. Indianapolis, IN: Liberty Fund.

———. 1982 [1763]. *Lectures on Jurisprudence*, ed. R.L. Meek, D.D. Raphael, and P.G. Stein. Indianapolis, IN: Liberty Fund.

———. 1982. *Essays on Philosophical Subjects*, ed. W.P.D. Wightman. Indianapolis, IN: Liberty Fund.

———. 1987. *Correspondence of Adam Smith*, ed. E.G. Mossner and I.S. Ross. Indianapolis, IN: Liberty Fund.

Snooks, Graeme Donald. 1993. *Economics Without Time*. Ann Arbor: University of Michigan Press.

Sobel, Robert. 1980. *The Worldly Economists*. New York: The Free Press.

Solomou, S.N. 1987. "Nikolai Kondratieff." In *The New Palgrave: A Dictionary of Economics*. Vol. 3, 60. London: Macmillan.

Solow, Robert W. 1965. "Economic Growth and Residential Housing." In *Readings in Financial Institutions*, ed. M.E. Ketchum and L.T. Kendall, 142–64. Boston: Houghton Mifflin.

Somary, Felix. 1986 [1960]. *The Raven of Zurich*. London: C. Hurst.

Soto, Hernando de. 2002. *The Other Path*. 2d ed. New York: Perseus Books.

———. 2003. *The Mystery of Capital*. New York: Basic Books.

Sraffa, Piero. 1960. *Production of Commodities by Means of Commodities*. Cambridge, UK: Cambridge University Press.

Stafford, William. 1998. *John Stuart Mill.* London: Macmillan.

Stigler, George J. 1941. *Production and Distribution Theories.* New York: Macmillan.

———. 1966. *The Theory of Price.* 3d ed. New York: Macmillan.

———. 1976. "The Successes and Failures of Professor Smith." *Journal of Political Economy* 84, 6 (December): 1199–213.

Stiglitz, Joseph E. 2001. "Information and the Change in the Paradigm in Economics." *2001 Nobel Prize Lectures* (December 8), 472–525. Sweden: Nobel Prize Committee.

Sweezy, Paul M. 1942. *The Theory of Capitalist Development.* New York: Modern Reader.

Sweezy, Paul M., and Paul Baran. 1966. *Monopoly Capitalism.* New York: Monthly Review.

Sweezy, Paul M., and Harry Magdoff. 1977. *The End of Prosperity.* New York: Monthly Review.

Tarshis, Lorie. 1947. *The Elements of Economics.* Boston: Houghton Mifflin.

Terborgh, George. 1945. *The Bogey of Economic Maturity.* Chicago: Machinery and Allied Products Institute.

Thaler, Richard and Shlomo Benartzi. 2004. "Saving More Tomorrow: Using Behavioral Economics to Increase Employment Savings." *Journal of Political Economy* 112:S1 (February), 164–187.

Tobin, James. 1965. "The Monetary Interpretation of History: A Review Article." *American Economic Review* 55 (June): 466–85.

———. 1992. "The Invisible Hand in Modern Macroeconomics." In *Adam Smith's Legacy,* ed. Michael Fry, 117–29. London: Routledge.

Tvede, Lars. 1997. *Business Cycles: From John Law to Chaos Theory.* Amsterdam: Harwood.

U.S. Department of Commerce. 2000. "Gross Output by Industry, 1987–98." *Survey of Current Business.* Washington, DC: U.S. Department of Commerce. June.

Veblen, Thorstein. 1994 [1899]. *The Theory of the Leisure Class.* New York: Penguin.

Viner, Jacob. 1965. "Guide to John Rae's Life of Adam Smith." In *Life of Adam Smith,* by John Rae. New York: Augustus M. Kelley.

———. 1972. *The Role of Providence in the Social Order.* Princeton, NJ: Princeton University Press.

Vivo, G. de. 1987. "David Ricardo." In *The New Palgrave: A Dictionary of Economics.* Vol. 4, 183–98. London: Macmillan.

Wallich, Henry C. 1960. *The Cost of Freedom.* New York: Collier.

Walras, Leon. 1954 [1874, 1877]. *Elements of Pure Economics.* Homewood, IL: Richard D. Irwin.

Weber, Max. 1930 [1904–05]. *The Protestant Ethic and the Spirit of Capitalism.* New York: HarperCollins.

Wesson, Robert G. 1976. *Why Marxism? The Continuing Success of a Failed Theory.* New York: Basic Books.

West, Edwin G. 1976. *Adam Smith, The Man and His Works.* Indianapolis, IN: Liberty Press.

———. 1990. "Adam Smith's Hypotheses on Religion: Some New Empirical Tests." In *Adam Smith and Modern Economics,* 151–64. Hants, UK: Edward Elgar.

Wicksell, Knut. 1958. *Selected Papers on Economic Theory.* London: Allen and Unwin.
Wicksteed, Philip H. 1933. *The Common Sense of Political Economy.* Rev. ed. London: Routledge and Kegan Paul.
Wilson, Edmund. 1940. *To the Finland Station.* New York: Harcourt, Brace.
Wolff, Jonathan. 2002. *Why Read Marx Today?* Oxford: Oxford University Press.
World Bank. 1993. *The East Asian Miracle.* New York: World Bank.
Yergin, Daniel, and Joseph Stanislaw. 1998. *The Commanding Heights.* New York: Simon & Schuster.
Ylikoski, Petri. 1995. "The Invisible Hand and Science." Science Studies 8: 32–43.
Yunus, Muhammad. 1999. *Banker to the Poor.* New York: Public Affairs.
Zarnowitz, Victor. 1992. *Business Cycles.* Chicago: University of Chicago Press.

Index

Abstinence theory of interest, 110
Aggregate demand, 153, 154*f,* 188–189
Aggregate demand management, 136, 137, 150
Aggregate effective demand, 158–159
Aggregate supply, 153, 154*f,* 188–189
Agriculture, 42, 43, 49
Alienation, 97
Alliance for Progress, 201
Alm, Richard, 33–34
Anti-American attitudes, 86
Anti-Samuelson, 170
Anti-Semitism, Marx and, 68–69
Antisaving proponents, 157–158
Apostles, 139
Aristotle, 38–39
Arrow, Kenneth J., 20
AS-AD diagram, 188–189
Associations, establishment of, 113
Austrian economists, 128–132

Balanced budget multiplier, 172, 176
Banker to the Poor (Yunus), 204
Banking, free, 36
Bastiat, Frederic, 47, 74, 151, 216
Bauer, P.T., 202, 204
Behavioral economics, 214*n*1
Berman, Marshall, 67
Birthrate, 52–53
Black, Joseph, 17
Blackboard economics, 55
Blaug, Mark, 55, 105*q,* 125, 167
Blinder, Alan, 20, 188–189
Block, Walter, 31
Böhm-Bawerk, Eugen, 93, 110–112, 180
Boulding, Kenneth E., 208
Bourgeoisie, 76
Bretton Woods agreement, 152
Brown, William Montgomery, 67
Buchanan, James, 209–210
Buckle, Henry Thomas, 12
Burning incidents, Smith's, 16, 17

Callaghan, James, 198
Cambridge school, 115
Cannan, Edwin, 15
Cantillon, Richard, 42–43
Capital
  accumulation and falling profits, 85–86
  forms of, 84–85
  marginal productivity theory, 120
Capital and Interest (Böhm-Bawerk), 110
Capital development, positive theory of, 112
Capital investment, 11
Capital (Marx), 68, 80–81
  money, 99–100
  transformation problem, 92–93
Capitalism
  benefits, 32–34, 98
  collapse predictions, 90–91, 101, 102
  crisis of, 86
  degrees of faith in, 26–27
  evolutionary role of, 99–100
  Friedman's view of, 196
  Heilbroner's view of, 202
  Keynes' view of, 135–136, 149, 153
  Marxist view of, 83, 85–87
  modern day, 97–98
  Protestantism and, 123–124
  threats to, 135, 138
  unstability of, 153, 172, 196
  Veblen's view of, 121–123
  Weber's view of, 123
  See also Economic freedom
Capitalism and Freedom (Friedman), 192, 197
Capitalist-entrepreneur, 111
Capitalists
  Böhm-Bawerk's view of, 110–111
  Marxist view of, 93
  risk taker, 111
  workers and, 93–94, 111–112
Carlyle, Thomas, 63
Carnegie, Andrew, 33
Catchings, Waddill, 157–158, 183

Catholics, 39, 103
Chamberlin, Edward H., 134, 215
Chirognomy, 141n3
Church attendance, 24n9
Churchill, Winston, 142
Clark, John Bates, 109–110, 117–120
Class conflict
  Marx, 85, 96
  Ricardo, 55, 57
  Veblen, 121–122
Class consciousness, 96
Classical model, 7
  abandonment of, 106
  dismal science, 50–52, 63
  imperfections, 134–135
  Keynes and, 149–150
  macroeconomics, 48–49
  principles, 18, 36–37
  recessions, 185–186
  recurrence, 206–209, 216
  See also Natural liberty
Coase, Ronald, 30, 55
Colander, David, 56
Collectivist Economic Planning (Hayek),
  200
Colonialism, 8, 86
Commerce, Montesquieu on, 40–41
Commerce and Government (Condillac), 43
Communism
  Marx and, 65–66, 87–89, 95
  See also Socialism
Communism and the Bible, 103
Communist Manifesto (Marx & Engels),
  75–76, 86
  revolutionary socialism, 88–89
  youthful fanaticism and, 66–67
Comparative advantage, 54
Compensatory fiscal policy, 172
Competition, 18
  imperfect, 134–135, 215
  Montesquieu on, 39
  Smith on, 30–31
Condillac, Etienne Bonnot de, 43
Condition of the Working Class in England
  (Engels), 75
Constant capital, 84–85
Consumer demand. See Demand
Consumption
  economic indicators, 182
  Keynesian view of, 150, 175, 181
  leaks, 180
  production and, 48–49, 184
  productive and unproductive, 186

Contradiction in nature, 87
Corn model, 57, 59
Cost. See Price
Cost, opportunity, 109
Cost of Freedom (Wallich), 201
Cost theory, 59
Cox, Michael, 32–34
Credit, Keynes' view of, 152
Critique of Critical Critique (Marx &
  Engels), 75

Darwin, Charles, 80
Das Kapital (Marx). See Capital
Debt, national, 176–177
Demand, 48–49
  aggregate. See Aggregate demand
  consumer, 106, 107–109, 185
  creates supply, 159
  effective, 158–159
  prices determined by, 109
Demuth, Helene, 78
Denby, David, 97, 98
Depression model, 162
Desai, Meghnad, 102
Determinism, 80, 87, 96
Dialectical materialism, 71
Diamond-water paradox, 50–51,
  108n1–109n1
Digression on Silver (Smith), 36
Diminishing returns, 53
Dismal science, 50–52, 63
Dissent, 101
Distribution, 106
  fundamental theorem of, 58
  law of competitive, 118
  linked to production, 109
Distribution of Wealth (Clark), 118, 119
Distribution problem, 117–118
Division of labor. See Labor
Douglas, C.H., 157
D'Souza, Dinesh, 29

Easy-money policy, 128, 130, 213
Eaton, John, 148n7
Economic and Philosophical Manuscripts
  of 1844 (Marx), 67, 74
Economic classes, disintegration of,
  93–94
Economic Consequences of Mr. Churchill
  (Keynes), 142
Economic Consequences of the Peace
  (Keynes), 140–141, 156
Economic determinism, 80, 87, 96

Economic freedom, 10–11, 18
  economic growth and, 31–32, 203–204
  effects of, 31–32, 34
  See also Capitalism
Economic growth
  Böhm-Bawerk on, 112
  economic freedom and, 31–32, 203–204
  keys to, 11
  Protestantism and, 124
  savings and, 179
Economic indicators, 182
*Economic Possibilities for Our
  Grandchildren* (Keynes), 152, 217
Economic theories
  pendulum approach to, ix–x
  totem pole approach to, x–xi
Economics
  blackboard, 55
  classical. *See* Classical model
  expanding role of, 209
  the imperial science, 209
  mathematics and, 55, 56
  moral behavior and, 30
  neoclassical, 106, 192–193, 199, 205
  as a social science, 113
  stagnation of, 106
Economics (Samuelson), 165–166, 169,
  170
Economics of Imperfect Competition
  (Robinson), 134–135
Edgeworth, Francis, 115–116
Education, 89
Effective demand, 158–159
Egoism, 27, 29
Ekins diagram, 180, 181*f*
Ekins, Paul, 180, 181*f*
Elements of Pure Economics (Walras), 107,
  116
Employment
  Keynes' theory of, 153, 154, 160–162, 172
  See also Unemployment
End of Laissez-Faire (Keynes), 149
End of Prosperity (Sweezy), 91
Engels, Friedrich
  death of, 83
  on Feuerbach, 71
  friendship with Marx, 74–75
  Marx's illegitimate son, 78–79
  revised views, 95–96
Enlightened self-interest. *See* Invisible
  hand
Enlightenment, 4, 6
Entrepreneurs, 48, 93, 111

Environmentalism, 214
Equation of exchange, 126–127, 196
Essay on Population (Malthus), 51
*Essay on the Nature of Commerce in
  General* (Cantillon), 42–43
Essence of Christianity (Feuerbach), 71
Everyday Stalinism (Fitzpatrick), 203
Exchange
  classical view of, 106
  equation of, 126–127, 196
  key to wealth, 9
  Marxist view of, 99–100
Experimental economics, 215
Exploitation, worker, 85, 86

Fable of the Bees, 39–40
Falling profits, 85–86
Faust, 72
Federal Reserve, 127–128, 160,
  194–195
Feuerbach, Ludwig, 71
Fiscal policy, 172, 208
Fisher, Irving, 125–128, 129
Fitzpatrick, Sheila, 203
Foster, William T., 157–158, 183
Foundations of Economic Analysis
  (Samuelson), 55
Franklin, Benjamin, 44–45, 174
Free banking, 36
Free markets
  degrees of faith in, 26–27
  post Soviet Union, 199, 204
  wealth and prosperity through, 13
Free trade. *See* Trade
Freedom, economic. *See* Economic
  freedom
Friedman, Milton, 3*q*, 191*q*
  on Great Depression, 128, 193–196
  honors and awards, 192
  on "invisible hand," 19–20, 192
  Keynesian opponent, 137, 192–193
  monetary rules, 198–199
  Phillips curve, 197–198
  quantity of money, 194, 196–197
Frugality. *See* Thrift
Fukuyama, Francis, 204

Galbraith, John Kenneth, 136
Garrison, Roger, 109*n1*
General equilibrium theory, 116
*General Theory of Employment, Interest
  and Money* (Keynes), 144–146
  capital instability, 135, 153–154

General Theory of Employment, Interest and Money (Keynes) *(continued)*
  German edition, 163
  monetary policy, 196–197
  Say's law of markets, 184–186
George, Henry, 119, 120n2
Gibbon, Edward, 5
God
  invisible hand and, 25–26
  Smith's references to, 23, 24, 25, 44
  See also Religious beliefs
Goethe, 72
Gold
  Great Depression, 194–195
  Keynes' view of, 150, 152
  mercantilism and, 8
  Mises' view of, 131
  removing from monetary system, 152
  Smith's view of, 9, 36
  See also Money
Government
  Friedman's view of, 196
  Great Depression and, 211
  Keynes' views of, 136, 150, 159
  size and growth, 212–213
  Smith's view of, 34–36
Great Contraction, 194, 211
Great Depression, 128, 132, 134, 163
  Friedman on, 193–196
  gold standard, 194–195
  Higgs on, 210–211
  money supply, 194, 195f
Great Duration, 211
Great Escape, 211
Greed, 27, 29, 97, 124
Gross domestic expenditures (GDE), 182
Gross domestic product (GDP), 158–159, 182, 212
Gutiérrez, Gustavo, 103
Gwartney, James, 31–32, 34, 205–206

Hahn, Frank, 20, 26
Hands, reading of, 141n3
Hansen, Alvin, 165, 167–168
Harmony of interests, 57
Harrington, Michael, 90, 94
Harris, Seymour E., 164–165
Harrod, Roy, 139
Harrod-Domar model, 201
Hayek, Friedrich
  on classical model, 106
  on *Fable of the Bees,* 40
  on investment, 183
  on Keynes, 192

Hayek, Friedrich *(continued)*
  on Mill, 62
  monetary crisis predictions, 128, 132
  on savings, 158
  on socialism and economics, 200
  stages of production, 131
Hayekian triangles, 131
Hazlitt, Henry, 192
Hegel, George Wilhem, 71, 87
Heilbroner, Robert, 25, 202–203
Hicks, John, 153
Higgs, Robert, 210–211
Historical materialism, 87, 96
History of Astronomy (Smith), 21
History of the Decline and Fall of the Roman Empire (Gibbon), 5
Hobson, J.A., 86
Human Action (Mises), 192
Hume, David, 6, 17, 24–25, 44
Hutt, W.H., 163q
Hutton, James, 17
Hydraulic Keynesianism, 174, 175f, 180

I, Pencil (Read), 10n2, 26
Illiad (Homer), 78
Imperfect competition, 134–135, 215
Imperfect market, 214–215
Imperial science, 209
Imperialism, 86
"In the long run we are all dead" (Keynes), 150–152
Income
  earned, 109
  national, 171–172, 182, 197
  See also Distribution
Income-expenditure diagram, 171–172, 186
Inflation, unemployment and, 187, 198
Inflationary booms, 130–131
Inflationary crisis, 186–189
Interest
  abstinence theory of, 110
  marginal productivity theory, 120
  market rate of, 130
  natural rate of, 130
  See also Savings
International development organizations, 201
Investment
  Böhm-Bawerk's view of, 112, 120
  Hayek on, 183
  Keynes' view of, 155–157, 162
  Samuelson's view of, 171–172, 174–175
  transfer tax, 162
  See also Savings

Investors, Keynes' view of, 153–155
Invisible God, 25
Invisible hand
    benefits, 19–20
    Fable of the Bees, 39
    Friedman on, 19–20, 192
    God and, 25–26
    interpretations, 22–23
    Keynes' critique of, 149
    mathematical models, 115
    Smith's references to, 21–22, 23
    Stiglitz on, 214
Iron law of wages, 58
IS-LM diagram, 153

Jevons, William Stanley, 46q, 107–108,
    114–115
Jews, Marx's anti-Semitism, 68–69
Joint-input problem, 118
Journals, 101, 113
Jouvenel, Bertrand de, 7–8, 11
Just price, 39
Justice, 18, 206

Kahn, Richard, 160
Kates, Steven, 49, 184–186
Keynes, Florence Ada, 138
Keynes, John Maynard
    on capitalism, 135–136, 149, 153
    chirognomy, 141n3
    dark side, 137–138
    death of, 147
    disdain for Marx, 147–148
    on *Fable of the Bees,* 40
    *General Theory. See General Theory of
        Employment, Interest and Money*
    on government, 136, 150, 159
    homosexuality, 139–140
    honors and awards, 191
    "In the long run we are all dead,"
        150–152
    on Jevons, 114–115
    life of, 138–147
    Marxist disdain for, 148n7
    misogynistic tendencies, 140, 156n9
    on Montesquieu, 41
    public works, 160–162
    recession solutions, 159–160
    on Ricardo, 56–57, 60
    on Smith, 149
    spending, 158–162
    stock market activities, 142–144, 155
    totem pole position, x, xif
    on uninvested savings, 155–157

Keynes, John Neville, 138
Keynesian cross, 171–172, 186
Keynesian economics
    comeback, 186–189, 213
    critics, 177–186
    revolt against, 192
    Samuelson and, 170–177
Keynesian revolution, 136–137, 163
Keynesian topics, 171
Klamer, Arjo, 56
Kolakowski, Leszek, 89
Kondratieff, Nikolai, 91
Krugman, Paul, 133q
    on Keynes' *General Theory,* 146
    on Keynsian economics, 138, 189
Kuznets, Simon, 158

Labor
    division of, 10
    marginal productivity of, 109
    value in, 59–60, 83
Labor theory of value, 54, 59–60, 83–84, 92
Labor unions, 119
Laissez-faire policy
    Bastiat, 47
    Keynes, 149
    Malthus, 53
    Montesquieu, 41
    Quesnay, 42
    Say, 47
    Walras, 116
Land, marginal productivity and, 119–120
Landlords
    Marx and, 84, 85
    Ricardo and, 57–59
Lassalle, Ferdinand, 77
Latin America
    Adam Smith solution, 104
    Marxist-driven ideology, 102–104
Law, The (Bastiat), 47
Law of comparative advantage, 54
Law of competitive distribution, 118
Law of diminishing returns, 53, 58
Law of markets. *See* Say's law
Law of nature, Malthus,' 52–54
Law of the falling rate of profit, 85–86
Lawson, Robert A., 31–32, 34
Lebergott, Stanley, 32–33
Leisure class, 121, 122
Lenin, Vladimir Ilich, 81, 86
Leontief, Wassily, 89
Liberation theology, 102–104
Liebknecht, Wilhelm, 77
Liquidity trap, 160, 177–178

Living standards. *See* Standard of living
London School of Economics, 113
Lopokova, Lydia, 140
Loss, price-cost margins and, 109
Lucas, Robert Jr., 198

Macbeth, 22–23
Machinery
  labor-saving, 11
  Marxist view of, 85, 86, 94
Macroeconomics
  classical model, 48–49
  Keynes and, 137, 153
  microeconomics linked to, 129, 137n2
  neoclassical, 205
  Samuelson and, 166
Macroeconomics (Mankiw), 206–207
Malthus, Thomas Robert
  dismal science, 50–52, 63
  population studies, 51–52
  sins of omission, 53–54
Mandel, Ernest, 90
Mandeville, Bernard, 39–40
Mankiw, N. Gregory, 191q, 206–207
Mantoux, Etienne de, 141n4
Marginal productivity theory, 118–120
Marginal utility, 108, 114
Marginalist revolution, 107–110
Marginality principle, 117
Market economy, invisible hand, 19
Market imperfection, 214–215
Market rate of interest, 130
Markets, Say's law of. *See* Say's Law
Marshall, Alfred, 112–113, 115, 133q
Marshall Plan, 201
Marx, Eleanor, 83
Marx, Karl
  an antieconomist, 94–95
  beard and Zeus, 78
  college radical, 70–71
  communism, 65–66, 87–89, 95
  *Communist Manifesto. See Communist
    Manifesto*
  criticisms of, 92–94, 110
  dark side of, 72–73
  Das Kapital. See Capital
  death of, 82
  and economics, 67–68
  and Engels, 74–75
  false predictions, 89–90
  illegitimate son, 78–79, 83
  influences on, 71–72
  Keynes' disdain for, 147–148

Marx, Karl *(continued)*
  life of, 68–82
  marriage, 73–74
  phrenology, 77–78
  poem about, 71
  poems by, 72–73
  police report on, 76–77
  poverty and wealth of, 79–80
  quotes, 64q
  recantation, 95
  religious beliefs, 69–70, 71, 89
  revolutionary socialism, 88–89
  Ricardo's influence on, 54
  Smith contrasted to, 64–65
  surplus value, 84–85
  totem pole position, xi, xi$f$
  transformation problem, 92–93
  youthful fanaticism and, 66–67
Marx, Laura, 83
Marxism & Marxists
  collapse of, 199–200
  Keynes' disdain for, 147–148
  modern-day, 90–91, 96–98, 100–104,
    213
  1930's, 135
Materialism, 97
Mathematics, 55, 56, 115–116, 168
McConnell, Campbell, 179
Meltzer, Allan H., 154
Menger, Carl, 107–108
Mercantilism, 7–9, 22, 44
Micro-credit revolution, 204
Microeconomics
  imperfect competition, 134–135
  macroeconomics linked to, 129, 137n2
  neoclassical, 205
Mill, John Stuart, 50, 61–63, 106, 122
Minsky, Hyman P., 153, 175
Mises, Ludwig von, 94, 128–132
  on Keynes, 151, 164, 192
  on socialism and economics, 200
  vindication of, 203
Modigliani, Franco, 179
Monetary crisis predictions, 128
Monetary History of the United States
    (Friedman), 193
Monetary models and policy
  Fisher's, 125–128, 129
  Friedman's, 193–194, 197–199
  government and, 213
  Keynes on, 196–197
  Mises's, 129–130
Monetary system, Smith's view of, 36

Money
  as a commodity, 129
  elimination of, 89
  Marxist view of, 99–100
  role of, 125
  See also Exchange; Gold; Monetary
    models and policy; Money, quantity
    theory of
Money, Interest and Prices (Patinkin), 178
Money, quantity theory of
  Fisher's, 126–127
  Friedman *vs.* Keynes, 196–197
  Hume's views of, 44
  Smith's view of, 36
Monopoly, 30–31, 86
Montesquieu, Charles de Secondat, 39,
  40–41
Monthly Review, 101
Moral behavior, 30
Multiplier
  balanced budget, 172, 176
  Friedman on, 197
  full employment, 160–162
  savings, 180
Musgrave, Richard, 209–210

National debt, 176–177
National income, 171–172, 182, 197
Natural liberty, 7, 10–11
  Keynes' critique of, 149
  principles of, 11, 18
  standard of living and, 31–32
  See also Classical model
Natural rate
  interest, 130
  unemployment, 197
Neoclassical economics. *See* Economics,
  neoclassical
New Left Review, 101
Newcomb, Simon, 126
Nordhaus, Bill, 208
Novak, Michael, 103–104

On Liberty (Mill), 61
*On Principles of Political Economy and
  Taxation* (Ricardo), 54, 56, 60
On the Jewish Question (Marx), 68–69
Opportunity cost, 109
Optimality, 116–117
Optimism
  era of, 46
  Smith and, 37–38
  turns dismal, 50–52, 63

Orbis Books, 103, 104
Oulanem (Marx), 72–73
Overworked American (Schor), 97–98

Padover, Saul K., 64q, 69
Paradox of thrift, 173–174, 179, 208
Paradoxes
  diamond-water, 50–51, 108n1–109n1
  thrift, 173–174, 179, 208
  value, 108
Pareto, Vilfredo, 115–116
Pareto optimality, 116–117
Patinkin, Don, 178
Pendulum, ix–x
Peuchet, Jacques, 73
Phillips, A.W., 187
Phillips curve, 187, 197–198
Phrenology, 77–78
Pigou, Arthur C., 178
Pin factory, 10
Plato, 38–39
Player, The (Marx), 72
Poetry
  about Marx, 71
  Marx's, 72–73
Pollution fees, 214
Poor people
  benefit from capitalism, 32–34
  Yunus and, 204–205
Popper, Karl, 96–97
Population studies, 51–52
Positive Theory of Capital (Böhm-Bawerk),
  112
Poverty of Philosophy (Marx), 96
Price
  determined by demands, 109
  determined by scarcity, 108n1
  determined by supply, 59
  stability, 127, 130
Price and Production (Hayek), 131
Price-cost margins, 109
Principles of Economics (Mankiw), 207
Principles of Economics (Marshall), 113
Principles of Economics (Menger), 107
Principles of Political Economy (Mill), 61,
  106, 122
Private property
  Marxist view of, 89
  Veblen's view of, 121
Privatization, 35
Production
  consumption and, 48–49, 184
  errors of, 185

Production *(continued)*
  factors of, 118
  key to wealth, 9
  linked to distribution, 109
  for profits and use, 106
  roundabout, 112, 131
  stages of, 10, 131
Production of Commodities by Means of
  Commodities (Sraffa), 55
Profit rate and value problem, 92–93
Profits
  falling, 85–86
  price-cost margins and, 109
  production for, 106
  use and, 109
Property, private. *See* Private property
Prosperity
  economic freedom and, 31
  keys to, 10–11, 18
Protestant Ethic and the Spirit of
  Capitalism (Weber), 123
Protestant Reformation, 123, 124
Protestants, 39
Public-choice theory, 209–210
Public Finance in Theory and Practice
  (Musgrave), 209
Public works, 160–162
Purchasing Power of Money (Fisher), 126

Quantity Theory of Money, 126–127
Quantity theory of money. *See* Money,
  quantity theory of
Quesnay, François, 41–42

Radical journals and organizations, 101–102
Rational expectations, 198
Read, Leonard, 10*n*2, 26
Real balance effect, 178
Recession
  1970s, 186–189, 198
  Keynesian solutions to, 159–160, 172–173
  Say's explanation for, 185–186
Reflections on the Formation and
  Distribution of Wealth (Turgot), 43
Religious beliefs
  Hume, 24–25, 44
  Marx, 69–70, 71, 89
  Smith, 24–25, 44
  Weber, 123, 124
  See also God
Religious freedom, church attendance and,
  24*n*9
Revolutionary socialism. *See* Socialism

Ricardian vice, 54, 55
Ricardo, David, 54–56
  dismal science, 50, 51, 63
  distribution, 57–59
  Marx and, 83–84
  Say on, 48
  value in labor, 59–60
Risk level, 111
Robinson, Joan, 135, 215
Rostow, W.W., 201, 204
Rothbard, Murray, 42, 192
Rothschild, Emma, 22–23
Roundaboutness, 112, 131

Samuelson, Paul A., 164
  AS-AD diagram, 188
  on *Capital,* 93
  criticism of, 169–170
  Economics, 165–166, 169, 170
  goals of, 171
  honors and awards, 166, 168, 169
  on Keynes' *General Theory,* 146, 153
  Keynesian cross, 171–172, 186
  life of, 166–167
  macro policy dilemma, 187
  on Marx, 69
  on Marxist economics, 94
  mathematical equations, 55, 168
  on national debt, 176–177
  on new global economy, 208
  paradox of thrift, 173–174, 208
  postwar predictions, 168
  revised theories, 208
  on Smith, 12, 174
  on socialism, 201
Saving American Capitalism (Harris), 164
Savings
  antisaving proponents, 157–158
  Böhm-Bawerk's view of, 112, 180
  economic growth and, 179
  Hayek on, 158
  Keynes' view of, 155–157
  Mankiw's view of, 207
  multiplier, 180
  positive side of, 180
  Protestantism and, 124
  Samuelson's view of, 171–175, 208
  Say's view of, 49
  See also Interest; Investment; Thrift
Say, Jean-Baptiste, 47–48
Say's Law, 48–49, 86, 92
  inverse of, 159
  Keynes and, 184–186

Say's Law and the Keynesian Revolution (Kates), 184–185
Schor, Juliet, 97–98
Schumpeter, Joseph, 60, 101, 200
Schwartz, Anna J., 193
Schweickart, David, 102
Self-interest
  meaning of, 27
  sympathy *vs.*, 29–30
  wealth and prosperity through, 18, 19
  See also Invisible hand
Self-restraint, 28
Selfishness, 29
Senior, Nassau William, 28n10
Shakespeare, 22–23
Sham-lecture, 13–14
Shaw, G.K., 189
Silver, 8, 9, 36
Skulls, reading of, 77–78
Smith, Adam
  advocate for the common man, 6–7
  burning of manuscripts & papers, 17
  burns clothes, 16
  customs agent, 16–17
  death of, 18
  economic freedom, 10–11
  on *Fable of the Bees,* 40
  famous remark, 38
  on government, 34–36
  hypotheses, 31–32
  invisible hand. *See* Invisible hand
  Keynes' critique of, 149
  life of, 12–18
  Marx contrasted to, 64–65
  natural liberty, 7, 10–11
  optimist, 37–38
  religious beliefs, 24–25, 44
  sham-lecture, 13–14
  shift back to, 205–206, 216
  sympathy *vs.* self-interest, 29–30
  totem pole position, x, xi*f*
  universal opulence, 6, 7, 10–11, 32
  view of greed and selfishness, 29
  view of trade, 8
  Wealth of Nations. See Wealth of Nations
Smith, Vernon L., 215
Smugglers, 16
Social Justice Without Socialism (Clark), 119
Social Security, 207
Socialism, 60–61, 200
  critics of, 203
  Heilbroner on, 202–203
  Marx and, 88–89, 95

Socialism *(continued)*
  Mill and, 62–63
  post WWII, 200–202
  Sweezy and, 101
Solow growth model, 207
Somary, Felix, 142
Soviet Union, collapse of, 199, 202
Spanish scholastics, 39, 124
Specie-flow mechanism, 44, 131
Spending, Keynes' on, 158–161
Spirit of the Laws (Montesquieu), 40
Sraffa, Piero, 54, 55
Stabilization policy, 208
Stages of Economic Growth (Rostow), 201
Stages-of-production, 10
Stagflation, 198
Stagnation thesis, 167–168
Standard of living
  capitalism and, 32–34
  economic freedom and, 31–32
Stigler, George, 14n4, 20
Stiglitz, Joseph, 214–215
Stock market
  crash of 1929, 127
  Keynes and, 142–144, 155
  transfer tax, 162
Suicide
  of Marx's daughters, 83
  Marx's fascination with, 73
Supply, 48–49
  aggregate, 153, 154*f,* 188–189
  demand creates, 159
  price determined by, 59
Surplus value, 84–85, 110
Sweezy, Paul M., 91, 100–101, 135
Sympathy, self-interest *vs.*, 29–30
System of natural liberty. *See* Natural liberty

Tableau économique, 41–42
Tariffs, Smith's view of, 8
Tarshis, Lorie, 175
Tax cuts, Keynesian view of, 172
Taxation
  land, 119–120
  Samuelson's view of, 176
  Smith's view of, 35
Teaching of Marx for Girls and Boys (Brown), 67
Theology, liberation, 102–104
Theology of Liberation (Gutiérrez), 103
Theory of Money and Credit (Mises), 129–130

Theory of Monopolistic Competition
  (Chamberlin), 134
Theory of Moral Sentiments (Smith)
  God, 23, 25, 44
  government, 35–36
  invisible hand, 21–22, 23
  sympathy, 29–30
  year published, 14
Theory of Political Economy (Jevons), 107
Theory of surplus value, 84–85, 110
Theory of the Leisure Class (Veblen), 121, 122
Thrift, 11, 36
  anti-thrift proponents, 157–158
  Böhm-Bawerk's view of, 112
  Keynes' view of, 156–157
  paradox of, 173–174, 179, 208
  Protestantism and, 124
  Say's view of, 49
  See also Savings
Tobin, James, 26, 162*n*11, 193
Tocqueville, Alexis de, 47
Totem pole, x–xi
Townsend, Charles, 15
Tract on Monetary Reform (Keynes), 142
Trade
  Bastiat's view of, 47
  Hume's view of, 44
  mercantilist restraint of, 8
  Smith's view of, 8–9, 16
Transfer tax, 162
Transformation problem, 92–93
Traveling abroad, youth, 14*n*4
Treatise on Money (Keynes), 143, 156
Treatise on Political Economy (Say), 47, 48
Tullock, Gordon, 210
Turgot, Jacques, 43
Twilight of Capitalism (Harrington), 90

Underconsumptionists, 157–158
Unemployment
  inflation and, 187, 198
  involuntary, 185, 215
  Mankiw's view of, 207
  natural rate of, 197
  wage cuts and, 178
  war and, 163–164
Unemployment equilibrium, 153
Union of Radical Political Economics,
  101–102
Unions. *See* Labor unions
United Kingdom, rise in income, 5*f*
United States
  standard of living, 33, 33*f*

United States *(continued)*
  stock market crash of 1929, 127
Universal opulence, 6, 7, 10–11, 32
Universities, economics departments, 113
URPE. *See* Union of Radical Political
  Economics
Utility, marginal. *See* Marginal utility

Value
  cost-of-production theory, 59, 106,
    108
  labor theory, 54, 59–60, 83–84, 92
  marginal principle of, 108–109
  paradox of, 108
  surplus, 84–85, 110
  in "use" *vs.* in "exchange," 108
Variable capital, 84–85
Veblen, Thorstein, 121–123
Viner, Jacob, 23
Voltaire, 15

Wages
  Böhm-Bawerk's view of, 111
  Clark's view of, 118–119
  cuts and unemployment, 178
  Malthus' view of, 54
  Mankiw's view of, 207
  marginal productivity of labor and,
    109
  natural liberty and, 11
  Ricardo's view of, 57–59
Waiting argument, 110
Wallich, Henry C., 201
Walrus, Leon, 107–108, 115–116
War
  employment and, 163–164
  Keynes' view of, 163
  Smith's view of, 35
Watershed years
  1776, 4–6
  1848, 60–61
  1948, 164–165
  1970s, 186–189
Wealth
  earned, 109
  keys to, 9–10, 18
  measurement of, 9
  Ricardo's distribution of, 57–59
Wealth, Distribution of (Clark), 118, 119
Wealth of Nations (Smith)
  editions, 15
  greed and egoism, 27–28
  invisible hand reference, 22

Wealth of Nations (Smith) *(continued)*
  objectives of writing, 7
  sympathy *vs.* self-interest, 29–30
  universal acclaim, 12
  writing and publication of, 4–5, 15
  See also Smith, Adam
Webb, Beatrice, 135, 200
Webb, Sidney, 135, 200
Weber, Max, 123–125
Welfare economics, 20–21, 115–116
Westphalen, Jenny von, 72, 73–74, 79
  death of, 82
Wicksell, Knut, 107, 130
"Woolen coat" example (Smith), 10, 19
Wordsworth, William, 46, 168

Worker-capitalist phenomenon, 93–94
  See also Capitalists
Worker exploitation, 85, 86
Worker revolts, 76
World Bank, 199, 201, 204
World War II, 163, 211
  socialism after, 200–203
Worldly Philosophers (Heilbroner), 202

Yeager, Leland, 189
Youth
  education, 89
  traveling abroad, 14n4
Yunus, Muhammad, 204–205

Zeus, 78

About the Author

Mark Skousen is a professional economist, investment expert, university professor, and author of over twenty books. Currently he holds the Benjamin Franklin Chair of Management at Grantham University. In 2004–05, he taught economics and finance at Columbia Business School and Columbia University, and from 1986 to 2003, at Rollins College in Florida. Since 1980, Skousen has been editor in chief of *Forecasts & Strategies*, a popular award-winning investment newsletter. He is also chairman of Investment U, one of the largest investment e-letters in the country, with 300,000 subscribers. He is a former analyst for the CIA, a columnist to *Forbes* magazine, and past president of the Foundation for Economic Education (FEE) in New York. He has written for the *Wall Street Journal*, *Forbes*, and *Reason* magazine, and has appeared on CNBC, CNN, ABC News, Fox News, and C-SPAN Book TV. His bestsellers include *The Making of Modern Economics* and *The Power of Economic Thinking*. In 2006, he compiled and edited *The Compleated Autobiography, by Benjamin Franklin*. In honor of his work in economics, finance and management, Grantham University renamed its business school "The Mark Skousen School of Business."

Websites: www.markskousen.com; www.mskousen.com

Email address: editors@markskousen.com